# THE UNIVERSE SPEAKS

## *A Heavenly Dialogue*

## Kimberly Klein

"*The Universe Speaks* is powerful proof that the 'veil between the worlds' is thinner than we think. Kim Klein's story of her daughter's death in a plane crash in Panama reads like fiction. But Talia's teachings from the spirit world after her 'death' provide the reader with hope, inspiration, and a new understanding of the reality of life."

~Jennifer Read Hawthorne, co-author, #1 *New York Times* bestsellers *Chicken Soup for the Woman's Soul* and *Chicken Soup for the Mother's Soul*

"Love and wisdom transcend the veil as Kim Klein's daughter on the other side reveals marvelous insights about the true meaning of life. *The Universe Speaks* brings hope to anyone who has ever lost a loved one."

~Randy Peyser, author of *The Power of Miracle Thinking*

# Dedication

*I dedicate this book to Talia, my sweet daughter, whose words, touch and love bring me joy and peace on a daily basis, and to G, whose love and dedication have helped bring Talia's words to me and to the world.*

Talia and Mom, our last photo together, taken December 2007
© photography by Helene Glassman/*www.imagerybyhelene.com*

For information about this title or to order other books and/or electronic media, contact the publisher:
Pretty Much Amazing Press, a division of PMA Content Group
Pahrump, Nevada
www.prettymuchamazingpress.com
1-800-650-6422

Library of Congress Control Number: 2011912911

ISBN (paperback): 978-0-9837750-2-7
ISBN (hardcover): 978-0-9837750-3-4

Printed in the United States of America

Cover and Interior design by: 1106 Design

Author Photo: Peter Palladino    Make up: Marie Augustine

# Table of Contents

# PART I

# Introduction

# The Dialogues Begin

On December 23, 2007, a small private plane carrying my thirteen-year-old daughter, her father and her best friend crashed into the side of a volcano in Panama, killing all on board except my daughter's friend.

Talia was my only child. For nearly three days the whereabouts of the plane—and the fate of my daughter, her father and her friend—were unknown. It was the most horrific and traumatizing time of my life. My mind and my body were not connected, and from the moment I realized my daughter was "dead," I have never been the same. My heart was ripped out of me, my emotions disconnected from my body, and my entire life torn apart.

Of course I will never be the same. Never the same because Talia is no longer "alive." But also never the same because all that I thought about life and death has been altered. In the midst of the worse time of my life I feel ultimate love and peace.

*Tell my mom I'm OK.*

Talia?

*Yes, tell my mom I'm OK.*

OK, I will when I see her.

*TELL MY MOM I'M OK!*

I will, I promise!

It sounded like an everyday message from a daughter to her mother—but it was really not so everyday. You see, Talia made that statement to my friend G on January 23—while he was on the way to her memorial service. She said it a month *after* she had died.

Now, I am not the kind of person who would readily believe that someone had heard my daughter speaking from the spirit world. In fact, I did not believe in the spirit world until recently. So why would I ever believe that those words, "Tell my mom I'm OK," were actually from Talia? It would have been much more rational for me to assume my friend had made up that message to help me deal with the overwhelming pain of losing my daughter.

But when G gave me Talia's message, I knew, deep in my heart, that those were Talia's own words. Yes, they were said to help me, but they were not made up; they were actually Talia's words, said by her, for me.

Who am I? you may be wondering. I'm Kim, Talia's mom. A forty-something, California-raised, well-educated, middle-class woman.

I grew up pretty simply, with no particular religious or spiritual rules to live by. I just lived my life my way, rationally and according to my own guidelines, which were pretty basic: Try to treat people well, don't lie, and be happy.

Because I didn't have any set religious or spiritual guidance growing up, I decided I didn't believe in God—or the spirit world. I was too independent to believe there was one supreme person or entity with a set of rules I was supposed to follow in order to go to heaven when I died. In fact, that idea annoyed me, because I saw so many religious leaders using their position to control the members of their congregations.

I felt that if there were a God, you should be able to pray to that God directly—he wouldn't make it necessary for people to go through an intermediary to get to him. There was no need to pray to a secondary source or confess to a human acting as God's representative, or do whatever a particular leader said you had to do. Nor did you have to join a church or temple as a means of getting to heaven. You could just be you, live your life, and speak to your God when you wanted to, on your terms.

But though I didn't believe in the God that most people I came in contact with believed in, I didn't shut myself off from the possibility of the existence of God either. Since the idea of God had not been pounded into me, and until recently I had had no mystical experiences or miracles to show me the existence of God, I had no reason to believe in either the existence or the nonexistence of God. But I was open to receiving proof of the existence of God or the spirit world. And I did believe in my own instincts, often "just knowing" something, which seemed to imply that I believed there's more to us than our minds.

I labeled myself *agnostic*—not believing but open to proof. I really believe it was this openness that allowed me eventually to see, hear, and experience the evidence I needed to prove that there is in fact a spiritual dimension and a power, a force that some people call God.

So when did I go from not believing to believing? It was just after I really understood that my daughter had been killed. I say *understood* that she had been killed, because even when I first found out, it took a while for me to really know she was gone. Gone from this earth the way I had known her. But once I realized she was in fact "dead," my entire belief system shattered.

This shattering was not like the shattering of a mirror, whereby when it broke nothing was left. It was like the shattering of a glass door that, once broken, allowed me to see into a world much more beautiful, perfect, and fulfilling than the world I was living in. My daughter's death is what shattered that door. From the moment I really understood she was gone, I went from not believing in life after death to absolutely believing in it. I knew that the messages Talia was sending me from beyond were from her, and so very real.

What made me believe? It was not that the words "Tell my mom I'm OK" in themselves changed me from a non-believer to a believer. Since the very moment I realized Talia was "dead," I began receiving many messages from her through various sources, all of which have built on one other and been confirmed by one other. When looked at both alone and as a whole, they have proven to me that not only is Talia actually telling people the messages they relay to me, but, beyond that, those messages are in every way totally, completely, and irrevocably Talia. I know, deeper in my heart and soul than I can even describe, that Talia is communicating to me and, most important, that she is not dead, but more alive and amazing now than she was with me here on earth.

✻   ✻   ✻

That moment—the moment when my entire belief system shattered—happened the afternoon of December 26, 2008, after I heard the news and really understood that Talia was dead.

I was lying down, drifting in and out of sleep, crying. Suddenly, I was startled out of my sleepy state by a definite sensation of pressure around my left wrist. I knew deep in my bones that what I felt was an actual touch, and my soul knew it was Talia.

I suppose you're saying, "OK, your daughter just died, so of course you are going to imagine things like her touch." Well, it was not my imagination.

Just minutes after I felt her touch on my wrist, my cell phone rang. It was my friend in Santa Barbara. She had just called Rebecca, a medium I had spoken to in the past, and during that call my friend said Rebecca had started to get messages from Talia that were meant for me. Rebecca told my friend that Talia was trying to show her "a charm or something."

I immediately knew what it was. Talia wanted me to get her bracelet from her wrist. This bracelet meant a great deal to both Talia and me. I had given it to Talia the previous Mother's Day as a thank-you gift for being my daughter. The bracelet was simple: just a gold coin on a black rope. It was her absolute favorite thing in the world and she never took it off, ever.

Right after I hung up the phone with my friend, my phone rang again, and it was Rebecca. "It's a bracelet! Talia wants you to get her bracelet with the gold on it!" Oh, my God! There was no way on earth this had been made up. No one knew about the bracelet or its significance, or that Talia had been wearing it on the trip—least of all Rebecca, who had never met Talia before.

My first couple of conversations with Rebecca after that were filled with short messages from Talia to me, meant to help me get over the shock of the accident. Here is a little of what Talia said. I will explain their significance as needed:

*Talia loves you. She's with her dad.*

*Talia and her dad stayed at the plane with Frankie [Talia's friend] to keep her safe until help came. They kept Frankie in a daze to keep her from panicking. They protected Frankie.*

*Talia said her dad guided Sam to help find the plane.*

*Talia wants you to get her backpack. She's worried about it.*

*Talia said she had the best life, a charmed life, and still considers it the same way.*

*Talia is concerned about the dogs and her male horse; he will be upset with any change.*

> Talia had two horses, a male and a female. Her male horse, Justinian, is an extremely emotional animal, and he was very attached to her. He reacts to change, so Talia's letting me know that she was concerned about him was significant.

*Talia is concerned about her awards and wants you to make sure to get them for her.*

> Talia had won numerous equestrian awards during the 2007 horse show year, and she was the number one equitation rider in her age group in our region. Talia had been looking forward to going to the awards banquets and receiving her awards in January.

*Tomorrow will be difficult for you. She doesn't want you to look at her this way. She had **no pain**.*

> The day after I got these messages from Talia, I was to go to the morgue to identify her body and to visit her in the flesh for the last time. No one knew that in the States. Only the members of my family who were with me in Panama knew. It was going to be a very difficult day for me, and in fact it was. I'll never forget the expression on Talia's face, ever. Talia didn't want me to remember her that way, and she was making a point of telling me that.

# The Dialogues Begin

*Talia said you were the best mother and will always be her mom.*

*Talia is with Stella. All passed family is with her. Stella has her by the arm, and she will be fine; she's there for you.*

> Stella is my grandmother, who died in 1980. Stella is not a common name, not one to be guessed.

*Talia wants photos and music as her memory. Said you know the song.*

> There is a particular song that was Talia's favorite at the time; I knew exactly which one it was. Also, Talia had many photos of herself riding that she was very proud of.

*Talia wants you to look for the hummingbirds.*

> The hummingbird message didn't have any significance for me when I first got the message in Panama, but as soon as I got home it did. I started seeing hummingbirds hovering by my office window, looking in, all the time. In one instance it was pouring rain, and this little hummingbird was outside my window. I said out loud, "Talia, is that you? It has to be, because hummingbirds don't usually fly in the rain."
>
> No more than ten minutes after I said that, I went to my back door, and as I was stepping out I saw, lying perfectly on the step, straight and centered, the same hummingbird I had just seen by my window on the other side of the house. It was wet and freshly dead. That was a confirmation from Talia, saying yes, Mom, it's me, and to prove it I'm making a statement!

*Talia told you to get her diary or journal.*

Besides the messages above, which I received right after Talia died, there were some remarkable events that further solidified my newfound beliefs.

Everyone I knew who was close to Talia and me, or close to Michael, her father, was clamoring for communications with them via Rebecca. One afternoon I was visiting a friend of mine, and we were talking about my upcoming birthday. I mentioned to her that my mom wanted to receive a message from Talia to find out what Talia wanted her to get me for my birthday. I commented that it would be amazing if Talia told my mom exactly what gift to get me and where to buy it.

Some friends of mine, a married couple, had a phone-in appointment with Rebecca no more than thirty minutes after the conversation I'd had about my birthday. During this couple's conversation, Talia said, "My mom's birthday is soon. I want you to get her a gift."

Talia then went on to describe the gift in detail, and where to buy it. What's remarkable is that she described not only the store, which had not even been in existence when she was alive, but the woman who had opened the store, where it was, and what it sold, giving the couple a detailed description of the item she wanted them to buy me. Right after they finished speaking with Rebecca, the husband got in the car and drove to that store, and on the table in the center of the room was the exact thing Talia had described. He bought it on the spot.

Well, my mom called Rebecca and left her request. While waiting for a return call, she started to search the Internet for a gift Talia might want me to have. She found what she thought was the perfect gift, and as she was looking at it on her computer screen, the phone rang. It was Rebecca returning her call. "Talia wants you to get her mom a glass heart." My mom almost fell off her chair. On the computer screen, at that very moment, was a photo of a glass heart. A pink glass heart.

Yet another unbelievable event happened to Rebecca while she was shopping. She was looking at some necklaces, and as she passed one in particular she heard Talia's voice say, "Buy that for my mom; it's her birthday." Rebecca asked, "Talia, is this you?" "Yes, buy that for my mom."

Rebecca bought the necklace, then called me and said she had something for me. I went to see her and had a reading, and it was then that she gave me the necklace Talia had picked out for me. It was made of crystals and stones; the meaning of one of the stones was "spirit manifestation." Another coincidence? Not in the least. It was Talia.

After hearing these messages and experiencing all of these "coincidences," and being blown away at the interconnectedness of them all, I had no doubt in my mind or heart or soul that Talia was sending them to me as signs that her consciousness was alive and with me still. As a reader who doesn't know Talia or me and has not lived our lives, you will never really feel the truth that I know so well. I'm telling you that before this time, I didn't believe in God, in the soul, or in the spirit world. To convince me that Talia is still here, communicating with me, took some really big substantiations. Really big.

# Before the Crash

EVEN BEFORE THE PLANE CRASH that killed Talia, events occurred that would reveal unseen forces at work.

Talia had just turned thirteen a few weeks before leaving for Panama with her dad for a weekend vacation, taking her friend Frankie with her. This wasn't the first time Talia had gone down to Panama with Michael—in fact, she had been there many times before. Michael went down to the islands at least twice a month, often taking Talia with him on his jaunts. Talia would surf, scuba dive, swim, explore, and commune with nature.

This particular trip was special to Talia because she was taking her friend with her. When I look back on it, what seemed like the beginning of a normal vacation was just a steppingstone on her soul's path, which she had walked throughout her life. A life that, despite ending in the flesh, has not ended in spirit.

On December 19, 2007, when Talia's dad picked her up for the weekend, I kissed and hugged her goodbye, as usual. I told her to be safe and that I would see her in a few days. That was it. I didn't consciously know that the hug and kiss I gave Talia as she left were going to be the last I would give her while she was living, or that this moment would be the last time I would ever see her alive.

I say *consciously* because when I look at some of my actions and thoughts in the weeks prior to Talia leaving, and when I think about what has happened since the accident, it seems I somehow knew that Talia wasn't coming home—at least in my subconscious awareness. There's no way I could have known consciously and not held onto Talia and kept her from leaving that night.

One odd thing that happened was that just a week before Talia left for Panama, I told her I wanted her to organize her jewelry. At this point Talia had her earrings and other miscellaneous things scattered in different drawers. I wanted her real jewels to be kept in one safe place so they wouldn't get lost. Most of her jewelry had sentimental value more than anything else, but it was important to me that she keep track of it.

So one night I gathered all her jewelry, and together we went through it, figuring out what was what. We put all the important pieces in a little jewelry box separate from her other things. That alone wasn't a big deal.

Then, a few days after Talia had left for Panama, I went to my safety deposit box and took out all my jewelry and other sentimental items and organized them, labeling everything for Talia—this came from her great-great grandmother, this was her grandfather's, and so on. If something happened to me, I didn't want Talia to be stuck with a bunch of things, mostly heirloom pieces, and not know the significance of each piece or who had given it to me and when. I cleaned it all up for her—or so I thought.

OK, maybe I was in an organizing frenzy or something. But looking at it now, there's no way I would have been able to go through Talia's jewelry after she died. It would have sent me over the edge, though at some point I would have had to. For some reason I was made to do it ahead of time. It seems very odd to me.

Then, while Talia was on her trip, I had a very strange "vision." I imagined Talia calling me from Panama and telling me that something had happened to her dad, but that she and Frankie were OK. I told her to stay exactly where she was; I was heading down to Panama right then to get her. I told her not to move—I would be there.

I figured this vision was just my imagination, and I actually forgot about it until soon after my return from Panama. But as I thought more about it, I realized it *had been* Talia, telling me she was OK, right after the accident. Her spirit letting me know she was OK. That made me very happy, because when I first got back from Panama, I wondered why I hadn't "felt" the accident when it happened.

There are so many stories of parents or spouses who say they had a strange feeling the moment an accident happened or an interesting visit from someone at the exact time the person died, and I wondered why I had not had that. I had even felt sad about not having had that feeling. But once I realized I actually *had* experienced it through my vision, I was a bit relieved. I can't explain why, I just was.

Of course, this vision was very close to what actually happened just days later. Except that Talia didn't call me; someone else did.

It was on December 23, one day before Talia was supposed to come home, that I got "The Call."

"Kim, this is Bob (Talia's grandfather). The plane that Talia and Michael and Frankie were on is missing." What? I literally went into a coma for a few seconds. My heart stopped. I couldn't breathe.

Needless to say, from that moment on I have never been the same. The details of the excruciating next three days are all described in my book *Hummingbirds Don't Fly in the Rain*. This plane crash changed my life, my belief system—and my understanding of death, the life that I led with Talia, and the life she is leading now.

# My Shift

How could Talia's "death" change how I look at the life we had together? Her "death" forced me to analyze every single decision I had made in raising her, everything we had done together, and every single word I had ever said to Talia while she was growing up. I questioned every single move I had made and how it related to her. Had I made the right decision letting her show her horse so much? Had I done the right thing saying no to this and yes to that? It didn't stop. I questioned everything.

Looking back, I realized that how I raised Talia made her the person she was while here with me and prepared her perfectly for the next part of her soul's journey, her life after the accident. In fact, Talia herself sent me a message letting me know that how I had raised her is what made her the person she was on earth and the spirit she is now; it gave her the ability to be at the level she is now, learning all that she's learning.

Here are the exact words she sent me through my friend G, the person whose conversations with Talia follow in this book:

*Tell her my time there was divine. She did everything in a perfect way and was (is) an awesome mother. She got me here perfectly.*

*My mom got me here perfectly. That's why she has no regrets, as she shouldn't, ever. She will share in this reward, and it's far beyond tremendous. There are no words to describe it.*

Those words are Talia's—but she was actually quoting me. A couple of days before Talia communicated this to G, I had told another person I had absolutely no regrets regarding my time with Talia. So when she said, "That's why she has no regrets," it confirmed two things for me: one, that Talia is with me all the time, listening to me, and two, that I was in fact the best mother I could have been to her. All my questioning stopped. This is what gives me a sense of peace.

# Talia

VERY SOON AFTER TALIA WAS BORN, her father and I got divorced. Now that I look back on my life, I see that raising Talia on my own was meant to be. Most of the lessons she learned in this life could not have happened if her dad and I had stayed married.

When I say that I raised Talia on my own, I really did. Her dad was around, and he did take care of his financial responsibility to care for her, but he was extremely busy and really did not see Talia much at all. The time that Talia and he were together was made up mostly of short weekend visits.

While I don't want to take away from his time with Talia, I do want you, the reader, to understand how much time Talia and I were together and how very close we were. Raising Talia was my destiny, my sole purpose in life. I was a full-time mom, and I loved it more than anything else in the world. I worked hard to raise her well and *consciously*.

It wasn't an easy job, though *job* is not the correct word; a truer word would be *honor*. It's not easy to teach, guide, and mentor a child from conception onward. Especially knowing that everything you say or do—and everything that child witnesses, experiences, and thinks about—will have a deep impact on his or her understanding and possibilities in this world and the next. Trying to give Talia information without giving answers, without influencing the direction of her thought or causing walls to be built around her mind, was the most difficult task I could have had. And I loved every moment of it.

Of course, at the time I was raising Talia, I didn't know that my influence and guidance would affect her life *after life*. I couldn't have known it then, because that was when I didn't believe in an afterlife. But I did know that her time on earth, with me in this life, would be molded by my every word and move. And because I wanted not to shape her thoughts and beliefs but allow her to grow and form her own, I had to be extremely diligent.

Teaching without limiting is the most difficult task there is. I watched over myself every second of the day. Each word, action, response—even the inflection of my voice—had to be used precisely to ensure that they were not influencing Talia's thoughts and beliefs but were merely stepping stones for her to walk on while forming her own code for life. My goal was to keep Talia's mind open and not to stifle her or cause the doorways of her mind, leading to all the universe offered, to close.

Looking back at Talia's life here with me, I'm confident that I accomplished my goal. I know this because Talia was an amazing child and person, an independent-minded, analytical, gracious, joyful, generous, and thoughtful girl who was wise beyond her years. Yes, I'm her mother, and all mothers think their kids are the greatest, smartest, most perfect kids on earth. But I'm not the kind of person to give credit where it's not due—in fact, I'm pretty critical. So when I say that Talia was everything I say she was, it's true.

Here's a portion of something the head of Talia's upper school said about her at her memorial. I think it really exemplifies who Talia was from an outsider's perspective:

"The first time I met Talia, I was struck by her extraordinary independence, her contemplative focus, her philosophic composure, and her unflappable maturity. She was *two* at the time!

"Every parenting book ever written, of course, refers to this time in the toddler's life as 'the terrible twos,' which makes my first memory of Talia all the more remarkable. Here was a child who, after being out of the womb and out in the world for just twenty-four months or so, comported herself with thoughtfulness, self-assurance, and grace—qualities that would become quintessentially Talia over the years. . . .

"When you're a teacher, you spend a lot of time wondering what your students will be like as adults. Sometimes it's difficult or even impossible to imagine what some kids will be like as grownups. This was never the case with Talia. She went about her business at Crane with such efficacy and aplomb that it was as though we had already had a glimpse of the adult Talia. Indeed, she figured out and accomplished more in thirteen years than many people do in a long lifetime."

Talia was true to herself. Everything she did was authentic and came from her heart, her soul, her true self. This is best seen through Talia's own writings. Here are some examples of her views about life, found in the autobiography she was assigned to write in school the year before the crash.

## My Life Messages

Some of my life lessons have really helped me through a lot of situations. It took me a while to compile a list because there is a lot of big life messages that everyone should follow, like be kind and don't kill, but I tried to think of other life messages that people often forget about or put aside more often. The ones I chose could end up being a lot more important than you think in the long run. Here is what I chose:

1) Life isn't fair; don't think it is.
2) Be an optimist; believe the impossible.
3) Never give up; fight till the end.
4) Do what you believe is right; even if it means not going with the flow.
5) Believe none of what you hear and half of what you see.
6) Listen to your instincts; follow your gut.

## Just One Day

I have thought long and hard about whom I would want to switch places with. I even wrote a paper on one person who I would switch places with. I read it to myself a couple of times. I decided that it was really horrible. I can't possibly imagine in my wildest dreams what it would be like to not be myself. I love my life so much I am lost when I try to think about what my life could have been.

Maybe for a day I could switch with the children in Rwanda so that at least for a day they could have a warm place to sleep, a meal, and clean water, so that they could live one more day. And maybe for one day I would really understand what it meant to suffer.

This chapter was the hardest for me but I am glad I did it. Maybe one day all little boys and little girls will have a warm bed to sleep in and food to eat every day. Not just for one day.

## TALIA

Lively, friendly, hyper, smart
Sibling of Zippy, Gunther and Layla
Lover of ice cream
Who fears spiders
Who needs chocolate chip cookies
Who gives laughter
Who would like to see and travel the world
Resident of Sterling Silver Stables
Klein

(The "siblings" Talia referred to here were her dogs!)

### Stop and Think: What is a Hero?

I think a hero is someone who is completely
selfless in all of their actions. Someone
who takes risks for others, and takes time
out of their own life for someone else's life.
I think that parents are heroes too,
because they raise us to be who we are
and put up with us when we're not so grateful.

Here's the letter Talia wrote to me when she was assigned to write a letter home, giving me a progress report on how she was doing in school.

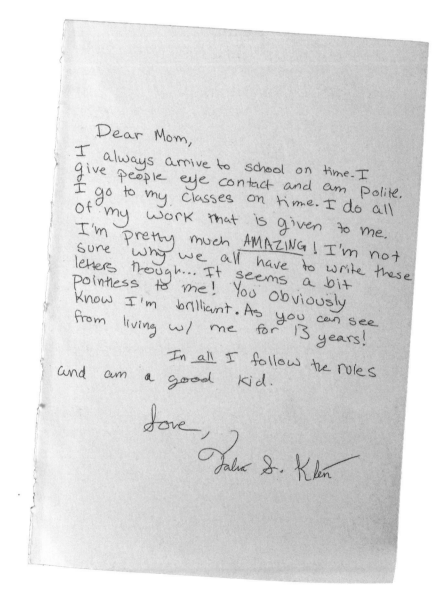

Dear Mom,

I always arrive to school on time. I give people eye contact and am polite. I go to my classes on time. I do all of my work that is given to me. I'm pretty much AMAZING! I'm not sure why we all have to write these letters though... It seems a bit pointless to me! You obviously know I'm brilliant. As you can see from living w/ me for 13 years!

In _all_ I follow the rules and am a good kid.

Love,

Talia S. Klein

Talia was truly a special person. Adults loved to converse with her. She was enthralled by conversations about the universe, whether there's a God, moral codes, quantum physics, music, literature, movies, food. She actually preferred to talk with adults than kids. But Talia was still a kid. She played sports, hung out with friends, loved volleyball, and loved riding her horses and competing in horse shows.

Talia also was a great student, and she loved school so much that she was torn between missing school and going to horse shows. One time I wanted to take her to Six Flags Magic Mountain on a school day, and she freaked out. No way was she willing to miss a day of school. It's not that I was a bad mom for wanting her to miss a day; it was just that Talia worked very hard and was always ahead in her assignments, so she was more than capable of missing a day of school for some good old fun. Even her teachers didn't mind that she "ditched" a day here and there for horse shows or whatever came up.

There was something unique about Talia. People called her an "old soul." Truly she was; she emanated wisdom.

Talia decided for herself that she didn't believe in God. That wasn't something I ever told her. Her father and I didn't believe in God, but I wasn't going to put my thoughts into Talia's head. She had to think for herself. It's interesting, though, that her belief system started to change as she neared thirteen.

Growing up, Talia would tell me that some of her dreams came true: sometimes she would dream that an event would occur, or that this or that would happen, and then it would actually happen, quite soon after her dream. She asked me if this was possible. Of course it's possible, I told her, because it's happening.

Well, those prophetic dreams of hers led her to start thinking about the possibility that there was more to us, more to the universe, than just our bodies. There was something else going on. Talia started to ask whether people could see into the future, and she said if that was possible, then maybe there were souls, or some sort of energy that enabled people to do this, since our regular bodies alone didn't have this ability.

Then Talia asked if I thought there were spirits all around us that we couldn't see but that animals could. This thought was spurred by Laura, an animal communicator I hired to "talk" to one of Talia's horses, Justinian, who sometimes acted up with her. When Laura "spoke" with Justinian and we heard what he had to say, both Talia and I were amazed. That conversation actually changed her understanding of the world and started Talia on an entirely new path.

When Talia realized that the animals were thinking, talking, and communicating with people and other animals, she concluded there must be a consciousness beyond the body. If that was the case, maybe there were spirits and other consciousnesses all around us, living in a world we couldn't see but that was truly there.

It was at this time that Talia asked about parallel universes—what were they, and did they exist? I told her I wasn't able to give her any real answers about whether they existed or even what they were, but there were scientists, quantum physicists, who were studying that very topic. Now that Talia was able to put a title to something she was so fascinated with, she decided, on the spot, that she wanted to become a quantum physicist instead of a patent litigator.

This revelation, as I called it, happened two weeks before Talia left on her final trip to Panama. It's amazing to me that right after Talia's mind opened to the possibility that there's more to the world, life, and the universe than what we see, she left her body and moved on into the realm she was so curious about.

The timing of Talia's death may seem coincidental, but, looking at the psychic preparation she went through and her interest in topics well beyond her years—even beyond most adults' thought processes—it seems that she was preparing for her next adventure: her life in the afterlife. In fact, now that I have the benefit of hearing from Talia from her new life, I realize that is exactly what she said had happened.

It's extremely hard for me to think that Talia was only supposed to be here with me for a short time. But when I heard from Talia herself that her life here was in preparation for her life there, I realized that my life's purpose was indeed to raise Talia in a way that prepared her for where she is now. Her true purpose in the afterlife is to learn and to transmit the messages and lessons found in her communications to me and to the world. I have no doubt that I helped her accomplish that purpose. In Talia's own words:

*My mom was very, very mindful of how she raised me. Do you see the fruit of it? She WILL share in the rewards of the fruit of my life, of my "being" who I am, because she was instrumental in it and a central part of my life. . . . It has nothing to do with my great honor of being her daughter or of my affection and LOVE for her as my mom. My love for her has no bounds and she knows this. I said before you had to be outside to see in; there are much deeper truths here than is readily apparent.*

*The life I lived WAS for an example. I didn't know it then and if you would have told me I would have laughed. I wouldn't have thought that was necessarily true, but it was necessary and it was true. You may not always know whom you are influencing. I influenced people then without noticing it. You're always more than you think you are. But to know that is to trust it, that you can be used in a divine way whether you know it or not.*

I know in my heart that because Talia was educated in a way that enabled her mind to remain open to the possibilities of the universe, she was able to enter the next phase of her soul's journey at a very high level. This has allowed her to learn the lessons she has learned so far extremely quickly, and it has enabled her to move close to the source of all things. This high level of learning in the spirit world is what allows her to know what she now knows and, even more important, it allows her to be able to communicate that information to us here, in this earthly realm.

**Talia; a few of her self portraits**

# "G"

T HE WORDS THAT FOLLOW in the dialogues (Part Two) are Talia's words—actual statements and information downloads that she has spoken and entrusted to my close friend "G" (abbreviated for privacy).

Who is G? He is my very dear friend. Since G was a young boy, he has been in touch with his instincts, always able to listen to his strong gut feelings. As he got older, these visceral sensations became stronger, and the more G listened to his body, the clearer and more definite his instincts became. Visions flourished as he began to hear and see the spirits. He also developed the ability to read people; at one point his ability to see auras around people was so pronounced he actually asked for that ability to go away, and it did.

Talia is not the first spirit G has heard or spoken to, but his communications with her have broken all barriers previously known to G and, according to Talia herself, the depth of the communications between her and G has never been reached before in any other spirit communications. The spirit world is in awe of their communications. As Talia said:

*Some won't believe it, but this hasn't been done before, not on this level, not in this depth. People have been communing with "spirits" ever since there were people in the physical realm, but it hasn't been recorded in this depth before. Mostly it has been bits and pieces.*

What is it that enables G to hear and communicate with Talia? As Talia says in the following pages, anyone and everyone is capable of communicating with spirits, but most people are simply unaware of this. Unaware because of the belief system they were raised with, were indoctrinated with, or have chosen for themselves. In some cases, their lives are just so wildly busy that they are unable to hear any communications that might come their way. Their minds are never quiet enough for the spirits' voices to be heard. But regardless of the many possible reasons for not being able to hear from loved ones or others, G is open and able to.

How does G hears Talia? Does he hear her voice in his head or does it come to him from the external world? What does her voice sound like to him? How does he feel when he is speaking with her? Is he in a meditative state or walking around doing normal things when he hears her?

Well, G has heard Talia, felt her, and seen her while in all states of being, from the very relaxed, quiet place that some would call a meditative state to going about his daily routine and all of a sudden hearing Talia speak to him as if she were standing right beside him. Sometimes he hears her actual voice; sometimes he hears her thoughts in his head. It does not matter what he is doing or how hectic his life is; what matters is whether or not his mind is clear and quiet.

If G's mind is quiet, he can hear and communicate with Talia regardless of what his outward world is like. There was an instance when Talia spoke to G while he was working. He heard her voice so loud and clear that he thought the people he was with could hear her as well. At other times, while in a meditative state, he has not only spoken to Talia but has seen her, touched her, and spent time with her. There are no rules as to how, when, and where G speaks with Talia. It just happens.

Talia's communications with G started off with a simple message meant to help me and evolved into hundreds of hours of actual discussions between G and Talia. Practically every word between them was carefully transcribed at the time they were heard or spoken. The date and time of each talk was kept from mid-April of 2007 forward.

Before April, Talia's communications with G were short and sporadic. We had no idea they would evolve into what they have become, and so, in the beginning, G simply scribbled some notes about his and Talia's communications for the purpose of telling me what Talia had said. Once we realized that Talia was not going to stop talking to G, and that their communications were growing deeper and more extensive, G started to keep a journal of all of their talks. As she spoke, he wrote; as he thought or spoke, he wrote. The conversations were written as they occurred.

In places, especially at the very beginning of the dialogues, these conversations will seem jumpy or disjointed—maybe even confusing—and sometimes rather personal. But in order for Talia's message to get out to the world the way she presented it, I wanted the conversations to be communicated the way they were originally written down at the time they occurred. I did not want to alter anything to make the text read better or to clarify or interpret what she said. I wanted to leave everything as close to the original as possible, with very little editing. So basically, what you'll be reading is exactly what was said and how it was said.

The only change I've made to the actual conversations was to remove personal information between G and Talia or between Talia and me. Not everything Talia said was meant for the world, and you will read her words to that effect in some of the communications where I left the original dialogue without deleting anything.

The reasons for some of the disjointedness are twofold. One, in the beginning Talia and G were actually learning to communicate with each other. Talia was new to multidimensional communication and was still learning how to communicate with us here. The ability of the spirits to reach us, and for us to hear the spirits, is a learned ability, which Talia speaks about in the dialogues themselves. Though everyone has that ability, the skill needs to be fostered, for us and the spirits. So as both Talia and G learn to communicate with each other, the conversations evolve and become much clearer and easier to understand.

Second, some of the questions G asks Talia are answered by her before he has had a chance to actually formulate the questions in words. Therefore, he has written Talia's answers, but they seem to come out of nowhere, when in fact they are Talia's response to G's thoughts, which she read before he even knew he had those thoughts.

There are things said and people mentioned that will make no sense to you, the reader, so where we thought it necessary to help clarify Talia's message, we have added some narrative, trying not to interrupt the flow of the dialogue. There is not always a reason or a lesson in the talks. Some are just friendly chats. That is part of what Talia wants the world to know: conversations between the spirits and us are as normal and natural as any conversation two people here would have. Communication with the spirit world does not have to be about meaningful, spiritual, "important" things; it can be just a conversation about day-to-day stuff. Just a hello or brief words of encouragement.

Yes, many of her messages are lessons—some of them deep and meaningful lessons about life and the universe—but not all of her messages are obvious. Some are very subtle.

But all of them are from Talia, who received this information from the spirit that moves through all things.

Regardless of whether you believe G is speaking to Talia in the spirit world or not, these writings are still important and intriguing messages that stand on their own, so please be open-minded when reading them.

So here we go. Here are Talia's words (in italics; G's words are in regular text). And here I am, Talia's mom, the previously devoted non-believer, now a believer. I don't doubt, I don't question, and I am not even a speck skeptical that the following words are indeed Talia's words, spoken by her to us, from where we call Heaven.

# PART II
# The Dialogues

# January 23, 2008

*The Day of Talia's Memorial*

*Tell my mom I'm OK.*

Talia?

*Yes, tell my mom I'm OK.*

OK, I will when I see her.

*TELL MY MOM I'M OK!*

I will, I promise!

And G kept his promise to Talia. That day, at the luncheon after Talia's memorial—her Celebration of Life, as I called it—G finally got me alone and told me that Talia was OK. When he said it, I looked at him and said, matter of factly, "Yes, I know."

G wasn't sure I understood exactly how sure he was that Talia was OK or whether I thought he was just placating me, so he said it again. "No, really, she is OK."

"I know!" I said, making it clear that I too knew. Taking a chance that he might think I was "out to lunch," I decided to tell G that I had been speaking to Talia through Rebecca, and that Talia had been giving Rebecca many messages for me letting me know that not only was she OK, but that she was with her dad and doing great.

G was excited and relieved. That's when he told me Talia had been communicating with him directly. That same night, once G got back home, he called me. Talia had another message for me.

*"Tell my mom that she will be OK, and that she is being healed."*

G continued to hear from Talia off and on for the next few months. As time went on, her messages to him and for me and others became longer, and their interactions, their dialogues became more detailed. What follows are those conversations between G and Talia that began in April 2008.

# April 2008

## *April 20*

Talia, you had a perfect life.

*It is even more perfect where I am now. My mom is being healed.*

## *April 21*

**6:20 AM**
Good morning, Talia.

*Good morning.*

Are you here?

*I am with my mom.*

*I like yellow. But my mom does not know that.*

Why did you tell me that?

*Just because you would know it was me and to tell you to believe yourself.*
*Always believe yourself.*

Talia telling G that she liked yellow was very significant
for me. Not because I didn't know about Talia's liking
the color yellow (I didn't), but because just a few days
before her telling that to G, I had put a bouquet of yellow
roses in her room. I feel that by Talia telling G she liked
yellow, she was really sending a message to me that she
was aware of the roses I had put in her room and liked
that I had done that.

## April 23

————◈————

Talia, sometimes I don't know if this is you or God speaking to
me, you sound so similar.

*We are so completely in agreement there is hardly any separation at all.*
*Where I am is more beautiful than where you are by like a billion times.*
*Where I am it's perfect, perfection. There are horses here.*

I want to be where you are.

*You have things to do. Nobody knows all the things you know . . . believe*
*in yourself . . . At Thanksgiving I saw who you were . . . that is why I*
*liked you. I told my mom I liked you. I wanted to talk to you too. . . .*

Talia is referring to Thanksgiving 2006. G and another
friend joined Talia, our family, and me for dinner. While
sitting at the dinner table, G had a very unusual, very
spiritual experience. He saw Talia in the spirit, in front
of a bronze-colored door, holding it open and looking

at him, inviting him to go through that door. What was beyond the door was blackness. She was wearing a crown on her head, and he heard a voice in his head, who he felt might be God, tell him, "She will be with me." At one point he looked down and noticed that he seemed to be wearing WWI clothes, although this vision disappeared the moment he acknowledged it. While G was having these visions, which I was unaware of, I noticed he had a strange look on his face. I just figured he was a bit uncomfortable sitting between two people he didn't know at the table. Little did I know!

So why didn't you talk to me more that day ?

*Convention. I could tell you were unconventional but I didn't have those words at the time. Tell my mom I love her.*

She knows.

*Just call her and tell her I love her. What is more important than that?*

### *April 29*

Good morning, Talia.

*Good morning.*

G was thinking about the Ginko tree that Talia's school had planted in her memory, and the words that were carved into the stone planter around the tree. Most of the words had been chosen by a friend of mine and me, with the help of Talia herself. I asked Talia to confirm to me, through Rebecca, that the words we had picked were the right words to use; she confirmed that she liked them and okayed them. Unfortunately, a couple of the words were changed by the parents group at Talia's school, who were paying for the memorial. My friend and I were not happy about that change, nor was G, and though Talia was not thrilled about one of the words that ended up being used, she understood why the parents group had chosen it. What follows is Talia's discussion with G about these words as G thought about her school and the special tree.

*That's why I want them to know about my life, to lead them to this place. That's important. My words are much better than their words. Much more precise and meaningful. They that are going to be touched by them, changed by them, will be. So why water them down and make them harder to understand? Did you not think I had help; they were born of the Spirit.*

*To bring forth fruit. To change people's lives. Their intellect traps them. Their thoughts circle in their heads until it becomes a prison. I want them to be free. There's nothing better than freedom.*

*My mom showed me how to be free, to think your own thoughts and not what people tell you to think. If you're thinking someone else's thoughts how can you be free? It's your birthright to be free. It's a yearning everyone has. So why would someone make a prison for others to live in?*

That's a good question.

*Yes, it is. We are all created in God's image. Is God free? He's only bound by his word. Which has no boundaries. People are enslaving each other on the earth. This needs to stop. Most of them aren't even aware of what they're doing to themselves and each other. He was sent to free you. Listen to Him; He is truth. The truth will set you free.*

That's what you've been trying to tell people all along.

*It takes responsibility and some work. That's what they fear. Which is another prison.*

*Tell her—Mom—wisdom is the PRINCIPAL THING; therefore, get wisdom and with all your getting, get understanding. Knowledge puffs up, but love builds up.*

## *April 30*

*I liked green tea. I had fun that day we tested the tea.*

> G thought this was a strange thing for Talia to tell him, but when he told me she had said it I knew exactly why she had mentioned it. It was a message for me! Talia and I both loved green tea, and one day we decided to do a taste test of many different types of green tea. There are dozens and they all taste different. So we tested about fifteen different types and found out exactly which ones we liked for hot versus cold tea. We had a lot of fun that day!

*Are you going to talk to me today? You don't have your pen!*

> G realized that he had no pen.

*Tell you what, I will walk with you and you do whatever you do.*

*Tell Mom to be patient; that is one thing she is learning. Tell her that her prayers have been answered.*

Just then the phone rang. It was me, calling G.

*That's Mom—she will ask you what's going on.*

G answered the phone.

What's Gunther doing today?

*Gunther can tell you all about me, though he's had a hard time coping with it all.*

> Gunther was Talia's and my German Shepard. At the time of this conversation with Talia, he was "dead" and with Talia in spirit. Right after the crash, after Talia "died," Gunther was so upset that he actually made himself sick. So sick that he died! When Gunther was sick I had Laura, the animal communicator, talk to Gunther to try to find out what was wrong with him, because the vets were not having any luck with their tests. Gunther told Laura that he wanted to be with Talia, and that he was going to be with her. As he was dying Gunther told Laura that he saw Talia surrounded in light and that Talia's hands were reaching for him.

*The things that I've told you are true. Every one of them. It's a waste of time to doubt.*

G was doubting whether he was hearing Talia correctly.

*Frankie will be all right; she just has to find her place of peace. It lies within her; she just doesn't know it yet.*

*My mom is excited about our communications. She just doesn't understand why she can't do it yet but she will. It's hard bridging the gap of the flesh.*

*I didn't hurt at all (the crash). I was received up into His arms and welcomed, then sent back to help Frankie.*

*My dad and I are closer now than we ever were. He thanked me for my prayers for him. He understands everything now. We have fun together.*

During the years before the crash, Talia's relationship with her father was not easy for her. Just a short time before the crash they were beginning to regain their closeness. So when Talia speaks of her being closer to her father now, it's very reassuring to me that, one, she and her dad are happy together, and two, that she is indeed speaking to G.

*My mom will be all right, He promised, and she will grow in understanding. I'm glad you have your pencil now.*

G is laughing.

*Laughter works well, like a medicine, and you need it sometimes. I'm glad to give it to you and that's what HE sounds like laughing through His people. He smiles a lot. He is all the fullness of the Godhead bodily and Pure Love without end. He is Everything and all there is without end. He is everything and ALL there is. There are so many words I want to say, and I'll keep talking with you.*

*Kim will be fine.*

Why did you use her name?

*That's what I was told. By HE who cannot lie. Who is All Truth, the Light of Lights. In whom is no darkness nor shadow of turning. These words are truth. I love you.*

You know I love you too.

*Thank you for taking my message. For your time.*

Talia, you know there's nothing I'd rather do.

*I know that and that's great! You know you can't share this with everybody—they'll think you are crazy.*

I know that.

*But I'm glad you're sharing it with whom you do.*

My pleasure.

*Mine is greater.*

*Tell her—Mom—that her prayer was answered today. She's always heard. Don't worry about the small stuff.*

*About that goddess stuff . . .*

> G was thinking that he now understood why so many cultures believe in gods and goddesses. People in the past must have spoken to various spirits in the way Talia is speaking to him, and their words, like hers, were so powerful they were made into gods and goddesses. He thought that Talia would have been called a goddess too.

*I can't really argue with you because we're all part of Him, so in that way it's true, but I don't really feel like a goddess, not the way you think. But I do absolutely feel AMAZING! World without end! There are so many truths, so MANY paths but only one true GOD. "Everyone will find ME in the end."*

*So much here is unspeakable. It's difficult for me to try to explain, to put it into words. This is a language beyond words.*

# May 2008

## *May 2*

---◆---

*There's no use telling you things you already know. But there's a difference knowing something in your **head** and KNOWING something in your **heart**, in your spirit, in your soul, deep down.*

*You have an unction from the HOLY ONE and you know all things. I'm just here as a reminder, a counselor through HIM.*

*You knew I was always going to be a teacher.*

No, I didn't know that.

*Yes, you did.*

Yes, I did—I remember now.

*Of course you do; you saw it, you just forgot.*

Now I remember, the power of the flesh.

> G realized that he did remember knowing somehow that she would someday be a teacher.

*The flesh has no power but the power you allow it to have.*

I can't argue with that.

*No, that would be stupid and you're not. So when you act stupid realize it's just an act. You're just acting stupid.*

*I always make you laugh.*

Yes, you do, every single time.

*I'm glad. It's such a tremendous pleasure helping others; if people realized that there wouldn't be so many problems. The payback is stupendous. Pass that on to people: THAT never fails.*

Thank you, Talia.

*My PLEASURE.*

*Thank you for being open to me. Mom too.*

I've got to go back to work.

*Yes, I know.*

*Your tears do water the path you walk. And they are counted.*

> G was reading a poem with those words in it when Talia started to speak again.

*Share the poem. That's a good line, and true. She'll like it; it'll touch her—Mom.*

*There are many deceivers; she'll hardly notice them. She's growing in wisdom. She asked to. Ask and you receive. People so overcomplicate everything. The truth is always simple and easy to understand once you boil it down.*

## May 2008

*Tell her my time there was Divine. She did everything in a perfect way and was—is—an awesome mother. She got me here perfectly.*

*You don't have to edit my words—she'll get it. Tell her to take care of HERSELF now. She's building something awesome now.*

You tie it together so . . .

*You can't help but tie it all together; it's all tied together.*

You know you're blowing my mind here.

*That's OK.*

You know I wish I could record this.

*Yes, wouldn't that be great.*

This is bizarre.

*Not really, this communication with the spirits has always been going on.*

I have to go.

*I know.*

*I don't have a watch.*

> G thought that was a strange thing for Talia to say, since you do not need a watch in the spirit, but when he told me about this I laughed because Talia never wore a watch unless she absolutely had to. She hated watches. G didn't know this about Talia. She didn't like the feeling on her wrist or the constraints of time. When Talia says these kinds of things to G, it's great because it not only confirms to G that he really is hearing Talia, it confirms that to me too.

*Go.*

I don't want to.

*You have to.*

*Go. I'm going out there with you. Of course I can be more than one place.*

**6:00 PM**
Thanks for the help today.

*Any time. I learn from what you are doing. I learn from everything you do. That's where the gods and goddesses came from, from us helping. We have to help; we're compelled to do it. How could we not?*

You could refuse.

*No, we couldn't. There's only joy and peace here, a peace so profound it surpasses all understanding.*

How long will you do this?

*As long as you need it.*

How did you become so wise?

*HE is.*

*The light brings understanding. The Light illuminates the words to quicken the understanding to that which is beyond words. Keep listening. I love to talk.*

*We—Mom and I—use to walk and talk a lot. Ask her what we talked about. That will make her think. RE-MEM-BRANCE. Tying all the pieces together into one coherent whole. Piecing it together. Nothing is really apart except for the contrast of the separation.*

## *May 4*

**7:00 AM**

*Write.*

What do you want me to write?

*Just keep writing. You're going to find out some things about your life you need to know. You don't need confirmation or validation, you just need the truth and the truth bears witness to itself. Your heart always knows what's true. You'll not be led astray. I know your heart.*

**8:04 AM**

Thank you for being my friend, Talia.

*THANK YOU for being mine.*

**2:28 PM**

Hi, Talia!

*Hi!*

How are you doing?

*You know how I'm doing . . . perfect. All things are yours. Spirits, this dialogue, this conversation, all things. Tell her—Mom—all things are hers too. Just tell her to claim it. She can do it.*

## *May 5*

---

**7:08 AM**

You're more alive than anyone I know.

G was thinking about some friends of his.

*I know . . . . They are cut off from their life, from the truth, by their thinking. As you think in your heart so are you. You are what you are by what you think.*

*People know. They sense the truth; it's just out of reach for most. What a source of frustration. Some people kill themselves over it, others live in desperation over the contradiction of being judged and misunderstood by what they are and what they are perceived to be. People should love one another and not judge one another. There is one judge; He does not need help.*

I have no doubt.

*As you shouldn't. Your lack of time is the push you need. You will never have enough of it there. Redeeming the time . . . The days are evil, in a manner of speaking.*

Talia, is there anything you don't know?

*Yes, lots.*

**12:45 PM**

While on his lunch break G thought about how excited he was about his communications with Talia. He thought about how the meanings of the words are so deep and multifaceted—there is no explaining it. He realized that what Talia had said, "They that are going to get it will get it and they that are not aren't; people that are not going to get it are not for a variety of reasons," was true mostly because people have prejudged her words and are closed off to them and their meanings.

So what do you think?

*Well said. See, Mom said you were articulate.*

G was laughing about this.

*I'm glad I can make you laugh. When you read this to Mom she'll laugh too.*

*I have not changed much, only grown.*

G started thinking about the color of green, noticing it more, and thought about the meaning of green as a color. He thought it meant growth.

*Yes, that is the meaning of green, growth. That's why I was pointing it out, and yellow and brown and gold. Any questions?*

And grey?

*Wisdom.*

And brown?

*Wisdom too.*

Why?

*Grey speaks of the maturity of wisdom.*

And brown?

*Brown speaks of being grounded in it.*

Let me ask the right questions.

*You can ask any questions you want.*

Inspire me.

*You already are. You should put this in your notebook.*

> G was writing down the discussion about colors he was having with Talia on a little piece of paper, since he was outside and not near his notebook.

OK, why?

*It's easier to keep track of.*

Let everything be done decently and in order.

*Yes, that is a good saying. Why do you do the things you do?*

I thought I was asking the questions.

*Yes, but that's a question you should ask yourself.*

You know you blow my mind.

*I know . . . I'm blowing your mind out of proportion, expanding it.*

I feel unworthy.

*Everybody's worthy, they just don't know it.*

*Think about "singleness of purpose."*

I'll have to think about that.

*Yes, please do.*

You totally blow me away.

*Thank you, I'm glad you think so.*

You know how humble that makes me?

*That's a good thing. The world could use a lot more of that.*

*I have to slow down to talk to you.*

> G knew she meant slow her vibrations down.

I'm glad you do.

*We don't mind, we just wish more people would listen.*

*There's not anything that's not interconnected with everything else.*

Is that true?

*That's absolutely true, and it can be proven. By mathematics, by inner vision, by intuition and by the Light. The Light that lights the life of all men. WHATEVER questions ANYONE has, the answers are there if they seek them.*

*You're going to find some things out you never dreamed of in the near future.*

I don't know if I like the sound of that.

*NO, it's good stuff.*

> G was thinking about how tired he was feeling.

*It does weary the flesh; your vibrations have to be faster. The whole universe is on a vibrational level for balance to maintain harmony. That's why it's easy to tell if someone is out of harmony; their very essence is not vibrating in harmony, and vice versa. It's a very delicate balance.*

*You're right about nothing being a coincidence and everything means something, although some would contend with you about that out of ignorance.*

Wow, that's pretty heavy.

*Yes, it is. That speaks of the Art of Life. That's an art you should study.*

I will.

*I know you will . . . I don't waste time.*

Thank you for sharing your wisdom with me.

*Thank you for listening . . . time to go.*

I know.

*Go ahead and go. I'll help you. You will feel me.*

### May 6

G was thinking about what I told him Gunther had said. Guther had told Laura that Talia liked to play games. Laura asked Gunther, "What kind of games does Talia play?" Gunther answered, "Like chess, only with people."

**8:09 AM**
Talia, I can't write down everything you say to me.

*Of course you can't—that would be unrealistic. There is a message here for certain people to MOVE them in a CERTAIN direction. It is like a chess game and it's a grand game, to move the pieces TOGETHER in a CERTAIN way. I KNOW what I am doing. It's far beyond this world.*

> G was thinking that he cannot possibly describe some of the visions he has while talking to Talia, or the meaning of some of the downloads he receives while talking with her.

*No, you can't describe what you're seeing any more than I can describe what I am being. Just let them flow. . . .*

You know what this means to me?

*Do you know what it means to me? This is IMPORTANT. Don't get hung up on the images and ashes.*

> G was looking at the small vial of Talia's ashes that he carries with him.

*They are pointing to something much grander. Your thoughts are more real than anything else there. They truly create. I see your questions forming before they are FORMED; that is why nothing's hidden that shall not be revealed. You are a tool to be used by the Creator. Fight a good fight, not against what IS going to be regardless. Of course he can use ANY THING to get his work done, but it's his good pleasure to give you the kingdom. This is a free gift to all who will receive it.*

Why are you doing this?

*I wanted someone to tell me these things when I was there but nobody did, even though there were some that could. I was astounded when I got here and found out the truth of the simplicity of it all, the obviousness of it all. It's a treasure not so well hidden. Why do people deceive themselves?*

Why do they?

*They bask in their pride. It's like a wall that blocks them off from the truth, from the obvious. After a while that wall is just as real to them as anything could be; remember, your thoughts create things.*

*When the sages talked of illusions, it was something REAL as illusions. It appeared to them as illusion because they knew that thought and methods of thought could dissolve what was perceived as real. Well, it IS real but created by the mind—that's about as REAL as it gets. So when people CHANGE their mind they change what was created by them so that it appears as an illusion. It's not an illusion, it's real. So when a person decides to change it, it changes and THAT is real.*

*That's a small blurb on the nature of reality. The nature of reality is living real. BEING true and speaking the truth out of a sincere heart CHANGES things. Alters the nature of reality: that's FLUID. It is not static. That is why they (scientists, true seekers) can't pin it down. It's not somewhere; it's everywhere and nowhere at once. It IS the true nature of being.*

Talia, you know I don't know these things.

*I know you don't, that's why I'm telling you! But you have perceived them.*

Yes, I know them but I don't know them.

*Yes, not in your head, few do, but they need to. This could change everything.*

Wow.

*Yes, that's MOM upside down. The revelation of the light of truth NURTURES, causes one to grow, straight and true. That's the change no politician can bring you, that's the change no politician can even promise you.*

*Yes, I am in POSITION to do this now; like the queen, I can move ANYWHERE.*

Which piece am I?

*Sometimes you're just a pawn. I don't mean that in a bad way, but you know that's true.*

I know.

*Now you're aware of it.*

Thank you. I can take your criticism.

*It's not criticism; it's just the truth. The truth will set you free, G.*

Talia, this is so absolutely awesome!

*I know, it's a true message of change.*

*I LOVE my friends and I'm sorry my going hurt them. It has purpose.*

> That day I had been speaking to one of my friends, a parent of one of Talia's friends from school. We were talking about the kids being hurt and missing Talia.

**9:22 AM**
> G thought about Talia's photos, covering them from the sun . . .

I don't want you to fade.

*I won't.*

*My ashes were my essence there.*

What does that mean?

*Think about it.*

Do you want me to carry them with me?

*Yes. My mom does.*

*She—Mom—asked for this to happen today. Tell her not to get distracted by the things of this world.*

**10:40 AM**
*Everything is tied together. It is one of the mysteries of living the ART of LIFE, realizing it's ALL tied together. World of One. You see how that truth has been twisted by the "well-meaning fools."*

Talia, there is no way I can express my thanks to you.

*I know, you don't have to pound your point across to me—I got it.*

OK.

*OK, now we're on equal terms.*

What do you mean?

*I mean, don't make an idol out of me. I'm not one.*

Is this chastisement?

*No, not at all, just a fact.*

Well, I've got to adore you.

*That's OK, I adore you too.*

Really?

*What do you think, I'm lying?*

No, I don't, you are cracking me up again.

*I know.*

I notice you always seem to get the last word in.

*You want it?*

No, not at all.

*That's you honoring me and I'm worthy of it.*

I know you are; why are you telling me this?

*It just came up in conversation and I'm putting things in perspective. You're worthy of honor too you know.*

OK, I've never had an experience like this.

*Me either.*

So it's new to you?

*Of course. Again, I'm putting things in perspective.*

### 12:43 PM

*Truth: sometimes it hurts, but it does bring relief, and healing if applied correctly. Don't be harsh or brutal with it.*

*She's—Mom's—been trying to get in touch with you.*

Why, did she call?

*No, the other way.*

> I have been practicing sending my thoughts to G tele-pathically, or spiritually, as I try to open up and learn to hear Talia.

Oh. I tried to call earlier. Why didn't she answer?

*She was busy.*

I thought so before I called.

*You KNEW so. Your emotional excitement spurred you too. Be careful with that.*

Your precision amazes me.

*Yours amazes me.*

Thanks.

*You're welcome.*

You're always so polite, so respectful.

*That is the way I was raised. Respect is a secret some people don't get.*

I know, a lot of them.

*That's one thing I tried to teach my friends.*

How many got it?

*Some. Respect opens doors where you would otherwise be turned away.*

I'm going to have to buy more notebooks.

*Looks like it.*

> G writes down all of his communications with Talia in
> spiral bound notebooks.

## *May 7*

---⬥---

### Early AM
*You're not going to talk to me today?* ☺

Good morning.

*Good morning . . .*

I wasn't going to.

*Why do you think I repeated how important this was?*

I figured because it was important.

*Yes, it is, but also I knew you would reach a point where you wanted to back off. Three is the number of power. Notice how many times I repeated things three or more times.*

*Let's talk about your training. You think it was a coincidence?*

There are no coincidences.

*Exactly. You were being prepared for just such times as these and what is to come. Your prayers have been answered; you're NOT deceived. I agreed and prayed with you on that. You know how to walk in this realm, but you must have confidence and faith. You do need some time to sort things out. This is a delicate balancing act. Do all the things you think you need to do because you need to do them. Go ahead.*

### 3:25 PM
*You have to be OPEN to me; fear stifles.*

*Self-pity doesn't serve you well. What have I told you that was wrong?*

Nothing. I just wanted to be sure it's you.

*Be sure, it's me.*

So now what?

*You're not really believing right now.*

No, I guess not. I'm sorry, Talia.

*That's all right, you need time.*

## *May 8*

### 9:00 AM

*Why do you doubt yourself?*

The way I was raised?

*Could be some other factors.*

*There are a handful of people that will receive this, a small remnant. They are the ones we are moving to accept this. The others will have to get it on their own. That's a circuitous route and time consuming. I'm trying to move them on a path of righteousness. That's the right path: to move them ahead. There are multiple levels and depths of understanding in this. The future is not written in stone; most of it's decided by the decisions of man. To accept or reject are close decisions.*

*You have a unique path of blending flesh with spirit into a harmonious whole.*

Some will absolutely reject this as heresy and the ramblings of a madman.

*Do you think you're mad?*

No, just a little crazy though.

*No, you are not crazy, but it sounds like it sometimes. Sometimes it takes an extreme to create a balance.*

## *May 10*

## 5:57 AM

You've got my attention, Talia.

*I told you not to edit my words.*

I wasn't sure it was you; it seemed too obvious. I don't want to add anything that's not you.

*That message goes much deeper than the obvious, it has to do with who she—Mom—is. It's all for the good. You're learning too, and if you hadn't left it out we wouldn't be discussing it now.*

> Talia is referring to something she told G about her death. She told G that it was her time to go. He didn't tell me that because he didn't want to hurt me.

What's the deeper meaning?

*The deeper meaning is really just as obvious, just deeper. You worry as much as anyone sometimes, so be careful who you judge or you will end up doing the same thing. Forgiveness is the key to freedom. You must forgive everyone no matter what they did to you or what you think they did to you. A key component is to be AWARE of it. Sometimes you can judge without being aware. What people do to you maliciously or inadvertently is for your learning, so how could you hold that against them. Also for me it was personally for her [Mom].*

> Talia was referring to the message that it was her time to go.

*I have so much AFFECTION for her—Mom—I could never fully explain it. So you see, if it [the crash] hadn't happened, we wouldn't have gotten into this because you wouldn't have been as open. You also do that to yourself. Your deeper self knows what you need, so when you think you're "screwing up" it's you doing it for your own good, for your own growth. See how exquisite that is. You cannot lose because EVERYTHING works TOGETHER for good to them who are called according to his purpose. You are called to the purpose; can you deny it?*

No, I know that.

*I know you do so don't deny it.*

Well, I really thought I screwed up by not telling your mom.

*You really didn't. You just left something out for a purpose—now it's right in front of your face.*

Wow, you really do know what you are doing.

*Told you.*

What about leaving the bracelet?

> I had a special bracelet made up that says, "Talia, Pretty Much Amazing," which I gave out to all of her friends.

G also has one that he wears, but he forgot to put it back on after he took a shower, and he felt bad.

*You knew you were forgetting something.*

I know, why did I do that?

*You'll see. You think you "screwed up." That was you teaching yourself again. You are your own best teacher.*

Am I going to ever quit being an idiot?

*You've never been an idiot, but you have acted like one before. People can easily convince themselves they're something they are not. They are made in the Creator's image. That inherently gives them the power and ability to create; therefore, they are in a manner of speaking the masters of their destiny. If people realized this they could change the course of their lives into anything they want. Most people don't know this. Most wouldn't even dream it was possible. Nothing is impossible to them that believe. Most people cannot receive anything so simple as ultimate truth. They think it must be complicated and ornate. That again is mainly their pride forming that perception so they can take credit for something that is essentially a FREE gift. You do not work your way into the kingdom; it is a free gift. It is gifted to everyone. That takes the eliteness out of the equation so that their own pride and selfishness can't accept it. They want to "do it on their own," and it just doesn't work that way.*

Thanks for the notebooks.

> Talia had a pension for writing and always had a hidden stash of empty notebooks ready to be used. I gave them all to G to use for his communications with Talia.

*You're known here.*

Really?

*Yes, really, you're real. We can't say that about everyone. Some people just aren't real, not even to themselves.*

That's sad, but I know it's true.

*Yes, it is "sad but true." It is no coincidence that that saying is so prevalent, because it's so prevalent. You've got to go to work.*

I know.

*A labor of love.*

This is.

*It all is, or should be. Do all that is in your heart.*

I never saw that deeper meaning of that until now.

*Now you do.*

Thank you VERY much.

*Thank YOU very much.*

**7:08 AM**

The biggest regret of my life is not having had more time to spend with you while you were here.

*Don't regret it. It's for a reason. Everything HE does is perfectly reasonable.*

Why won't she—Kim—answer the phone?

*It's for a reason.*

You crack me up; you are killing me!

*I'm killing what you don't need.*

### *May 11*

———✦———

**AM early**
*Tell her hi . . . and I love her. This is her first Mother's Day without me.*

*You have questions.*

Nothing springs to mind; I don't know where to start.

*You want to ask about my life, of how I got this way.*

Yes, I did.

*He knew me before the foundation of the world—before all you know to exist was. He fashioned me from an image of pure thought, from pure and holy love, and established me a place in his kingdom. We ARE all an aspect of God, of his holy vision. Remember he said without a vision the people perish. This is His vision for His people that without they perish—His vision is that none would perish, but that all would come to Him, to come back to their very source of being. He clothes himself in darkness to show the contrast of his light. HE said, the Kingdom of Heaven is WITHIN you. And yet are not people clothed in darkness? Aren't most blinded to the very light within them, that surrounds them?*

*THAT'S God clothing HIMSELF in darkness. He lives WITHIN you; his pure essence is the ONLY LIFE there is; that is why he said, "You can do nothing without me."*

This is mind-boggling.

*Well, it shouldn't be. He said you have the mind of Christ, who understands all things. The only confusion is by the darkness that surrounds you. He is the light; he is the illumination of all understanding. All you have to do is receive Him, not reject him, and believe him. The simple truth to set you free.*

*No analyst will figure this out; it's a gift to receive.*

*Most of the things of this life are like charms to keep you idle, to keep you from receiving this gift.*

*When you see through this illusion to the meaning of these things, these "charms," it always points back to the truth. People receive these messages all of the time but most ignore them as a stray thought or their imagination. Yet when they begin to awake they realize that these messages are messages of truth. Now it's their decision to pursue this or fall back into darkness and sleep. MY message is to wake people up, to awaken them to a glorious new world that is THEIRS to walk in. THAT'S when they will be fulfilled. ALL that they want is here and all that is here can be realized within them.*

I'm . . . stunned, really.

*That's what the truth does to people. It's stunning. There's SO much more.*

*This book has something to do with everything. The interconnectedness of ALL things.*

How can we apply this to our lives?

*By believing.*

## *May 12*

### 6:07 AM

*People are afraid of what they might find out about themselves. What others may find out about them. It shakes the foundation of their perceptions, about what they believe. It's intimidating for them to accept that as truth. It would change their thinking, of what they are comfortable with. To accept the "true tracks" would be to accept all that the Spirit teaches as real, for it is a doorway to the spirit.*

"True tracks" is a term used to describe the floor of tracks left by animals or people while walking. The true track is where you find the individualization of the one who left the track.

*That vision [at Thanksgiving of Talia holding the door open] you had WAS my invitation into the mysteries of the spirit. Am I not revealing them?*

Yes!

*Yes, and revelation entails responsibility. Who wants more responsibility?*

But how can I . . . ?

*Baby steps. Your enthusiasm pushes you too fast sometimes. You must present it as they can accept it. If they are not willing to take baby steps it's no sense trying to get them to run a marathon. How many did you get in Martial Arts?*

One.

*Yes, one. Sometimes one is enough. Sometimes one is all you need. Remember, God is one. Even the master himself only had twelve. Twelve out of all the people he met and touched and healed. Only twelve willing to follow him, forsaking all. And what did he promise them right up front? That he had no place to lay his head. That's that truth that astounded them. That's the hook that caught them. And they WERE fishers of men because he "made them to become." That's awesome, isn't it.*

Yes, that's awesome; you said you had to be clever.

*Yes, clever in the spirit. Look what those twelve did. Talk about a place of honor, well, they really do have it. THE rewards are UNSPEAKABLE.*

## 7:50 AM

*Why do you think he said, "Thou shall have no other gods before me?" Because there ARE NOT other gods before Him. They are all false idols who only cause pain and misery. He came that you might have LIFE and that more abundantly.*

*You HAVE been chosen for this. You think this was haphazard? I have the most amazing counselors here.*

## 3:24 PM

Who's going to get this?

*There are many factors involved in whether a person gets this or not, but primarily it's a personal decision, a choice. The dynamics of choice can never be understated. To climb to the mountain top you have to WANT it. I also made wise decisions during my life; that's how I got "here."*

*This is fun! I love communicating with you.*

G thought as he walked, *I don't want you to take over my life.*

*Don't worry, I'm not going to "take over your life."*

G thought she said that kind of cheerfully; I think it was kind of funny to her.

It was funny to you, wasn't it?

*Yes, it was.*

## May 13

Talia, I don't know where to start.

*Just write.*

I feel like I'm full of questions.

*You are. You're a person to help us get our message out.*

Direct me.

*Direct yourself.*

*Yes, I was having fun. I wouldn't have told you if I wasn't having fun.*

*My life went perfectly. Perfectly.*

*You CAN'T write down everything I say to you or show you.*

*You're getting glimpses of the whole message. I could show it to you in an instant but you couldn't contain it; the natural mind would wash it away. Everything I say to you isn't a message for the masses; I'm your friend. The message for the masses isn't even a message for the masses because the masses aren't going to get it. The message is for those who ARE going to get it. The option for freedom is ALWAYS before your face.*

What about the three Native Americans?

> Some time back, while G was driving across the country, he had had a spiritual experience in which three Native Americans came to him and told him of their plight while still here on earth.

*The three Native Americans were like a conference call to you. They were not all in the same place on the same level. They are poor souls whose circumstances of their life created much bitterness in their lives. They wanted an audience to air their grievances and you gave it to them. It will take much "time" before they move on, but they will.*

*You sensed the grandness of the message. That is as a full-course meal. The milk, the meat, the drinks, the dessert—everything of a splendid full-course meal on earth, only lasting and much more. Some prefer a buffet, to pick and choose. Some choose to settle for the crumbs from the table. Some just are not going to eat at all. AND it's a free meal, except for the effort.*

*My being seated at the head of the table at Thanksgiving WAS a symbol of royalty and of my being able to move anywhere.*

*All the circumstances of your life too, have put you in a position to receive this.*

*So you see, your life too is perfect in every way.*

*Thanksgiving, I saw you then as being a bit tattered and war torn, a glimpse of your grief and struggles and something far beyond that, the light of life. You seemed somewhat a contradiction; a part of me was just as fascinated with you as you were with me.*

Just as?

*Just as.*

> G had a vision while sitting next to a pond of seeing a
> silver dolphin statue with children around it. At about
> the same time G had the vision, I was having a discus-
> sion with a sculptress about a fundraising project she
> was working on, whereby parents of departed children
> could sponsor a small dolphin sculpture, to be included
> in a much larger installation, in memory of their child.
> But G didn't know about my meeting until later that day,
> and then he questioned Talia about his vision.

So what about the dolphins, Talia?

*The dolphins are not about buying "me" a dolphin. The dolphins are
about redemption, about redeeming the time, about the joy of life,
about the fellowship of play—it's about working together in harmony.
Dolphins ARE like children. Dolphins are intelligent—but they never
misuse it. There's much more about the dolphins, but everything isn't to
be written, but just to know.*

Well, again it's nice to know I don't have to write everything.

*No. Anyway, all the books in the world could not contain it all.*

*All the things people tell you are not true.*

Why are you telling me that? I certainly know THAT'S true.

*You certainly do, but you certainly do not know who is not telling you the
truth at times.*

Is this a warning?

*Yes, it is. Just beware—be aware.*

Thank you for the heads up.

*That's good—keep your head up.*

G thought about alertness. Looking to the SOURCE.

*Yes, the LIGHT. The light is a sword of truth that cuts through the darkness in any direction you wield it. It's being used right now to cut to your heart to illuminate your soul to the truth of life.*

Then G thought about how he receives downloads of information from Talia and how he then just knows, like osmosis.

*The absorption can be instantaneous or VERY SLOW. The light quickens. The light was EVERYWHERE the day you visited [at Thanksgiving]. You saw me moving in wisdom.*

Absolutely, yes.

*You see how many people saw that?*

Kim and I got a glimpse?

*Pretty much.*

*And yet there were seeds planted. Everybody pretty much knew something was going on. You can only be conscious by what light you are walking in.*

This is . . .

*Yes, the whole meal deal. I'm a part of everything.*

THAT is an astonishing revelation!

*Yes, so are YOU. So is everyone.*

*NOTHING hidden that shall not be revealed.*

*The time of subliminal messaging is over! We want to get it out there.*

You were reading my thoughts a while ago when I was thinking that you seemed to be everything, when you said to me that you were a PART of everything.

*Yes, why did you think He said, "Love your neighbor as yourself?" You are ALL a part of the WHOLE, the Oneness of God and all there is, because there ISN'T anything else.*

This is earth shattering!

*Yes, the dust of the earth in whom is the Breath of Life. Why do people look for miracles? Tell them to look in the mirror. The negative connotations people look to others with is the darkness speaking, a misunderstanding, the voice of darkness. Give it no place. Your spoken word creates.*

*This is one of the most important works you will ever do.*

I love so much being a part of this.

*You're a part of everything.*

*To know the length, the breadth, the depth and the height. Nothing is hidden that shall not be revealed. Your face is the face, or reflection, of God on earth; why do you think a smile goes so far?*

I wish I could give people the understanding of what's behind those words.

*Only they can do that. There are people using these powers for ill, but it will never really work.*

I didn't think so. Nice to know.

*Yes, it is—that's why I told you. Their threats are empty.*

You know I love this bracelet.

G is speaking of the "Pretty Much Amazing" bracelet.

*I know, and not as a physical object but what it symbolizes and the direction it points.*

When will this all stop?

*Never. You heard the franticness, the way the world "ties your time." You've been given time to do this.*

I've noticed throughout this you've mentioned time a lot.

*That is because it's important. It's important to understand it. Time is flexible. It CAN be distorted and bent, just as gravity bends light. Light is NOT a constant. That's man's understanding of the physical nature of light. That's incorrect as they will discover (some know already but they want to prove it). A direct KNOWING is always more efficient than scientific proof. Scientific proof is merely a demonstration of what is already known.*

I know you are not dogging science, are you?

*Not at all, but there are "two sides to every coin." There are actually infinite sides to everything, but we won't get into that.*

Do you know how much I appreciate this?

*Yes, I do, completely.*

Who is the little girl?

While visiting Talia in the spirit, G saw a little girl with her. When he told me this I immediately remembered that Rebecca, the medium I speak to Talia through sometimes, saw Talia with a little girl as well.

*I'm her teacher. She is a beautiful, beautiful soul.*

I saw that.

*What bothers her most is she is so missed. She's dealing with it wonderfully; she's coming to understand.*

What is her name?

*Names are not important, unless you want power over something.*

That has so many meanings on so many different levels.

*Yes, it does.*

Mind-boggling.

*Your mind needs to be boggled from time to time to get the trash out.*

Never heard it put like that.

*Shaken around, part of the "great shaking."*

*I will show you things to come. Now we're going to get it right. Now's the right time. For everything there IS a season. Now it's my great honor to be a part of this.*

You told me a while ago to stop here and do the things I need to do. We kept going. What's with that?

*Do all that is in your heart. Time doesn't mean much here. Time is important THERE. What would you rather spend your time doing, because you ARE spending it.*

*The power of the Spirit is beyond words. Indescribable, undeniable. It is Living.*

*Time has many parallel dimensions running at the same time. That's how you experience two experiences at once. Future and present now. Past and present now. Future and past in the PRESENCE now. It's all one, the oneness in Him. He is, the only reality that is. Time as you experience it is an illusion. The separation of things and places is an illusion as you experience them.*

*You see how the frustration arises, the discontent? You see how the peace rules in your heart, the absolute contentedness? It is a matter of consciousness, or walking in the light of the fullness, or walking the darkness of despair. Walk in the light—it's so much easier.*

This whole experience is beyond anything I ever imagined.

*And YOU have a vivid imagination!*

I'm sure a lot of people will say that when they read this.

*Oh, they will.*

### May 14

**5:37 AM**

*Opportunity is a doorway. Sometimes you have to get through it quickly. That's where the quickening comes in. Without it you'll not have the necessary speed to manage it or even recognize it: that the doorway is even there or exists.*

Can you open it yourself?

*Not by the works of the flesh; the quickening is a gift of the spirit. Seizing the opportunity is a choice, a decision of the higher Self, who always knows what is best. That's why most people miss it; they're not in touch, in tune with their higher Self.*

I've heard of the higher Self but never really thought in those terms.

*I just want you to know it exists. That's the self I told you to believe in. I was blessed on earth to be in touch with my higher Self so that my steps were directed. That's why my confidence was so high.*

> G was thinking that Talia was answering his questions even before he had a chance to form them into words.

*Yes, I'm answering your questions during, before, and after you ask them. Here there's no time. It's all at once, therefore I have to slow down to more clearly perceive the timeline or this wouldn't make much sense at all. You get it?*

Yes, I think so.

*As you think, so you are.*

Then I get it.

*Bravo, excellent choice. See how easy that was?*

Not a problem at all.

*There really are no problems, only lessons to be learned.*

So problems are another misnomer?

*Pretty much.*

*I'm influenced by the people around me; everybody is. You're influenced by the company you keep. Walk circumspectively, not as fools, redeeming the time.*

There's time again.

*Yes, bend it by the force of your gravity; you know how to do that.*

I've done it before.

*Yes, from the ground up, the foundation, blended with the quickening of heaven.*

Hardly anybody's going to understand that.

*No, hardly anyone will. That's something you have to experience; the intellect will never get it. But you've done it and it was a sign to others.*

*She—Mom—is a very special person whose eyes have been opened to this. Greater love has no man than this.*

> Talia is referring to my shattering, and my new unwavering belief in the afterlife.

*He's already given everything. Past, present and future are yours. You CAN change the past. That's another misconception people have. That you can't change the past. Well, if it's all happening at once you can certainly change the result of the past, and I've already given you the key: Forgiveness. That's the ultimate gift anyone can give another. The healing properties of that are truly beyond description.*

*Remember your friend who called you true blue? He saw into you. He asked for that because you were a mystery to him and he had doubts about you. That put his mind totally at ease. Remember the light in his eyes when he told you? That was the light of life. That was the light of revelation. That was the true light in him bearing witness with the true light in you. Face to face. No man has seen God's face at any time. To see God's face is to die. To die to the Self.*

*To die is to live.*

*Help others. How can you help others when you're tied up, wrapped into yourself.*

I guess pretty poorly.

*Yes, poorly—you've not been given poverty.*

*Who is the King? Who do you serve? Yourself. Or are you friends with the King?*

I'm friends with the King.

*Exactly, now live like it.*

I'll try.

*Don't try, do.*

*That's why we're getting into a more detailed description of some things here. For others the simple truth will suffice. No matter what we do here, some are just not going to receive it. Some will look for an ulterior motive. That's the darkness in them looking, groping really, for the darkness in others.*

How can you help them?

*They have to help themselves. God will not remove your choice, but he will certainly compel you in the right direction.*

Why do people fight so hard against Him?

*That's their flesh struggling against death. They know that to see Him is to die. They love their lives, no matter the misery. It's all they know, so they think that's all there is. They know it's not, but that shakes their very foundation to where it seems to them like they are dying. Like they are going to lose their lives. But He said that who loses his life will save it and he who saves it shall lose it. The fleshly mind can't handle the contradiction of that so they fight against it. It's all very simple, see?*

Yes.

*We could get into it, the myriad of facets of it, much more deeply, but if they didn't get that, more is not going to help them either. They have to help themselves. They ARE the masters of their own destiny.*

Strict rules.

*No, the laws of life.*

G was thinking about art . . .

*People who don't understand artists, don't understand themselves—we're all creative. The Art of Life encompasses all of the arts. Gives place to creativity. True art also inspires. I was interested in art.*

*The deception is because of scrutiny. The truth can bear any and all manner of scrutiny; a lie cannot bear the light at all.*

Boy, this is good stuff.

*Isn't it though.*

This whole art thing is fascinating.

*How could it not be?*

Good point.

*It's a perfect point. It's a perfect pointer, a perfect pointer to truth. Why do you think people are so in awe of art? Because it's inspired, it inspires, it's inspirational. It can TRANSFORM people to other levels. Haven't you been inspired to push some of the things you do to the level of art?*

Yes.

*That's being inspired, doing something inspirational even before it's art. That's the goad you need sometimes to take things to another level. Remember what your dad said, that "there's an art to everything." That's a truth he speaks a lot. He's right; there IS an art to everything. You've had a hard time understanding people that don't want to make things into an art, to take it INTO the next level.*

Yes, I have.

*They have just as hard of a time understanding you. ART is not easy without the flow, the flow of the Spirit, which is the only true inspiration. Without the spirit you can do NO thing. Remember, He said "be ye perfect." A lot of people have struggled with that. Even become discouraged. He was told, "These are hard sayings Lord; who can hear them?" What a question! Now THAT is a sacred question. Man's spirit strives to be perfect; it's imprinted within them. That's the struggle, that's the fight, and yet when he yields himself to Him, the fight is over. He said, "Take my yoke upon you, for my burden is easy," because he LIVES within you.*

Boy, there's more to this, isn't there?

*Of course. A LOT more.*

*It's the very crux of the nature of man, of ENTERING INTO REALITY.*

Wow!

*Yes, wow indeed.*

Thank you for this.

*You're welcome, always.*

> G was thinking about having dinner with some friends . . .
> eat, drink and be merry for tomorrow we die. . . .

*That's THE ANSWER.*

Point being?

*Look at what you just said. The answer to every question is within the very question itself. It's not so much a riddle as a solution when you look at it, see it, perceive it on a multi-dimensional, holographic, spherical-like structure. You got that revelation before.*

Yes, but I didn't have the words, and when I tried to explain it, people looked at me like I was crazy, like I had two heads.

*That's because only the light reveals it. Words without it are just words, dead. "Everything is spherical," you said.*

Yes.

*And how could you expect them to understand that, without the light of direct knowledge?*

Yes, I came to realize that but it was still frustrating.

*Well, now we have some words to explain it somewhat. You think this is deep. And it is, but these are baby steps. Don't you think I feel some frustration here trying to get this ACROSS?*

I thought of that, but I didn't really think you would be frustrated there.

*We have the same feelings here, just more perfect. You can feel my frustration now trying to get this across in words that are easy to be understood.*

Yes, and I've been a bit frustrated at times.

*This is not an easy task. There IS a great gulf. This takes tremendous energy. The good news is that there's no lack of it. Tapping into it is a trick I'm trying to teach.*

Trying?

*Trying means exactly that, it's trying. We're DOING it, but it is trying. There's a difference.*

This is phenomenal.

*Yes, it is. All things are possible to them that believe. You see some of the multi-level lessons behind every word, which you can't express. That's the main source of your frustration. Remember, art is true expression. Expressing yourself on that sublime level is true art. No matter WHAT you are doing.*

*The more you get rid of what you don't need, the more you can "have" what you do.*

**11:47 PM**

*All that frustration you are feeling from them—your friends—already is the strivings of the flesh. "Much ado about nothing," as it were. Don't get caught up in it; it will just bog you down. "Be ye separate."*

Yes, it's hard to really take it very seriously.

*Take YOURSELF seriously. YourSELF knows all things and is moving you into another plane. Where all things are possible. Seize the moment.*

I never saw it like that before.

*Yes, capture the moment.*

Time again.

*It's a large issue. It's a real paradox. There's a lot of it, there's not enough of it, and it really doesn't exist. Some places anyway. Every place is at the same place. It's been placed in Him. That's the only place that is.*

*Time is a creation of thought, of higher thought, to create "separation" for learning so we can bring it all back together again into an even more perfect whole.*

You're not going to tell me that's not heavy, are you?

*No, I'm not. How astounded do you think I am daily?*

Oh, man, I can't wait to see you.

*We just talked about time.*

## 1:14 PM

*You see how we change here just like we change there. IT has to do with PURPOSE, with inspiration. The pieces I'm moving are to change them. Change them for the better. To inspire them to change. Anyone can change—it's up to them. Yet art inspires. To express your true self is to express the light of life of the only Being that is, the Creator of all things. You are created in His image, from perfect thought. That makes you a creator. You CAN change things. How many times have you heard it said, "Can't change it." That's a lie. And as it's been said, a lie is but for a moment, but the truth endures forever. Seize the moment, break the lie by the sword of the light of truth. The Kingdom of Heaven suffers violence and the violent TAKE IT by force.*

*To be a child of the King is your birthright. There's no earning it. You're BORN to it. I was born to it from the very beginning.*

*J's dream; I put it in a context he understood.*

> Talia's Uncle J had a dream that Talia called him on his cell phone. He heard the ring, answered it, and heard Talia say to him, "Hi, Uncle J, I am all right." When he woke up he knew deep in his heart that it was really Talia that had come to him to speak to him. G then spoke to Talia about the dream J had had and then told him about this discussion with Talia.

*Thank you for confirming that to J.*

## 9:20 PM

What about that sense of urgency you have?

*That's my knowing: there's not much time there. Time is short—how many times have you heard that?*

A lot.

*Yes, and it's true, time is always short there. It's just not long enough to do all the things you need to do. That's why I'm spurring you on, in a manner of speaking. You're tired, weary.*

Yes.

*You need sleep. When you're this run down it's hard for us to communicate.*

You had a lot more you wished to communicate today.

*Yes, I did. Don't worry, we'll get into it in depth. My message will not be detoured.*

So we're going to stay on the right road.

*You bet.*

*Of all the misconceptions, death is the biggest myth of all.*

## *May 15*

Personalities.

*The differences are intricate, sometimes subtle, sometimes very contrasting. There's a reason: it's learning the difference. If you're in total agreement what difference does it make?*

**2:43 PM**
*You don't have to edit anything I say, but you can distill the message.*

*The world needs more than sages now, it needs a revolution.*

> Talia, I feel like I want to explain what you are saying to people, but sometimes I do not even know how to explain it to myself.

*You can't always explain what I am saying, any more than I can always explain what I'm saying.*

*This message is far beyond me.*

*If the eye is skewed it skews your perceptions.*

*You must have an intense desire, a passion even to achieve enlightenment. What many consider enlightenment is merely knowledge. Enlightenment is walking IN the light.*

*If your perceptions are skewed, soon that divergence from the path becomes greater, eventually leading to deception and even delusion. And yet if you yield yourself to the path of light, it becomes the perfect path in which you can do no wrong. The perfect law of life is the law of liberty in which there is no law.*

*This is the way of wisdom. Few know this path. Did I not say "there would be few to find it"?*

> Talia, this did not sound like you. It sounded like another spirit.

*This is who I serve. There's many personalities, all aspects of God. God is infinite, unending; He expresses himself through us. That's His art.*

### May 16

**1:03 PM**

Talia, who were all of the sages? The wise men?

*Truly the sages, as you call them, are one, even though they are far and few between.*

*No one knows them but they know each other.*

*He reveals himself in His creation. He is countering the dogma of the day by revealing Himself in this way.*

Talia, I wish I could spend more time with you.

*The time you spend with me will be returned to you many times over. This is giving in its most perfect sense.*

Whoa!

*Whoa! We're just getting stated.*

## 5:32 PM

*His art, his children, the apple of His eye, is what is closest to His heart. There is an expression, "Seeing through the eyes of God." That's a perfect expression.*

*One worthy of all attention.*

*This is to SEE all things.*

*This is to KNOW all things.*

*This is to BE as all things.*

*This is to be all things to all men that some might be saved, delivered from all darkness and delusion.*

*The choice to enter INTO the darkness results in an end result of delusion. Is not this the definition of insanity?*

*Choose to enter INTO the light. For in the light are ALL things seen.*

## *May 17*

**6:46 AM**

*What fellowship has light with darkness. The darkness will never and cannot understand the light. So don't resent the message; be thankful for it.*

**11:20 AM**

*Every day there's options, choices set before you. Rarely is the case "I had no choice."*

*The decision is yours. Wisdom is profitable to direct. (You don't have to be a part of a game you didn't subscribe to).*

*He that is offended for not getting their own way is going to be offended anyway.*

*In all labor there's profit, but beware of entering into a game that doesn't edify.*

*Putting yourself first is often putting everyone else first too. This is meat that you're understanding. Be not darkened.*

**12:37 PM**

*You should notice a common thread, a common theme throughout all this. That's ONENESS. A cohesion of the whole. The dark, negative, repelling force is just as much a part of bringing all of the parts into a cohesive whole as its counterpart.*

**4:35 PM**

This is a labor of love.

*For me too.*

**6:43 PM**

We talked of gravity before.

*What is always present along with it?*

Magnetism?

*Magnetism is a force that both attracts and repels. That's one explanation of the conflict you see between people for no apparent reason. It's also an explanation of the mysterious attraction some feel for one another. This in people is a spiritual force. The reason I started with gravity is that it's the foundation, rooted and grounded in love. Love is a force that NEVER fails.*

*Another reason I began with gravity is to let you know you have it. It's a force you can learn to use for good. Meditate on the meaning of this and it will become clearer. All things are possible to those that believe.*

*Electricity has both positive and negative aspects. All this is tied together in a most intricate manner. Suffice it to say that all things are held together by the word of His power.*

**7:20 PM**

*You're weary; you have to be up for this.*

Sorry.

*No need to apologize—recharge.*

How?

*Time off, rest.*

## *May 18*

**7:53 AM**

G thought to himself, *I am going to be late for work.*

*This is not just a job; it's an adventure for you. It's an opportunity to touch people in a positive way.*

Good morning, Talia.

*Good morning!*

Your excitement is contagious.

*I hope so.*

*She—Mom—slept well last night. She has good instincts but her head gets in the way sometimes.*

Why are you telling me this?

*So you can pass it on. Today will be a good day for you.*

It doesn't feel like it now.

*Goes to show you can't always go by feelings. Go by truth. It's time.*

I know.

*It's important to know the times.*

Wow.

*Exactly.*

It's already turning into a good day.

*Told you.*

**1:10 PM**

My air-conditioner quit.

*It's for a reason.*

What is the reason?

*It's all hooked into the system. Don't rely on their system. See how comfortable it is? It's not about just being lulled to sleep, it's also about comfort. See how fast your body adjusted? It's also a choice of a mental direction to acceptance.*

Thank you, Talia.

*No problem.*

**2:33 PM**

*Your whole attitude changed that situation for good.*

### May 20

Talia, it's been a while since I have heard from you.

*Yes, it has. You've been very busy and you had to recharge.*

I don't know where to start.

*There's really no starting and stopping since there's really no time. It's just continuing.*

That's the way it feels.

*That's the way it is.*

I feel like hardly anyone's ready for this.

*No one hardly is. That's OK, their hearts are being prepared. This is to receive the message of life in the continuance of all things. All things will continue whether they are prepared or not. Preparation is yielding, not resisting the Spirit.*

*I lived my life as an example; I didn't know it at the time. Now it's clearly manifest. That was the spirit living through me. The credit is all His and to reveal His glory upon the earth. He does this continually.*

Oh, wow.

*Oh yes, an instrument for His glory. He alone is worthy of praise and honor. He alone is the One true God.*

How can I know this is you?

*How can you not?*

Well, it's just sometimes I hear your voice so clearly I know it's you without a doubt, and sometimes it's indistinct.

*Know thyself. That's my answer.*

### *May 21*

**7:00 AM**
Good morning, Talia.

*Good morning. You still haven't grasped what it means, me being a part of everything. You still haven't grasped what it means, you being a part of everything.*

*The spider takes hold with her hands and is in king's palaces.*

*I said the violent take it by force.*

*People are largely opposed to violence. Generally they should be, but that's not what I am speaking of here.*

*He rebuked the wind and it stopped.*

> There were unbelievably strong winds that night. G yelled out to the wind to stop.

*You rebuked the wind last night and it slowed, paused, according to your faith. According to your faith so be it unto you. According to your faith so you hear. According to your faith so is the level of your understanding. Without faith it's impossible to please Him. Every man's been given a measure of faith. Use it. Nothing's more pleasing than pleasing Him. Why would you hinder your own faith? Why do you fight against yourself? There's no winning warring against God. He is and all there is. Walk in faith.*

I believe.

*Yes, the devils believe and tremble.*

What are you saying?

*I'm saying the lessons are never-ending.*

I'm missing something here.

*You're missing a lot. You want to get to the end. There is no ending. The race is not to the swift or the battle to the strong. You think you're strong;*

*there's only one source of strength, and you know where the speed comes from. You've studied it. Time to study some other things. All things are yours. You know where you got the speed, now get what you need. Strength is easy to misuse. Remember you have to be clever. Being clever is being in balance. If you're out of balance you fall.*

*Yes, you got that before but you forgot—that wasn't very clever. Take hold with your hands like it was hidden treasure, because it is, absolutely.*

You seem not so chipper today.

*There's a time to be chipper and a time to cut to the heart of the matter. Now's the time to cut to the heart of the matter.*

*I'm exactly who I was yesterday, only more.*

That's beautiful.

*Exactly.*

*We know who we are. If you knew who you were almost all your so-called problems would disappear instantly.*

How do we know who we are?

*I've already covered that, sufficiently. Remember I said don't judge. You're just as dense as those other people, just ON another level. That doesn't make you ANY better than them, just dense on another level.*

How do you change this?

*I've already covered that too.*

*You see in His light; you see light. If you do not walk in the light you have, how can you see more light? That's where the lessons seem to end. They don't; they are just waiting for you to catch up.*

*Yes, I said we had work to do.*

I'm sorry, Talia.

*You don't have to be sorry to me. You can't hurt me. You can concern me, but you can never hurt me.*

Thank you for your patience.

*Thank you for yours.*

I'm very grateful.

*That's good, being grateful is good but being graceful is better. Yes, only by the grace of God.*

You are FILLED with this message.

*Yes, I am. It's like being pregnant, pregnant with Words of Life. I WILL deliver this message and it WILL bring forth life.*

Singleness of purpose.

*Perfectly.*

*You're getting more undense by the moment. This doesn't have to be a long process—it can be instantaneous.*

You couldn't speak a lie if you tried.

*There's no way I could here. There's no way to even try. That's as senseless as anything you can think of. The whole foundation of everything that means anything is truth. Nothing is more absolute, no footing firmer. The truth is the beginning and the end, yet it has no end or beginning— that's the truth. How could it ever be otherwise?*

I don't know.

*Yes, you do.*

Nothing can hold this message back, can it?

*No, nothing will. Nothing is NO thing; how could it hold it back? Nothing doesn't even exist. You see my meaning?*

Yes.

*Nothing can ever work against you because nothing is no thing. It doesn't exist except as a construct of your mind. There is nothing to come against you but yourself. When people get this the wars will end, whether between nations or within us.*

*My life will never end, and I will succeed in all I do because He always gives me victory. This is something I know as an absolute concrete fact.*

*This is something you should confess for yourself. Because it's TRUTH and the TRUTH never fails.*

I know truth and love are synonymous.

*Yes, that was revealed to you before; now walk in it.*

Time to tighten up.

*Time to tighten up by shaking away the loose ends you don't need. Time to burn away the dross by the light of truth.*

This seems easy.

*It is! But again it takes a great effort, intense desire. This intensity is the flames I speak of, the flames of truth, flames to burn away all that can be burned so all that is left is that that cannot be burned. That's all that is going to remain anyway. Ashes to ashes, dust to dust—all that is left is perfection, which is really all there is. So you see, "be ye perfect" is not such a hard saying after all.*

*He will "cause you to become"; your job is to let him. SEE—not so hard after all.*

"After all" means something.

*Yes, it does.*

*After all the work and there's none left to do, the real work will begin.*

I don't really understand that.

*No, you don't; it's not time.*

But it's prophecy.

*Yes, it is.*

"It's not time" means more than it looks like too.

*Yes, it does. Things, meaning EVERY thing, are leading you in the direction you need to go. Did He not say, "My sheep know my voice and they follow me and another they will not follow?"*

Yes.

*Do you think the Shepherd doesn't know what he's doing?*

No . . .

*No is correct—yes he does.*

*All the promises of God are "yes" and "so be it."*

I . . .

*Don't worry about the future or dwell on the past. These are lessons that are happening right now. All things are yours. You don't really get that.*

I'm trying.

*IT'S trying. Stop trying, receive it! It's only the separation in your mind that confuses. Oneness of mind is no confusion. If you know how fragmented you were you'd be devastated. But your faith, your higher Self, KNOWS he's bringing it all together and cannot fail; therefore, it's true that you shouldn't be too concerned. You're helpless to pull yourself together anyway. It's enough to know he will cause it to happen.*

**4:18 PM**

OK, I keep seeing diamond shapes everywhere.

*The diamond is a stone born of fire, intense pressure, and gravity. It's VERY hard. And a stable currency. But primarily it bends or channels light to reveal colors that symbolize moods, personalities, ministries, mysteries, and clarity. Also the beauty of purity. These things—the beauty of purity—cannot be had or manifested without fire and intense pressure, also polished by the hand of man. See you are part of this.*

**5:17 PM**

You told me once that animals talk there where you are, but I didn't write it down.

*No, because you thought it was too outlandish and might compromise the credibility of the message and dialogue. You've since learned otherwise, and everything I've said to you has been confirmed in one way or another. It's all part of the process.*

Did I disappoint you?

*No, because I know the answer as soon as I think it, although it's not quite like that either. This really can't be explained in earthly terms.*

I heard you say that colors there were much more vivid.

One of the things that Talia told me when I went to see Rebecca was that the colors where she is are much more vivid, vibrant and amazing then they are here, with us.

*You KNOW they are! And crisp. You can smell them, hear them if you want to, and even taste them. There's nothing like it, not in your shadow world.*

Wow.

*Yes, wow!*

*There it takes faith, here it just is. There are really NO words I can use to describe it.*

That sounds . . . wonderful.

*WONDERFUL! It is, a WORLD of WONDER beyond ANY description.*

Then it's no sense asking you to describe it.

*No, no sense at all, but I could describe elements of it to you.*

Please do.

*ANYthing you want is here. It just IS and there's no end to all you can do here. One is NEVER tired but filled with hope and a sense of Purpose. The expectations burst forth! There is no within or without. There is no sorrow, pain or suffering. Those are like a distant memory. Your life on earth is SO short, no amount of suffering could ever compare to the glory that is to be. The deepest doubts you ever had there you could compare to a mist, hardly noticeable. Here you are totally, absolutely and completely fulfilled. No thing missing. Everything that there is, is here to behold—beauty unspeakable. Words just fail.*

**7:16 PM**

G was looking at Talia's ashes.

*I'm not there!*

> G and I were discussing reincarnation. I was curious whether or not Talia would tell me if it was real or not, so I asked her and then asked G to ask her about it.

**9:47 PM**

Reincarnation. Is it real?

*It's real—if you want it to be real.*

## *May 22*

**9:43 AM**

*I know you have things to do. I know you have your life to live and so do I.*

> G was walking, thinking back to when Talia told him that she was going to give him a special ranking, when Talia popped in . . .

*You're thinking they are physical skills. The physical skills are a doorway to the spirit.* **THIS IS THE ART OF LIFE.**

**12:50 PM**

How's the little girl?

*She's doing better, much better. She's accepting all things as they are.*

I can feel your excitement and joy.

*I LOVE this—His—work! We HAVE to use multiple meanings, otherwise it would make no sense.*

Because it's a multi-dimensional universe?

*That's right. That's one reason.*

I wish I had the words to describe you.

*There are no words to describe me. You could describe elements of me or partial aspects of me, but to define me is to define the universe. To label all that is. How could you ever label all there is? But to describe ANYONE would be the same. We are all made in His image, so to describe anyone completely would be to describe Him, He who is ALL there is.*

Yes! Wow!

*Yes, wow!*

*That's actually a pretty good description.*

I'm cracking up here.

*I know you like to have fun, so have fun with it.*

I am.

*I KNOW you are.*

    G prayed for Talia.

*That was . . . very powerful.*

I . . . didn't know it worked both ways.

*Yes, it does—it works ALL ways.*

That was like spontaneous combustion or something.

*That's the Spirit bursting forth for truth.*

*The times of these forced games are over for you.*

> Doing what other people expect of you, acting the way people expect you to act.

Good.

*Yes, indeed. You were chastised for your boredom many times. They pushed you to have interests in something that had no interest for you. You resented that because of the force used to remove your choices. Often when you were inspired to the correct choice you were chastened. This was very discouraging for you. It also showed a blatant lack of respect for you as a person. If the authorities, the ones you were taught to respect, showed none to you, how could these teachers expect any response but rebellion. That's your free spirit rebelling against the spirit of slavery forced upon you. You saw most just go along. You saw a part of them secretly hating it, and yet they went along with the program AND were rewarded! Now there's something to puzzle a child. You saw what really was versus what was happening, and it didn't add up. As a matter of fact you were called stupid for speaking about it and not going along with it.*

*Where are these people now? Some will read this and weep—with realization; some will read this and laugh—with disdain.*

And some will just scratch their head.

*Most won't read it at all. Their minds have been made up. That's the process of this world: to make up your mind.*

So you'll fit the program.

*In a manner of speaking, yes. But if one can see through this delusion one will be free. Men's hearts yearn for it—that's why it's spouted off so much—but it's mostly used to bring them back into bondage. That's the power of this world. The power to break the human spirit, to crush the spirit is to have a defeated foe, a slave. The truth WILL set you free.*

*Now, think of that alternative. That's what they are doing! Using the law to bring into bondage. Matters not whether it's a religion, a government or an individual; the process is the same.*

This is perfectly cogent to me.

*Yes . . . never depart from the simplicity, which is IN the anointed one! He came to set you free! He came to GIVE you life, liberty and that MORE abundantly. You see, the counterfeit cannot compete.*

Talia, is this you?

*That doesn't matter—it's US.*

*Of course I'm here. Time to remove yourself.*

Time to remove myself?

*Yes.*

What do you mean?

*Just exactly what I said.*

Remove myself from what?

*Remove yourself from the kingdom of darkness—and all that entails— into the kingdom of light.*

That's where the true Authority is, isn't it?

*Yes, of course. You CAN do anything, you know.*

Is that true?

*Of courses it's true. One should compromise when one should. And one should not compromise when one shouldn't. That's pretty obvious, isn't it?*

Yes . . .

*You asked about compromise and that's my answer.*

This could go on and on forever, couldn't it?

*It will. I'm growing up into Him IN ALL things; so are you. Just wanted you to know.*

Well, that's a confidence builder.

*Yes, it should be.*

That seems like such an everyday answer, and yet there's multiple meanings again.

*Yes. Always.*

There you go again.

*I'm always going.*

You're having fun here too, aren't you?

*Every bit and much more.*

That's great.

*Yes, that's Great!*

Talia, the queen.

*I don't need a servant, yet to serve me would be to serve the King; a friend WILL work just fine.*

That's an awesome answer!

*How could it not be?*

Guess it could not.

*No, it couldn't. EVERYTHING here is awesome!*

*You know, unless people look at this as a hologram, the meaning will be obscured. Their minds have to be open to do this. Most minds have been forced closed by what we discussed before.*

That whole timeline, like writing "before" or "earlier" is so odd. It's hard to write it because I know it's happening in the NOW.

*That's just to frame it to help them understand. It's exactly what we were talking about—viewing this as a hologram—holographic point of view. The One Point sees all points of view. To perceive this, one must see it. This has nothing to do with the natural eyes. This is also far beyond what the natural intellect can grasp. The truth has no conflict with itself; that's man's ideas thrust upon it.*

What am I going to do with this discussion, this journal of mine?

*You're going to publish this. Great is the company that publishes this.*

Help me.

*You already are.*

Double meaning again.

*Oh, many more than that.*

*I'm among a Great Company now. We WILL fulfill our purpose.*

There's some hard times coming.

*There's some interesting times coming for sure.*

**7:24 PM**

*You have an explanation?*

About what?

*About it all or pick a subject.*

Talia, I don't want to do this if it's not you.

*You don't want to do this if it is me.*

Why not?

*Your personal pride. You fear it. Just burn it away with all the rest. Remember what I said: fear stifles. Now write it down.*

Why?

*Because I asked you to.*

All right.

*Of course it will be.*

*You think you know no one else will see through it like you do. That's an assumption you shouldn't make.*

I just don't think there's very many that will be able to connect the dots.

*That's true, there won't be very many, not for a while, so . . .*

So I guess you know what you are doing.

*Of course I do. I've already told you that. I know EXACTLY what I'm doing.*

I'm just trying . . .

*What's with the struggle? That's funny; you're trying to explain it to yourself!*

I'm sure there's a lesson here.

*I showed you the lesson I'm attempting to get across here in an instant— now you're resistant.*

No, I'm just trying to explain it to others.

*No, you're trying to explain it to yourself, and it's YOUR explanation. You've GOT to see the humor in that.*

Yes, perfectly.

*That's where it comes from. You're afraid of acceptance. That's silly really, that's just a concept. You know this—why the insecurity? Let me tell you one reason for that. It's because you've judged other people for striving so hard to gain acceptance. You know that's a vain show. That's why I said BE AWARE of judging others because when you do, you do the same thing yourself. So when you see people making mistakes, if you can correct them, correct them; if you can't, then do not judge them.*

Thanks for the correction and the explanation.

*You're welcome. Now let's get on with it. There's a lot more to do yet.*

Ok, here it is.

> Talia asked G to read a poem. He didn't know why, but
> he did it anyway.

*An Explanation* (7-24-04)

I'm roaming on the landscape of a dream
My surroundings dark and unreal
Sparks of passion devour
Pass like mist of the moor at twilight
Words fail to tell
As they so often do
Ask again
"Explain it to me"
You explain it to me
What you fail to see
What you can't hear
What you won't smell
What you refuse to touch
What you choose not to understand
What you decide to deny
What for you is impossible to feel;
All our hearts are fashioned alike
So for a change
Explain it to me.

*Now if you read those words it encapsulates everything I've been saying.*

Really?

*Yes, really.*

How so?

*Read it again.*

    G reads the poem again.

I really do think I see what you mean.

*Of course you do—every time you read them it's clearer. Hidden in plain view.*

*Science is struggling with understanding the non-locality of mind, but the answer's right there in the words you wrote, not to mention mine. Not to mention mine. The answer's still revealed in yours. The hidden wonders of the revelation of creativity. It's right before anyone's face wherever they go. They just don't see them.*

Why?

*They are blocked off for nearly any number of reasons. But . . . mostly pride. I mean, "What would people think?"*

Talia, what if I get up there and you tell me half of this stuff was not you but me?

*Then we'll have a big laugh.*

You don't seem to be worried about being misquoted.

*I'm not worried about anything. I AM concerned about getting the truth out.*

I KNOW *THAT'S* you.

*That's why I said you sometimes must walk by faith, not by sight and not always by what you KNOW to be true. We all know in part but we will KNOW even as we are known.*

I know that's you too.

*Pleasant to know, isn't it?*

Yes, it is.

*The promises of God are the promises of God. Remember that when you must walk by faith. Anyway, you and I are One. In Him. How could we ever be wrong?*

That's a heavy statement.

*That's a statement of fact. So, if you and I are one, and we agree as one, how could one contradict the other? We are one in Him. How could we ever lose?*

Your clarity is splendid.

*My clarity is yours.*

I can see how someone could twist this around.

*If they are going to twist the meaning of these words around, they're going to twist it around from a twisted mind. That's no concern of ours. You are part of this. You are part of everything. You are connected with all things, with all there is. That's why I say "we," "us," "our." This is our message—not just mine but ours. You have ownership here. You felt at times you were being used.*

But it's such a joy to be used.

*But that's not really what's happening here. This is your message too.*

I suppose I didn't realize that.

*Now you do. To realize is to live real. Live real; anything, everything else is phony.*

Nobody's ever put this so plain, so clearly.

*Everyone knows all of this already; there is nothing new under the sun. We're just reminding them to wake up! It's wake-up time!*

That's a fact.

*You bet it is.*

That's a bet I'll take.

*You already got it. See—it's already in the bag. What are you working for? You already have all you need.*

There's some stuff there I'm going to have to think about.

*Please do. That's some good advice you just gave yourself.*

I've often wondered what it would be like to have someone you could ask anything to and they would have the answers.

*You've always had someone like that.*

But I didn't know it.

*Now you do.*

And I know it's not you either.

*No, it's not. We are not going helter-skelter here in any direction for curiosity's sake. We have a message and that's "singleness of heart."*

That's the first time I've heard you use that term.

*That's the first time I've used it.*

What does that mean exactly?

*What it means we've already discussed elsewhere in other terms in some depth. What it means exactly is, singleness of purpose is the "doing." Singleness of heart is the "being." For out of the heart are the issues of life. Out of the abundance of the heart the mouth speaks. Diligence is needed here, and a close watch. Words are life and death; choose life. I ALWAYS chose life. It's all there is really. So the choice is easy and simple.*

Awesome!

*Yes, it is, isn't it.*

## *May 23*

Talia, the day we met, you were sitting at the head of the table, and at one point I saw a crown on your head. When I looked down I saw myself wearing an old tattered, dusty uniform—something like from the civil war or WWI. Could you tell me about that?

*Yes, I could.*

*What we wore symbolized our future relationship in the NOW. Not only is a crown placed upon your head by someone else, it speaks of your thoughts. It's also a symbol of your treasure stored in heaven for you, and kingly authority. Your clothing spoke of your past trials and tribulations, your present battles and your calling. Remember what your friend Ken said. God showed him about you, the same thing the spirit showed you about you.*

In the mouth of two or three WITNESSES shall every word be established?

*Go to work now. Remember I said don't ask if you don't want the answer. That's why I pointed to your watch. We don't really have the time for this now. We'll speak more about this later.*

*You see now how you can call the answers unto yourself. That's being creative.* **That's the Art of Life.**

Splendid.

*Yes, it is, totally.*

When you total it all . . .

*Yes, exactly, you can never come up wanting.*

## *May 24*

———————————❖———————————

Talia, you can do so much more where you are than where I am.

*It's not only that I can do much more here; I can do ANY thing here. The truth's never that complicated. It's just that things are not always as they seem or appear to be. Do not pre-judge what you think is. We have specific things to write about here.*

When your message is out, will you keep talking to me?

*No matter how deep I move into He in whom all is, I will still talk with you.*

*It seems I'm pointing to a faraway shore; it's really not so far away.*

*Be mindful not to hurt others, for what you do to others you do to yourself.*

*I already know what you're going to ask before you ask it. The questions are just to frame it for your SELF. All are one.*

*You already see how my Game is moving people.*

Yes, I do.

*Of course you do, I'm affirming to you what is real. The only thing the false world offers is pain and suffering.*

*I do like pushing the envelope. That's why it's hard to keep up sometimes. Now that you see the truth as a hologram, you see past, future and present just is.*

Pushing the envelope again.

*That's part of my job.*

### May 25

**6:17 AM**
*Write!*

Good morning, Talia.

I want to record what happened last night, but I don't know where to start.

> The night before, I was explaining to G what Talia's touch felt like to me. As I was telling him, I felt Talia's presence very strongly, and as it persisted, G began to feel Talia as well. The feeling he had moved deeper until he felt as if his pains were being taken away by Talia. Her energy was healing him. He no longer had any pain!

*Let it absorb awhile.*

That was awesome.

*I know, for me too.*

I didn't know you were a healer.

*Me either.*

You either?

*No. I know all things are possible, but that was a new experience for me too. Do you feel my great joy in helping others?*

Yes.

*That's everyone's gift.*

*My mom feels on a VERY deep level, and I'm healing her too. She will always be able to feel me. You see the light in her eyes? That's not a mistake or your imagination.*

That's the light of life, isn't it?

*Yes, of course it is.*

I really didn't expect that, your healing.

*Yes, well expect the unexpected. Most people expect the things they conjure up in their minds, and that is what they get.*

Masters of their own destiny.

*They are creators; most just do not realize it. They should be co-creators with the Creator—that's easy enough. Instead they create their own misery, for themselves and others. What could be a more simple choice.*

**7:10 AM**

*Presence of mind IS the issue. That's a large part of Singleness of Purpose. This direct focus is where you see the miracles. Presence of mind is a term you've heard before; now think of what that really means.*

I think I know exactly what you mean.

*You do!*

But how can I put that in words?

*Again that's something that must be experienced. We could discuss it in depth until you ran out of paper and still barely scratch the surface of what that means, but what's the point.*

Another multifaceted answer contained in the question.

*Yes, you are a quick study; I heard that about you.*

That's precious, and sweet of you.

*How could it be otherwise?*

Point taken.

*Exactly!*

*You see all the many directions we could take here.*

Yes, like many paths leading up a mountain.

*Yes, MANY paths and they ALL lead to the top. His ways are more than the sands of the sea.*

Literally, I was told that years ago.

*I know, I'm quoting you quoting Him now. You saw the look you got when you told people that.*

Yes . . .

*Again, it must be experienced—not in word but in power. That was a small portion you experienced last night.*

I really don't have the words for that.

*Of course you don't. There aren't any really. But you heard the silence, the stillness. That's where we LIVE.*

*Yes, indeed. That speaks of the promises of God: his contract with his people. You have a contract of everlasting life with the Creator, IN WHOM nothing was made WITHOUT Him. You see all things are WITHIN Him. How could you EVER fail, He ALLways GIVES us the victory—in Him. Now these are some concepts you're not completely grasping right now, but you will.*

How can I ever repay . . .

*There is no repaying; it's a free gift. You're not quite getting that yet either. You think you have to work for it. I'm telling you there is no work to do; it's already been done for you. Completed, finished in Him.*

So we just receive it.

*Yes, what happened last night? Did you work for it?*

No.

*No, not at all, you just took the wine.*

> Talia uses the term "wine" to explain the gifts G receives from her.

## 7:16 AM

*You see how to obey is better than to sacrifice?*

Yes.

*And how He fulfills his promise to give you all the desires of your heart?*

Yes.

*This is a lesson told in the earliest parts of human history.*

Cain and Abel?

*Yes, you should reread that. That's God Himself revealing His true nature. That story also reveals all the so-called problems of man. No use to rehash it here; it's plain as DAY. Yes, wherever you go it's right in front of your face. Face to face. Look in the water, in a placid pond: THAT'S your answer. That's why so many people look to others to fulfill them. They can't believe they HAVE all the answers contained within them. There are no OTHERS.*

Oneness.

*Yes, to most that's just a word, without meaning. Again it has to be experienced. God is an experience. Most people think it's just pie in the sky! The PIE is within you. The Kingdom of Heaven comes not with observation.*

*The invisible God.*

There's way more to this, isn't there.

*There's no end. Rooted and grounded in Him growing up into all things! THAT'S gravity.*

Last night all I heard you say was "Hi," and as for seeing you, that isn't meant to be.

*I told you we would speak of it later.*

I know. I just wanted to record it.

*It already is, it's ALL recorded, in the Book of Life. NOTHING compares with THAT book. It contains everything. Some think it's a figure of speech. It is every word ever spoken. Some think it's just a list of names, because that's how they see it as described. It is a list of names, of natures, natures of life. All the nature of life, of being is contained therein. If you could just see the cover you would weep. I did. With joy. The beauty of life is unspeakable.*

Wow!

*Yes, wow! Remember that word's inverted; that's the nurturing spirit of the Mother, giver of life. The sweet Holy Spirit.*

I'm out of time again.

*Told you you'd never have enough of it there.*

Must feel nice to be always right.

*You think you know what it feels like.*

Is that a dig?

*Yes, sort of. Just wanted to give you a laugh before you went to work.*

Well, you did.

*Good.*

You are the most—wow!

*Yes, I am.*

> G was getting dressed and got a long-sleeve shirt to wear.

*Short sleeve. Sometimes less is more.*

*Remember you're a pathfinder. Remember who you are. I'm always reminding you who you are.*

**10:24 PM**

Well, Talia, I guess you proved how cool you were last night.

*You were talking about it with Mom, my touch. I just confirmed your truth. You know the universe confirms YOUR truth too. This isn't a one-way street; as a matter of fact they go in EVERY direction. These are paths of truth; these are the laws of life. These paths will lead you out of bondage and into Liberty.*

What you did last night—that was so precious and beautiful.

*I always am.*

## May 26

**6:34 AM**

Talia, your name is so beautiful.

*That's because that's who I am. That describes my very nature: "Heaven's Dew." You experience me. You experience me in my truth, my living my truth. I live UP to my potential. Anyone can do it, live UP to their potential. That's a free gift too.*

*When you experience me you experience a part of Him who is in all, through all and in you all. See how that works? It's his great pleasure to reveal Himself in his people.*

You ARE just like Heaven's Dew.

*I am. Again, you don't have time for this right now. You'll never have enough time to do the things you need to do here. You could use that sense of urgency also. You have much to do and so little time. Use what you have wisely.*

Death as an advisor.

*Life makes a much better advisor, life in the pure sense of the word.*

**1:23 PM**

G felt Talia's touch.

That WAS the sacred silence wasn't it?

*Yes, it was, not in words but in deed and in truth.*

Out of time again.

*Yes and no.*

**10:23 PM**

Hello, Talia.

*Hello, G.*

I'm tired.

*I know; just write.*

You said I had to be UP for this.

*You do, you are.*

OK.

*You think we can't transcend the flesh? We can do all things. There are no limits here. Remember what your grandfather said about fatigue: it can work for or against you.*

Figured he said it for a reason.

*Everything's for a reason. I already told you that.*

OK, let me have it.

*You already do—you just don't know it yet—but you will.*

Do you see all things?

*I see all things that I see, you see.*

Yes, I see what you mean.

*That's why they were called seers: they SAW. They couldn't always articulate either, but they saw. They put things they saw in their own words for the people. It wasn't for themselves, the seers. You're a messenger for your people; give them the message.*

What's the message?

*To reveal the Art of Life—that's living it. Like I did, and do.*

You are a shining example.

*Yes, I am, always. What do you fear? Rejection? You've already been rejected in every possible way, and you've already been accepted in every possible way. What's there to fear?*

Nothing.

*That's exactly right. Fear nothing. You've been given the gifts. Use them, don't quench them. Don't think: do, write, flow.*

I can do that.

*Of course you can. I don't waste words. You should know that by now.*

I do.

*Yes, you do.*

Then I will do by being in Him.

*Now you're getting it. See—it is easy. Your struggles are an example for others. Your victories are an example for others. You've never been one to beat your chest anyway. We appreciate that even if you have suffered the scorn of others.*

I'm writing!

*Yes, you are—see how they flow, the words of life. Lived impeccably they bring forth fruit everlasting. Why are you stopping?*

I'm just amazed.

*It is amazing, always and forever. Pretty much amazing.*

> Talia using the words "pretty much amazing" has a special meaning to me. Those are the words she used in a letter she wrote while in school, describing herself to me! When G heard those words he thought he was imagining things!

*You think you're thinking this up? If you are you need to work for RAND (a think tank).*

I don't think they'd have me.

*Believe me, they would stifle your creativity, then want to dock your pay. You know how that works.*

Oh yes, I do, the old set up.

That's one of those "experiences" I hate.

*It's for a reason.*

Figured.

*You've figured right. You don't need their kind anymore. What could they add anyway?*

About the only thing I can think of would be money.

*Money's nice to have, but it isn't the god they make it to be.*

I know that.

*Then why worry about it? They don't know who you are, but I do. You know who they are, but they think you don't.*

Spirit on the water, darkness on the face of the deep.

*That's exactly right; those kind of people will never get it. That's their lot in life and they have their reward. You don't need them, they don't need you, but they call you indispensable.*

They lie.

*Yes—you know it's true.*

Yes, I do.

*Yes, you do. Now, without them what do you have?*

Everything.

*Yes, everything. Trust us—we're here to help you.*

I trust you, I trust you.

*Good, now let's go on. Leaving those things behind.*

*Yes, just drop them. Remember, the company you keep.*

Then I will keep you with me.

*And I will always be there for you.*

## *May 27*

**12:14 AM**

*You stopped.*

Just tired.

*Why?*

Probably lack of sleep.

*Yes, and other things: trinkets in your way.*

A test.

*It's all a test. I told you that.*

I just know when you're tired you make mistakes; that's how the brain operates.

*Your brain has very little to do with what we're doing here now—it's a tool to use. Just don't be overly reliant on it.*

Well, that's a mouthful for a girl so smart.

*You know where that comes from, and it's not brain power. This causes a lot of problems.*

I've certainly seen that.

*Yes, you certainly have. Keep your HEART with all diligence, not your brain. You have to be somewhat out of your mind to do this.*

That's funny.

*Yes, it really is, isn't it.*

I feel a little achy.

*Well, that's all temporary.*

Guess everything is here.

*No, not everything. What counts is forever.*

That's beautiful.

*Yes, it is.*

How's that little girl?

*She's wonderful, just wonderful.*

That's great.

*Yes, it is great.*

*She's understanding now. I've explained a lot of things to her now and she accepts them. She trusts me completely. She is a VERY precious soul. Lovely. She's smiling now. She says hello, and she likes you.*

Why can't I hear her?

*She doesn't know how to do that yet. She's still learning. The lessons here are never ending; they just go on and on.*

*Go to bed now.*

Sounds like a plan.

*It is.*

Goodnight, Talia.

*A goodnight to you.*

**7:24 PM**
Talia.

*Yes. You had a good time today. That was a nice thing you did today. You know, just spending time. You really were not thinking of yourself today.*

No, come to think of it, I guess not.

*You were open today to help others.*

Yes, I guess I was.

*That was not so hard now, was it?*

No, not at all, quite pleasant really.

*It always is. Even just being open to help others really says it all.*

Well, I appreciate your approval.

*You walked in your truth today and you really didn't even realize it. See how effortless that was? That's just letting Him live his life through you. That's the Art of Life and the Art of Peace, letting the Creator live His life through you.*

*And you were just talking this morning about the obliviousness of people and their capabilities of moving in the spirit, another part of them they are not even aware of . . . at play.*

*That's completely true. That's their innate curiosity moving what they really ARE. How could they not do this? It's their very nature as spiritual beings. Matters not their level of awareness of it or their remembrance of it. They are going to do this anyway. Everyone does this. We are all fashioned alike and have been born by the very breath of life. Who have you seen proud and puffed up for being born?*

Can't say as I met anyone.

*No, you haven't, yet how many have you met puffed up about having the breath of life within them?*

I guess a lot.

*Yes, you have. You've even done it yourself a time or two. Almost everyone you've ever met has at some time, and yet none of the credit is theirs; it just is. That's the gift of life. A lot talk about it; few know what it is.*

Never heard it put like that before. That's boiling it down to the brass tacks.

*And I've never heard that statement before. ☺*

*Never waste time. You don't have enough of it.*

But can't I bend it?

*You saw it warp a couple of times today—when you took it by force. You said "it's mine" and it was so. You ARE a creative creature. You ALL are. We ALL are. How could we not be? We are created IN his image. Some think that's in likeness of; nothing could be farther from the truth.*

Why?

*BECAUSE THAT TAKES AWAY YOUR POWER AS A CREATIVE BEING.*

*They're under the impression that that also relieves them of some personal responsibility. It doesn't, of course, but that's a subconscious perception they adhere to for what they believe is personal gain. That is another ploy of enslavement. If they convince you you're powerless to change your circumstances without their help, what are you to them.*

A slave and a dunce.

*That's exactly right.*

This is some heavy stuff.

*When has it not been? I told you this is a message of freedom. Many want a process of A B C, but it just doesn't work that way. You were born free. You don't have to "do" anything. You just have to "be" in Him.*

Boy, that smacks of humility.

*And your pride will smack you down every time.*

*Now to answer your question, "How can we verify this to others?" Everyone already has access to truth—they were born by it. Honesty with themselves is one access or doorway, pure honesty. Another is by the quickening of the spirit, revelation by the light of self of He who is all. His ways to reveal the truth are numberless. There is no way I could even tell you an untruth. It just isn't possible. This path, this truth WILL set you free.*

*There is just no way for us to discuss ANY thing here without it leading to more freedom. I told you nothing was better than freedom . . . in Him. I can only point in the one direction because that's ALL that is. I told you of many paths. These are many ways, and the number of his ways are numberless. Your friend Ken has the revelation of numbers; no use covering it here—ask him.*

> G called his friend Ken to confirm some things he had told him.

*That was a good call and confirmed to you everything we've been talking about here.*

Yes, it did.

*I'm glad you agree.*

I do.

*I KNOW you do. We MUST agree; what else could we do? Nothing. We could do nothing without agreement.*

*Yes, now agree with him on what he says about you, because what he says about you I'm totally in agreement with.*

## May 29

**7:35 AM**
Talia?

*Yes.*

Good morning.

*Good morning. The words aren't going to jump on the paper—you have to write.*

I feel we're behind.

*We're not behind; we're right on time.*

I just feel you have a lot to say.

*I do.*

Then could we get started?

*We already have.*

You're playing your Game today, aren't you?

*Yes, I am. I'm moving people in the direction they need to go, including you. You're going to find out some things today you didn't expect.*

Like what.

*You'll see.*

I'm expecting the unexpected.

*No, you're not, not really. You think you know the direction your life is taking you. You really don't.*

What do you mean?

*What I mean is that the words that I'm speaking to you are spirit and life; your natural mind can never understand them.*

I know that.

*You know that on an intellectual level. That's not what I'm talking about here. As long as you're SELF-CENTERED you can't grasp this. It's when you look OUTWARD to others, when your pride dissolves, then you can receive—to overflowing.*

That's perfect, simple truth.

*Of course it is. That's intellectual knowing—now live it. It's easy to start thinking about this and miss the point.*

I think that's because I've judged others for living trapped in their brain.

*That thinking's correct. Now, let it go, just release it. It's that easy.*

> G spontaneously took a deep breath, just like the other night during Talia's "visitation."

*Like a breath of fresh air, wasn't it.*

Yes, it was.

*And nearly instantaneous, wasn't it? That's how quick it is for you to make a decision to change. Now that's using your brain as a tool, as it's meant to be used. You see the design of this all?*

You are a chess master.

*I'm FAR beyond that.*

It's such an honor to know you.

*It's such an honor to be known.*

Wow!

*Yes, again the world turns things upside down. When you see "beyond the veil" you see the nurturing spirit, for the "growing up into Him." Then everything seems a gift. That's the true nature of our father. There's variance of natures but one spirit.*

It's really not so complicated.

*No, it's really not.*

Talia, you are totally awesome!

*Yes, I am and always will be. Unchangeable.*

### *May 30*

**9:30 AM**
*Everything you do correlates with everything else you do. That's what you learned yesterday that you didn't expect. I told you this Life, this ALL was an intricate web. A luminous web of life. It's everywhere.*

*That's why it feels like it's all happened before—because it's all happening at ONCE.*

*You were just speaking the other day about where Solomon came from.*

*All things work in your favor, for your good, ultimately.*

*How could you judge someone for screwing up—it's all for their learning. Everybody's on a different level of learning in the same place. Unless a person has given themselves over to pure evil and is doing pure evil.*

Why do you call it pure?

*Because that's what it is: pure undiluted evil. That's easy to see. That determination on your part you ARE meant to judge, without being judgmental or judged yourself. You know who they are because they have chosen to become that. They have decided in no uncertain terms to become that that they are not.*

*This is meat.*

This is meat?

*This is meat. You have to chew it well, then give it time to digest, then it brings forth life.*

This whole message seems to be becoming more condensed.

*It is, absolutely. They HAVE been spoonfed and pampered long enough. Time to grow up into Him in ALL THINGS. The voice of Truth echoes throughout the universe, bearing witness, reflecting itself to itself.*

When you put it like that, it's amazing anybody could NOT get this.

*Isn't it though. That's why I said, "Choose life"; it's ALL revealed in the light. There is no other truth. It's a real struggle to walk in darkness.*

*Asleep to truth. Some are far off the road; many of these are leaders. You see how humanity is where it is.*

Why did you call this path a road?

*Because there's room enough for everyone.*

*You ask the right questions—that's one reason you were chosen for this.*

Yes, I used to drive some of my teachers crazy with my questions.

*Well, you're not driving us crazy, but unlike most of your teachers we DO have the answers.*

This is way beyond cool.

*Yes, it is, off the charts in every direction, all leading in the same direction.*

Thank you, Talia, thank you so much!

*Thank YOU so much. So many struggle so hard trying to become what they are not. This is a LOT of work. Yet, if they yield themselves to what they are, the struggle ends.*

This is self-evident, isn't it?

*Yes, evidenced by the Self, of who they really are. Society generally attempts to force people into being what they are not. You see the misery this causes, the deep discontent. Because that's all based on a lie. People instinctively know this and yet most accept it as truth, instinctively knowing too, that truth is freedom. When they don't get the expected results they either resign themselves to their fate or they try even harder with the program they've been taught. The conflict comes with what they know to be true and what they have been told is truth. This IS a craftily woven lie intertwined with truth to appear as true. This is the sell to acceptance of it. No lie is of the truth, yet to deceive one must use the truth in a twisted fashion.*

So if they were to tell the truth it would sound something like: we want to enslave you so we can have complete power over you, right?

*Yes, something like that, and who's going to buy into something like that.*

Nobody.

*No, believe it or not some still would, but not nearly enough to matter to them. These I speak about want ultimate power. They will never get it, of course, but that doesn't detour them from trying. Nothing will ever be enough for them—that's what makes them so dangerous to the common man.*

"Nothing" and "common man?"

*Nothing is what they get. Nothing will ever satisfy. That's why they work without ceasing, trying to find it. The IT they seek doesn't exist.*

*Common man is exactly that. The common man is powerless to resist. They have the stranglehold on now. Haven't you felt it hard to breathe sometimes?*

Yes.

*That's the interconnectedness with all things. When one suffers you all suffer. That's why it's important to help others. That's what we're doing here.*

*Time IS short. Now is the time for man to DECIDE to intend the outcome. The choice is simple, so very simple. Yet strong delusion IS sent because man chooses a lie instead of the truth. REMEMBER the saying, "Choose this day who you will serve." The choice is simple and not so very hard at all. Use what you have to make you into what you want to become. People are going to do that anyway. The lie they tell themselves is: "I don't have the things I need to become what I want." That's completely false. They have within them everything they need to create everything they are to become, and that's what they really WANT. They want to become what they were created to be.*

You are so far beyond me.

*I'm not so far beyond you. We are one. I'm Part of you, you're Part of me, we are a Part of the whole, which is one in all. Remember singleness of heart, singleness of purpose. This is that singularity which is the ONE, the Whole, Creator and Creation in one.*

There's a huge emphasis on this.

*There's a huge emphasis on this because that's all that is.*

I notice you mix milk with meat a lot in this.

*It's nice to have something to drink with a meal.*

There's not going to be a lot of my narrative here, is there?

*There doesn't need to be. If you were a writer you could weave a colorful tapestry of background to all this, but we're not interested in that. We are interested in the forefront, the forefront of truth. This is the cutting edge. This is what changes people's lives. As I've said, some of this is just for you. Not that you've been singled out as special or something—it's just that it's just for you personally. Not that the residual benefits will not benefit others if you live them, because they will.*

*Some things are not lawful to speak. "Lawful" meaning the "laws of life." You were told before, and not by me, that many things are unlawful to speak unless they are already walking in that light. To confirm it for them, that's His prerogative, to be first. The first born among many brethren. The first to reveal that light.*

*Your enthusiasm is commendable, but wisdom is profitable to direct.*

## 5:15 PM

*Strong meat is for those who by use have their senses exercised to keen discernment. You asked whom that was for. That's my definition of "them." You always liked advanced classes anyway. If you had your way everyone would be beyond you anyway. That is the selflessness I speak of.*

So, I'm not a totally lost case after all.

*You've never been a lost case, although you have been totally lost before.*

Redemption.

*Yes, exactly, you have been bought with a price.*

Talia?

*Yes?*

I just remembered I was told I would write a book.

> Years prior to this, G was in his yard when he heard a voice tell him that he was going to write a book. He blew it off, thinking to himself, *I am not a writer.* But now, after all of these communications with Talia, and Talia telling him that these dialogues should be published, he remembered what he had heard years prior.

*You were and you did not believe it.*

No, I didn't.

*Now do you?*

Well, like you said, the truth is right in front of my face.

*It always is.*

I can still feel that you're like pregnant with truth about to burst out of you.

*I am! I am waiting on you.*

Then let's do it.

*You're not ready yet.*

I'm just taking notes here.

*That's not exactly true. It's not just audible. My spirit has to co-mingle with yours for you to clearly receive this message. It's not just you taking dictation; that's how you see it, but it's more than that. Our minds have to "click" together by the quickening of His spirit. Sometimes you're "far away" from where I am. It's not that I'm far away, it's that you are. It's not difficult for you to get here, but it's difficult for you to "stay" here. That's that very quiet place in the center of your being. That's where we live; we dwell in the peace. This is a difficult place to describe with words for none are needed here. That is That That Is.*

Well that's a mouthful and no mistake.

*No, no mistake at all.*

*These are some things people have been asking about, begging to know. It's time they knew them.*

*The last enemy to be destroyed will be death. That's what we're attempting to get across here, that myth, that illusion of separation. There really is none. A lot of people know this. A lot of people think it's mere fabrication. The fabrication is the walls they've built with their mind. Matters not whether they believe they are creative beings or not, the fact is they ARE; therefore they ARE going to create no matter WHAT they believe.*

You're also the deepest person I know.

*You should get around more.* ☺

You're ageless, aren't you?

*There is no age; a person's "essence," what they really are, is without time. Time OUT OF MIND. The age you speak of is an outward appearance or a chronological timeline. It doesn't exist here. It is realized as a concept, to be used here to put things in context to be understood there.*

Now that's something I never heard before.

*Nor would you there. Either they do not know it, or if they do conceive of it, they have not the words to really explain it in understandable terms. It's just a concept to them, a picture or snapshot of truth. What's important is that we're "trying" to move you out of concept and into reality. Reality is realizing the truth. Of "being" in it. It's true living, not false death.*

*Death, as you SEE it, is real. Death, as you UNDERSTAND it, is a myth, a concept. This misunderstanding is what hurts the most. That's why I told you, as you looked at my ashes, "I'm not there," because I'm not; I'm "here." I am as you said the most alive person you know. That's why you've never heard me talk about my dying—because I never did. That's an illusion and a myth, a very convincing one, by the way. It will be used to dispel all the myths just because it is so convincing.*

It does hurt.

*Yes, it does.*

I remember years ago when I was told about writing a book I questioned what it was going to be about. The answer I got was "everything." That's when I really blew it off.

*That's why I told you that you could ask any question you wanted.*

**8:49 PM**
> G was thinking about the time to come when Talia's words, these conversations, are published, and how a lot of people that do not believe in spirit communications might think he is crazy.

*You'll be ostracized in certain circles.*

I've been there before, and I really couldn't care less about those circles. I don't care to move in them anyway.

*Just letting you know.*

OK.

*It's going to hurt a little.*

Been there too.

*I know you have. I'm just getting you prepared for a little more. It is for your growth.*

Guess it's time for me to grow up.

*You have said you're a late bloomer.* ☺

*They that are going to reject this are going to reject this no matter what we say. You cannot save them all, G.*

## *May 31*

**9:35 AM**
*Thinking about on-the-job training?*

That's where the real learning takes place, isn't it?

*Yes, Einstein wasn't joking when he said the biggest thing that got in the way of his learning was his education. He was smart enough to wash away what he didn't need. And THAT'S one of the biggest lessons he left.*

You didn't go with the flow of conformity, did you?

*No, I saw through it, instinctively.*

That's amazing. I mean especially for your age.

*I take no credit for it. I've already explained my walk there. As for age, again, there is none here.*

Wisdom born of God.

*Exactly. How could one take credit for a free gift?*

> G was thinking about some of the things Talia has been saying and had written down his own interpretations of some of it, when Talia spoke up.

*You wrote your thoughts around the revelation like a commentary. It wasn't bad, but it wasn't very precise either. To be perfectly precise it must be born of the spirit. That's what's different about what we're doing here: the perfect precision. Like a surgical instrument cutting to the heart of the matter—which is just energy slowed down. Now, if your energy slowed down, what does it take to speed you up to reveal the energy being you are? Something to think about, isn't it? There are enough commentaries out there.*

Ah. . .

*We just don't need elaboration, that's all.*

Well, thanks. It was just a free flow of consciousness, stream of thought thing.

*No, it wasn't. It was what mattered, slowed down, like a stutter step— it didn't feel at all the same to you, did it?*

No, not really.

*Not really, exactly.*

*It's not that it was bad or even wrong, it's just that that's not what we're doing here and it's not needed. Now you see how you could never do this on your own?*

Yes.

### 11:25 AM
*You've got something else to do today. Go and look at things from a different perspective, a different point of view. You've looked at it from your own point of view, now release it and see it with new eyes.*

Where.

*Just follow.*

### 9:47 PM
I don't feel that I got that much out of today.

*Yes, you did; you just don't know it yet. Some things serve you and some things do not. You need to be with me to do this.*

I know you don't like to hear this, but I'm trying.

*Stop trying; BE. We can't go much further if you don't stop doing what you're doing and be what you are.*

I don't feel very inspired today.

*I do.*

Well, let me have it then.

*It's already yours; that's what you're not getting.*

Oh, I see the multiple meanings of that.

*Now you're getting it.*

I'm staring at the page waiting for you.

*And I'm staring at you waiting for you.* ☺

All right, I'm ready.

*Are you really?*

I think so.

*You think . . . so?*

I'm not following.

*No, you're not. You need to lead now.*

What are you getting at?

*The truth, always. The truth is you ARE on the cutting edge of darkness.*

I've been told that before, twice.

*That's because that's the truth, confirmed in the mouth of two witnesses.*

What does that mean exactly?

*It means that light is expanding, and you're right on the cutting edge of it.*

I feel this, but it's like deep down and vague.

*That's all right, the light will reveal it. When you walk in it you will see more.*

This must seem like elementary school to you sometimes.

*It does, but it's still just as fascinating as it can be.*

Just as fascinating as it CAN be—wow, that's unreal.

*It's just as REAL as it can be too.*

What would you like to talk about?

*Everything.*

Well, as Grandfather said, "That's a lot."

*Yes, it is; it's everything. Everything is in Him really—there is no other.*

That's a nifty doctrine, and I'm sure it's true, but it's hard for us here to really conceive of it.

*You have been conceived BY Him. Forget the doctrine—he's WAY bigger than that, and you can be sure it's true. We're going to move beyond now.*

What does that mean?

*We're going to move Beyond, NOW. We're beyond where we were then. Now we're Beyond now again. You have to SEE it to understand it; words aren't going to make sense.*

Oh, man, there really is no explaining it, is there?

*Not in words.*

It's a wave formula, isn't it.

*Something like that.*

Time, light and gravity are waves?

*Time, light, and gravity are physical phenomena, parts of which are made up of waves, but there's much more to it than that. The physical is not what we're speaking of here.*

So there's a mathematical equation for this, a language made up of symbols so the mind can see it?

*That's one way.*

# June 2008

———————✦———————

**7:23 AM**

I saw it as a wave circling around behind you. It seemed about to
push you from the back, and it was full of colors of all kinds, some
I'd never seen before.

> G had a vision of Talia, with the most incredible colors
> swirling in the wind around her and behind her.

*That's the wind of the Almighty pushing us to new places. That would
be the easiest way to describe it. Although no words can do it justice—it
just is. The colors are His blessings, unending. There is no end to the colors
or His blessings. It's His good pleasure to give us the Kingdom. God IS
love and love never fails. He will not fail in what He has set out to do,
and that's to bring us all back into his fullness. Can you feel the joy of
anticipation?*

Beyond that!

*Oh yes, I told you there were no words for this. You've heard it said there was no new thing under the sun, and there's not. He completed his work there and declared, "It is finished." There are two correlations here, one in the Story of Creation, after which He rested, and one in the finished work of the cross. Look closely at this. This ties everything we've talked about here together. I can tell you there's no end to the new places here. He said He will do a new thing in the earth. I will tell you to look for it—watch.*

I see in both places he said it is finished.

*It is!*

I keep thinking of Joseph here.

*Joseph wore a coat GIVEN to him by his father, a coat of MANY colors. What did his brothers do?*

They threw him in a pit out of jealousy and were going to murder him but sold him into slavery instead.

*Sold him INTO Egypt. What happened?*

In the end he ends up feeding his brothers and saving them from famine.

*What I'm trying to get you to see here is he FORGAVE them.*

And there's a famine in the land now?

*Yes, there is, a famine of His word, of his true Voice. Remember the five-course meal I told you about?*

Was it five?

*It was five; you just didn't write it down. That's what we're doing here, laying out the meal. So they that have ears to hear CAN partake and be strengthened and move on.*

I remember you saying five now, but I didn't want to limit. I was reasoning I guess.

*Anyone can talk themself out of most anything. There are no limits to any number—it's just a symbol. People look at numbers dispassionately; it is a language and it's full of passion. Remember I told you if it came up to explain his revelation of numbers.*

G's friend Ken has a theory on numbers and their meaning.

Ken said there are really only ten numbers.

*There are and there's no end to them.*

Everything that can be contained, which is everything that is, is contained in 0.

*Although that doesn't explain it exactly either. Contained is a gross term, slowed down; nothing's really contained, you have to SEE this. There are no words to describe it.*

This is hard to grasp.

*There is no "grasping" it; you must be in it.*

> G thought about an incident in kindergarten. G was in art class and he asked his teacher for more colored crayons, because there weren't enough colors out. She told him there were plenty of colors out, and he said, "No, there aren't; I need more colors." She said he had all the colors that existed. G again said, "No, there are more colors." The teacher was exasperated and began to walk away, and while doing so asked G in a sarcastic tone, "So, you want your mom to buy you more colors? Are you jealous of the kids that have more than you? You can make do."

G thought, *No, that's not it. It's just that I see more colors than I have to use.*

Now, that's something I haven't thought about since the day it happened.

*There are LOTS of lessons there, aren't there?*

Yes, there are.

*You see, they train you to see what they want you to see and nothing else. It works too. Until you break through and see what's really there, which isn't what you were told at all. You remember we talked about the prison of the mind? Those are manmade bars.*

Well, now I feel like my parents got their money's worth out of kindergarten.

*You did.* ☺

I wish I had known then what I know now. I would have called her on it.

*You were five.*

There's that number again.

Whoa! Talia. Thank you for this! This is priceless!

*Yes, it is priceless.*

I'm thinking precious . . . there are no words to describe you, are there?

*No, there are not. That would be like describing the infinite.*

It always comes back in a circle because it's spherical.

*Yes, it does, because it is.*

My mind is blown here.

*And that's a good thing.*

Blowing the bars right off. I just feel like jumping up and down screaming.

*You can.*

I feel like running out, holding this over my head and screaming.

*If you do, you are going to get some looks.* ☺

*I'm giving you the last word today.*

Why?

*Because I'm honoring you.*

Thanks.

Guess that pretty much says it all.


**11:28 AM**
I feel when I get up and walk out of here into the world with other people everything pales by comparison.

*It just seems that way. It doesn't. You can still walk in it when you walk out of here. Remember, it's just distractions, trinkets.*

That all there is here, isn't it, just trinkets.

*That's all there is to distract you. See through it.*

I noticed you said before every man's been given a measure of faith. I know it says THE measure, but I wrote it like I heard it. But I've been wondering about that.

*You heard right. Every man's been given the measure of faith, but what he receives is A measure of the measure. Told you we were here to establish Him in the present truth.*

So the truth is changing, but it's unchangeable.

*No, not really. The truth is the truth, unchangeable, but it is established presently.*

Well, that's kind of hard to understand.

*It would be unless you're walking IN it, established IN the present truth.*

**6:38 PM**
Talia, you're SO awesome.

*And just think, I'm a very small aspect of God.*

No . . . that's TOO much to comprehend.

*You must surrender yourself to that that cannot be comprehended.*

Thank you for choosing me, God. Thank you for choosing me, Talia.

*You were "open"; you chose yourself.*

## *June 2*

------◆------

**9:21 AM**
Talia, I just read through nearly all of these dialogues so far, and it seems like the building blocks of life.

*That's a perfect description, because it is really.*

Can't help but notice the image of an infant.

*Well, that's understandable. That's pretty much where we are really, but we're growing, fast.*

We?

*We're all in this together. If people understood that, the fighting would stop. When someone looks to someone else, that's when the fighting starts. When someone looks to someone else and sees themself, that's when the fighting stops.*

*What can someone give you that you don't already have?*

*OK, we could discuss this in detail, but we already have. Again, all things are yours, already. You already have all things you need. Seek it like hidden treasure, because it is. Seek and you will find. He cannot lie. Now, that's an equation that balances itself perfectly. And the answer is within you. When people do the math the war stops. There's nothing to take from anyone because you already have all you need.*

Now I understand why math is a perfect language.

*It is! And perfectly logical. Perfect logic is perfect. The problem with logic is people's imperfect use of it, which is of course illogical becoming the exact opposite. Yet some cling to their view with a tenacity that's nearly unbelievable.*

*Again, the universe is spherical; when they cannot or will not get outside their mind it just circles in their head. You ARE a microcosm of the universe, you know. Therefore you can know all things just by knowing yourself.*

If people knew this . . .

*People in reality* **DO** *know this. We're just reminding them—RE Minding. People also know the unknown can be known. This is a seed or spark within them that creates the desire within them to search. How many do you see searching, seeking for something they just can't put their finger on? That's the unknown but not unknowable that they know; if they knew, all their questions would be answered and they would be fulfilled. That's what they WANT. But for most their brain has been washed to another direction. They accept being called consumer; they wallow in it really. Wouldn't it be better to be called givers; wouldn't that be something to aspire to?*

Oh man, Talia.

*Good stuff, isn't it?*

Oh yes, it is!

**1:51 PM**

*I told you this wasn't so much a job as an adventure for you, to touch people in a place they deny to themselves exist.*

Cool, sounds like a Navy slogan.

*It's an ocean of consciousness. You're teaching them to navigate though the sea of the universe, which contains all things. Everyone's trying to get there in their own way; most just don't know it.*

*The infinite is within them; that's something else that is hard to comprehend. But it's there! That's why I say it's right in front of your face, in the mirror. There's a certain fascination to people when they hear the words "behind the looking glass." That's another pointer, pointing to hidden truth. But you do really have to look behind the looking glass to see it.*

Holograph!

*Yes, outside of yourself looking back into yourself.*

A reflection of what truly is.

*That's it.*

I have to go look in the mirror.

*Yes, please do.*

*What did you see?*

One thing, you can track a man's "times" by the lines on his face.

*Yes, every one's there for a reason. What else?*

I see what's going on inside is reflected outside.

*And what's going on inside is a small part of everything that is, all happening at once. Now do you see what complex beings you are? How could you belittle another?*

That would be foolish.

*The height of foolishness. A fool is known by his multitude of words. Most of what you do that really counts is without words. How many words did we speak the day we met?*

Not very many.

*But look what happened and look where it led to. Look where our relationship, our friendship is leading us: fruit unimaginable.*

That's wonderful to know.

*Yes, it is. You knew you had something more to do. I just reminded you.*

Well, thank you **VERY** much.

*You are always welcome.*

## June 3

### 8:03 AM

I'm not feeling it today, Talia.

*How many times have you done things without feeling like it?*

A lot.

*So what's different with this?*

I just don't want it to be me. I want this to be you.

*It is me; it's us. Moving in Him. You don't always have to feel it; as a matter of fact, not feeling it is for a reason.*

Faith.

*That's part of it. You're interested in the credibility of this, and I appreciate that. I know it's hard and it's not easy; it's also NOT hard and it's one of the easiest things you've ever done. It takes effort, sometimes great effort. It's also one of the most effortless things you've ever done. It's a real struggle, and it's not a struggle at all. The flesh wars against the spirit and the spirit against the flesh, and those are contrary one to the other. But He always gives us the victory.*

Thank you for that.

*You're welcome. Are you ready to move on?*

Yes.

*Good.*

> The night before, I took G to visit a friend of mine from high school who was in town for a short visit. I knew that she would be fascinated and amazed by Talia's words, and I wanted G to tell her about the communications.

*That girl you met last night. You said she had a sweet spirit, and every time you thought of her you thought of that, that she had a sweet spirit. Well, that's true, she does. And when you said she was on a good path, you saw the mountain with many paths on it. That was a confirmation that what you spoke was true. You helped her navigate by what you spoke to her about. You even said you saw the light in her eyes. That was the true light. You honored me by what you spoke to her about last night, and I want to say thank you.*

You're welcome. Talia, you're teaching me about honor.

*That's something you asked about years ago and not so long ago: "What is honor? I'm just not seeing it here." That prayer was honored. Prayers are present. Prayers are never ignored. Ask and you shall receive. He SAID,*

*"You have not because you ask not. Ask and you shall receive." And He cannot lie. He is truth and joy unspeakable.*

You're honoring Him here, aren't you?

*He is worthy of all honor and praise and glory. He is the source of all things, but He is not just the source of all things, He IS all things. There are lesser beings of God, but He is all Beings.*

You can only see it to understand it.

*Absolutely.*

How do you point things out?

> G is referring to how Talia causes G to see, or focus on, or think about something.

*That's just energy, easy as can be. You can do it too, you know. It's thought condensed to a small pulse. You send it with intent.*

I "see" it.

*That's the only way you can know what I mean.*

There's electricity involved.

*It's spiritual energy. The brain and nervous system receive it as an impulse; that's why you feel it.*

But would you still feel it without the body?

*Of course you would, but the vibrations are on such a higher level that you don't need to. It just is—things are just known.*

*That was sweet what you did last night. That was true sharing, and you curbed your enthusiasm to a perfect balance. You didn't try to convince anyone of anything; you knew it just is. That is a fine way to present truth. Present the facts with true passion. That's authentic. That's felt by people and that's what they'll remember: the passion of truth. Out of her own mouth she said, "The truth will set you free." She knows that to be true and has claimed it for herself; therefore, it is so.*

*All true knowledge is the knowledge of Him, the building blocks of life. How often has He mentioned buildings? Man loves to build. They are "made" in his image. You are a holy temple. He is building you. To become what He is. In all things.*

That's awesome!

*Of course it is. And, He cannot fail.*

Then, why do we worry so much?

*THAT'S a good question.*

## June 4

**7:43 AM**
Good morning, Talia.

*Don't think, write.*

Talia, there's no way for me to express my gratitude and deep, deep appreciation of what you've done and are doing and are being. You're truly changing me from the inside out.

*I told you this was a message of change. Of course it's changing you— you're listening. You're listening in the quietness of THAT THAT IS. Of all things. All things are yours.*

Wow, I never saw it like that before.

*I also told you to look with NEW eyes. He is doing a new thing UPON the earth, meaning you, meaning all who will listen and are willing to see with new eyes. You see things differently now. You're starting to see things as they really are, endless fascination. All things are placed in Him to bring you back to Him. That's where you came from in the very beginning anyway. See, it is all spherical, from and back to Him.*

No one has ever put it like this.

*This is the Pure Word of truth. This is given to me, and I'm just sharing it with you.*

I saw the little girl last night (the little girl that Talia is taking care of), and she was grinning from ear to ear, and her face was glowing, with light all around her face. She looks so different.

*She IS different now. She completely understands now. Understanding brings joy unspeakable. You see so many people struggling to understand. That's another pure desire placed in the heart of man. They too instinctively know that to truly understand will bring joy unspeakable. With partial understanding things seem complex and sometimes troubling. With complete understanding comes peace!*

You're explaining everything!

*You were told this would be a book about EVERYTHING.*

Yes, I even saw it with a capital E.

*And THAT was for a reason.*

This is everything I ever wanted.

*Of course it is. You wanted a DIRECT LINE. It doesn't get more direct than this. You'll notice I don't filter anything, and yet my personality comes through clearly.*

That's something to think about.

*Yes, it is. God has never meant to remove anyone's personality but to enhance it. We are all unique in this way, beautiful aspects of what He is. That's part of this message, to reveal that. When someone attempts to stifle your personality that's their hatred or misunderstanding of the pure. That's them warring against God.*

*You see how time seems to distort when we're doing this?*

Yes.

*It doesn't really. Time is linear in man's thinking, in man's view. When man thinks of the eternal he thinks in linear terms. This is a completely false assumption. Time, like space and everything else, is spherical. But even that doesn't explain it: it is and yet it is not. Time, really, is a concept. It is not; it is nowhere. It seems to man it's everywhere and just is, and there is nothing you can do about it.*

He just can't change it.

*There is nothing to change about something that is not. How many times have you heard, "Time just seemed to stop?" This is an event of pure experience where perceptions were replaced with reality.*

*That's another "trick" not to be distracted, to "focus" your mind. Time itself is a distraction.*

**6:47 PM**

That was a real surprise when you spoke to me while we were working.

*Why would I not? It was fascinating to me. I told you I learn from everything you do. I jumped at the opportunity. I "seized" the moment and I enjoyed it immensely.*

Well, you are welcome any time.

*Thank you. I'll take you up on that.*

You ARE crafty.

*It's far beyond a craft. This is an Art.*

The Art of Life.

How did it go with Frankie today?

> Frankie and I met with Rebecca, the medium. Frankie wanted me to go with her. She wanted to hear what Talia had to say to her.

*Good. Not as good as I had hoped, but better than it seemed.*

Did she receive it?

*Yes, she did. She has a lot to learn yet, but she'll get it.*

Excellent.

*Yes, it shall be.*

*Why don't you call and find out. You're distracted by it anyway.*

OK.

> G kept thinking about Frankie's and my meeting today with Rebecca and really wanted to hear about it from me. His desire to talk to me about it was distracting him from speaking with Talia.

**8:06 PM**

I don't know what to say.

*You got a message you didn't expect today.*

> While I was with Frankie at a meeting with Rebecca, Michael, Talia's father, came through and told Rebecca that he really liked G.

That was nice of him.

*He's a nice man.*

That makes me feel bad, for judging.

*Don't worry about it. There's nothing to worry about. I'm just pointing out that your thoughts are real; they create. They can create chaos and misery or peace and joy. Peace and joy are better, you know.*

My thoughts being real have never been this real to me before.

*Again, this in an experience. You just experienced it.*

Yes, that hurt a little.

*It was a good hurt. To change you. To change your mind.*

I'm glad it's changing.

*It is. We just changed it.*

I feel it.

*How could you not? You've trained yourself to be sensitive to so many things, how could you not be sensitive to this, that your thoughts affect people. Good or ill, that's just the way it is.*

Makes sense to me.

**10:43 PM**

> G was having a beer, relaxing.

*How's the beer?*

The wine's better.

> G is referring to Talia's touch and her healing of him, which he calls "wine." When he mentioned wine, Talia told him that she had tasted some wine while here, in her body.

*I tried it. I didn't like it.*

Does your mom know?

*She knows.*

*Everything won't be resolved every time we talk about it.*

I figured that.

*You're a strategist; you would.*

Never thought of myself like that.

*You do it all the time.*

OK.

*Yes, it is.*

Kind of has a sneaky connotation.

*Not at all; you're just crafty.*

I said that to you today.

*And I said it was Art. I'm trying to get you to move into that level. Most I'm trying to do this with are unconscious of it. Do you see what I was dealing with today? Filled with distraction.*

Never thought of that.

*Now you can.*

Must be frustrating.

*It is. Beyond words.*

I'm with you.

*Yes, you are.*

You are absolutely, totally, and completely awesome!

*Yes, I am. You could admit that about yourself, you know.*

THAT wouldn't seem right.

*But it would be. We're speaking of your higher Self here, not what you see as imperfections or mistakes. Mistakes are just learning experiences anyway.*

Well, if you put it that way.

*I do. To speak it is to declare truth. It also hastens its being. Words are life. Choose life. Speak words of life; they're life giving. Also declare this about others. Show them who they really are. See the change. Words are life. Are not the words I'm speaking life?*

Yes, they are.

*Then use them. Speak into being. You CAN create life. "Having your loins girded about with truth." I've already told you this message wasn't just for you—time to get it out there. You've seen the signs, undeniable.*

Talia, if only one other person gets this . . .

*Oh, there will be way more than that. You've already seen people changing from this.*

Yes, I have, without a doubt.

*Then bring them the message.*

## June 5

**8:16 AM**

You said you had things to say today, and I had something to do. Now I'm back.

*Quiet yourself.*

Talia?

*Yes?*

You have an appointment today, I guess right now.

> I had a phone appointment with a famous medium in New York. Though I hear from Talia through G, and Rebecca, I wanted to see if this other person was able to hear Talia differently and to pick up on different messages for me personally.

*I don't have an appointment. There are places for us to be and we are. It's not here and there; everything is. All at once.*

So you're not distracted by this?

*Not at all, but you are.*

I'm thinking ahead.

*Yes, and you're trying to categorize things. It doesn't work like that.*

Then I need to quit that.

*Yes, and let things be as they are. Be in the Now. That's all that is.*

What about character?

*Character is a byproduct of everything we've talked about here. If you walk in it, if you live it. As a matter of fact, it's a very small issue when you compare it to what were discussing here. Most use the words "character" and "work ethic" as a banner to carry proudly. I tell you it's not that important to talk about: either you have it or you do not. What difference does it make to talk about it?*

Then let's move on to something else.

*Yes, let's.*

What's the issue?

*The issue is perfection. That's something most will not talk about because they think that they know it's out of reach for them. But it's not. They can't do it alone though, and that's what disturbs them. I'm telling you it's not out of reach at all. It's right before you.*

You're saying you have to "see" it.

*Yes, it's within you, but you have to see it. Remember I told you without a vision the people perish. They just wither on the vine. The vision is right before you. You just have to claim it. He does the work. He said He would finish what He started—the Author and Finisher of your faith. Your job is to let Him.*

That seems simple enough.

*It's all simple enough, more than simple enough. I told you people nearly always complicate things. That just muddies up the waters. Who wants to drink muddy water? You are made from the dust of the earth and have the breath of life. You can muddy the waters or you can let them flow clear.*

And I see that when you do muddy the waters, if you are still it will settle and be clear again.

*Sometimes you can't help but to muddy the waters, but that is a lesson too.*

On that note I've been wondering about something.

*Ask it.*

When I got back from my walk, when I didn't have my pen, once I got it you said, "I'm glad you got your pencil." Did I hear you wrong or what?

*You heard right. I wanted you to know you could change things in the past, that you could erase them. People carry burdens of the past with them like baggage. It's back breaking.*

That's awesome!

*Of course it is.*

Yes, you SAID you had some things to say today.

*Yes, I did.*

Did I hear you right earlier when I asked you about the mediums, psychics, etc., when you seemed to say they're rusty?

June 2008

*Yes.*

Why?

*What causes rust?*

Oxidation?

*Lack of oil.*

The anointing.

*Yes, many are called but few are chosen. It's not that they don't have a gift, it's that they've left their first love. It's not that they can't be used either, because they are. The anointing is a protection, a power. The kingdom of God is not in word but in power. There is nothing sweeter than the Holy Spirit and there is no faking it. Why take a Model T when you have a BMW.*

That WOULD be slower.

*A circuitous route. The truth must be quickened to bring forth fruit and only the Holy Spirit can quicken.*

Wow!

*Yes, it nurtures too. Nothing can possibly be gentler.*

You DO move me.

*Yes, I do. I move everybody I can. I move them in a perfect direction. You've seen this.*

Yes, I have. I just don't know how to describe it.

*There are no words to describe it. You can see it or you cannot. You can feel it or you cannot. There's no faking this either. You see people suppressing their emotions. Emotions are another tool in your arsenal to be used.*

Why did you bring up emotions?

*Because that's part of the message. People have been taught to suppress them long enough. I'm telling you to use them. They come from the essence of what you are, so to deny them is to deny yourself. This causes MUCH sickness. And the doctor's cure is to treat a physical ailment.*

That IS stupid.

*It's ignorance. Yet they will spout off about their education, never suspecting they've been taught wrong.*

Hmmm . . .

*I'm righting some wrongs here, with the sword of truth, which is a light to shine on the darkness. The darkness in them really hates that, unless they're ready, unless they are prepared to move on. Most are stuck in the mud of their own making.*

You don't pull any punches, do you?

*Why would I? It's either all or nothing. You know what He said about being lukewarm.*

What is the void?

*That's everything that is not. Everything that is has a counterpart that is not.*

That's hard to understand.

*Yes, it would be, wouldn't it? You asked.* ☺

## 11:06 AM

Now I know why you didn't answer me when my thought had completely formed, *Were you prefect on earth?* It was ignored and you kept going. You answered it at the same time through someone else.

> It was not a coincidence that Talia brought up the issue of perfection with G when she did. I had just been talking to G, and I had told him that I thought that Talia was pretty perfect while here with us. Then, while I was on the phone with the medium in New York, Talia told him that she wanted me to know that she was not perfect while here with me.

*Yes, I did. All of your questions will be answered.*

Well, I'm seeing the perfection of imperfection.

*That's something not many see, but that's true, there is. It all has purpose, meaning.*

Everything means something.

*Absolutely, exactly, everything. When someone says "don't mean nothing," they're just not seeing it.*

We've got to see the invisible.

*Exactly. You MUST look to those things that are not seen. Anyone can do this; as a matter of fact, everyone does. We're dealing in matter of facts here. Time to go.*

## *June 6*

---

Talia?

*YOU NEED a DAY off. This is your day off. You know if I need to say something to you I can get through to you.*

**10:09 PM**

*You're getting it! You're getting it!*

> Right at the moment Talia said that, G and I were having a conversation in which we were speaking about and contemplating all of the things Talia had told us about energy being Truth. Right at that moment we realized that energy is all there is, that we are energy beings, pieces, parts of the one source of energy.

**11:04 PM**

Talia, you can show me what you want to show me here.

*It's not time.*

**11:42 PM**

I heard your friends were acting out.

> I had just found out that some of the kids in Talia's class, her friends, were beginning to act out at school, and get into some trouble. One of the kids admitted that he was depressed over Talia being gone, and that was why he was acting out in the manner he was.

*My gravity held them together.*

## *June 7*

—————◆—————

### 7:13 AM

*You act like it's not enough time.*

You said there wasn't.

*Exactly.*

Boy, it's going to be another one of those days.

*It's a perfect day that the Lord has made.*

His mercies are new every morning.

*Of course they are. Everything is new every morning, everything is being renewed always. I told you it was ALL energy. Energy from every thing that is. The scientists have noticed a piece of energy here acts on a piece of energy there instantaneously, but that's not exactly true either. That's as they see it. In reality there is no here or there, and instantaneously isn't correct either. It is all now. They will discover that matter is energy slowed down by focused thought. That time is a perception. And that thought creates. They've already discovered that just to observe something acts upon it. That's why I've said so many times to look. Looking at something acts on it to reveal it as it really is. I said you were a creative being. "Ye are Gods."*

*You've said yourself that the eyes project energy. What did my eyes do to you the day we met? They changed you; they acted on you to reveal who you really are. The light of the eyes rejoices the heart. This IS the light of Life. Have you not captured someone with your eyes? They also capture the moment when you see it. So you see there is also more to this seeing that I've mentioned than you saw. In His light shall we see Light. And all of this can be proven by mathematics also. The passion of truth never fails. The precision of perfection is focused thought to reveal truth that will set you free. I told you, you have a part to play. That's why I call it a Game. Games are fun.*

Talia, you just—wow.

*Yes, I just wow.*

*Go now; this will never end. Never ending. Always.* ☺

## 12:47 PM

*Mental blocks of memory are always self-imposed or accepted. No one has power over you unless you allow them to have it. Thinking is an attempt to freeze time, which always causes confusion.*

G is thinking about a big test he has the next day.

*What's important is what you get out of it, not what you get from it. Many are not only missing the big picture, they are missing the little pictures too. There is really only one picture.*

G thought to himself, *I'm quickened.*

*I told you that's not me. We're quickened together. All this is yours. The revelation of the knowledge of truth. You asked to know what everything really was, what everything really meant. I told you prayers were "present," and the honest prayer of faith was honored and answered. So it is.*

I'm overwhelmed.

*You need to be.*

I need to "BE."

*He supplies ALL YOUR NEED. I cannot lie. I am as an embodiment of Truth. How could it EVER be otherwise?*

It cannot.

*That's correct.*

*Because your confidence will be shaken. You know why.*

So that that cannot be shaken will remain.

*Exactly. We are dealing in exactness here. Like dealing cards, you get to choose. It's a GRAND game. A game of truth in the inward "parts," to complete the whole.*

*My mom got me here perfectly. That's why she has no regrets, as she shouldn't, ever. She will share in this reward, and it's far beyond tremendous. There are no words to describe it.*

> Hearing this really touched me. Talia telling G that I should have no regrets was a confirmation to me that Talia is really with me, always, and that she responds to what I ask her or say about her. Just a bit earlier that day, I was on the phone with a friend of mine and I told her that I have no regrets with how I raised Talia, at all. Then to hear Talia say this was to me a wow moment!

*Thank you for telling J (Talia's uncle) I love him.*

And you said he would receive it.

*And he did, perfectly. That was sweet of you.*

That brings tears.

*They're all counted.*

"I am as" an embodiment of truth?

*"I am as." There is one body; we are images of it. What you see on earth as a person is an image of that person. That's why there is no death. That's a physical body ceasing to function. There IS no death. That's why I call it an illusion. Like a mirage in the desert, of water. The water is not there. The water—which is life—has moved on.*

Perceive those things that cannot be seen. "Look" to those things which are not.

*Energy is invisible unless it's slowed down enough, acted on enough, by an outside force or an opposite force to be seen, but you can always perceive it.*

Always?

*Yes, always because you ARE energy. How could you not perceive yourself? Nobody's THAT cut off. That's just something that is, and that's all.*

**1:55 PM**
I know why you were chosen for this.

*It was revealed to you; respect.*

*Don't judge anybody for anything by outward appearance (age, looks, social status, etc.), but judge with righteous judgment, which is spiritual judgment, spiritual discernment.*

*You could talk about your service in the "intelligence community," which is a real misnomer. Now you're in the REAL intelligence community.*

**6:00 PM**

Why did you bring that up?

*Because you like shining the light of truth on the darkness of ignorance.*

I'll bet it ties into some other things.

*I'll bet it does.*

Talia, it looks like I have a few minutes.

*When it's all over that's what it will look like.*

When my life on earth is over I will look back and it will look like a few minutes?

*Yes, that's what it will look like, like a flower of the field.*

"Behold the lilies."

*That's right.*

Guess there is not much to get hung up about.

*You can only hang yourself up by the false images in your mind.*

Thought creates.

*Pure focused thought creates reality, in its many splendors.*

*You were bought with a price and His servant you are to whom you obey. You'll notice most people obey whoever pays the most. You are not your own; you have been bought with a price.*

"The lamb."

*The Lamb of God. I told you I was going to talk about a lamb.*

I remember.

*"He is the One."*

Someone that read some of this dialogue said that "he sure skips around a lot."

*THEN they should ask themselves: A) Who is the "he" they're talking about? B) If he skips around a lot, it's for a reason, and C) If they're not tying it all together then perhaps they are not seeing it. I tell you, this must be seen holographically. To really make sense of it, their eyes must be opened, by being open.*

Some say, "You can't open your mind to every conceivable point of view."

*There's only one point of view that matters.*

### June 8

### 6:12 AM

*I'm glad you're going to my tree dedication.*

I'm glad too.

> Talia's school planted a very special tree in her honor and memory, a Gingko tree that was the same age as Talia when she "died," thirteen. The tree was planted in a stone planter, and around the edges of the planter special words were engraved. Words that describe Talia: Amazing, Authentic, Gracious, Joyous, Insightful, and Athletic. As soon as the planting and stone engraving were finished, the school had a special dedication ceremony presenting the tree to the school community and to me.

**7:45 AM**

You told me awhile back, "It was my time," and I said I'm not going to tell your mom that. If you want her to know you can tell her through someone else.

*That was for you to know.*

Then you did tell her through someone else.

*Then it was time for her to know. You said yourself, "Things take time." I told you there is timing in everything.*

Vibrations.

*Yes, and other slower rhythms.*

I can see it.

*Yes, and you've heard the music.*

I have.

*Think of the scale of sound your ears hear. Just as narrow as sight, yet some think all they see and all they hear is all that is. It's blatantly obvious that it is not. Their very logic is flawed to death. I told you people create whether they want to or not.*

I have felt you, touched where you are at, smelled you and even tasted it that day you healed me. I've seen you and I hear you now. Nothing is more real to me really.

*All you sensed in a harmonious whole. You're no different in that way than anyone else. Most of your problems are unconscious. I'm here to raise your consciousness. "Your" meaning everyone that takes the time to read these words and to listen to the voice of truth.*

That's awesome!

*We will not fail. I have seen the End and it's a Beautiful Beginning.*

*Passion creates quality.*

*You asked about it.*

**1:35 PM**

You know, I thought the poem I wrote, "Explanation," was pretty stupid at the time.

*That's because it was over your head. I'm telling you people do not realize their capabilities. I'm saying to you that there are no limits. When people realize who they really are, all limits are transcended and there are no limits.*

Sounds good. How do we do that?

*By being who we say you are.*

That sounds like a pat answer.

*Again, you want a method of A+B+C. Let's skip A (the beginning) and C (the end) and just BE.*

That even outdid the other answer.

*You ARE down today. Snap out of it. That's the problem.*

I feel like the walking dead.

*You are experiencing a bit of that today.*

Oh man, there's some irony here.

*Sure is.*

*You want to be up all the time, and that's not going to happen. The downs are just as important as the ups.*

Well then, I guess I should rejoice always.

*Of course you should. Be at peace; all things are going to work out just fine.*

It does not feel like it.

*You can change it in an instant.*

Thought is faster than light.

*Thought is focused energy. Study this.*

OK.

## *June 9*

**5:15 PM**

> G was thinking to himself: I remember when I traveled through Santa Barbara when I was younger. I heard a voice say to me, "There is a girl from here who is going to change your life." My response to this was basically, whoopee! And then the voice said, "But she's not born yet." Needless to say I was a bit crestfallen at hearing this. Not to mention slightly doubtful! But then I KNEW what I heard. At the time I just filed it away. That night I slept very peacefully. I continued on my journey the next day north along the coast, through the redwoods into Washington, then back down through Nevada. I had some very interesting experiences.

**7:00 PM**

*Maybe you should share about the sleeping bag.*

Why?

*Because that's another "in your face" example of how He supplies all your needs.*

**9:20 PM**

G kept seeing a very particular kind of flower in his mind. He saw it so many times he finally asked Talia about that vision.

What is the meaning of this flower?

*It means I love my mom.*

G tried to find that flower in books and on the internet but could not. Then out of the blue, I showed G the vase that Talia, through a friend of mine via Rebecca, had given me for my birthday. The vase was blown glass, and the pattern and colors were exactly the flower that G has seen in his mind. It was then that G understood what Talia had meant by her statement, "It means I love my mom."

### June 10

After I met that girl, Kim's friend, you said, "It was a fine way to deliver it." It was because of where SHE was at, wasn't it?

*When you see they are not receiving it, by a spirit of resistance, say what you've got to say and move on. She was in a place to receive it. She was OPEN to receive it. She has strived to get there.*

Rebecca said you had mastered multidimensional communications.

*I have but there is much to learn yet.*

## June 11

**3:15 PM**

*"It was beautiful."*

Talia said that to G right after her tree dedication ceremony.

## June 12

**11:25 AM**

Talia, I hope I can live up to your expectations.

*I don't have any expectations. I expect you to be who you are.*

*We know in part, and we prophesize in part, but when that that is perfect is come, that in part shall be done away with. The Kingdom of Heaven is within you.*

**5:54 PM**

Talia!

*Yes!*

I've missed our time together.

*So have I. I'm glad you were at my tree dedication.*

I'm glad I was too; it was an honor.

*It was an honor for me that you were there.*

This is humbling.

*Good, that's a good thing. You just need to know who you are.*

I'm trying to find out.

*So you are.* ☺

Yes, I see what you mean.

I heard that Frankie said she felt you there very strongly, and also afterward when she got home.

Frankie wrote Talia a letter after the tree dedication.

*She did and I'm so glad. I want her to know I'm all right and that I'll always be with her and that we will always be friends. She is very, very special to me. She always will be. She told me she felt me and that she misses me. I don't want her to be sad. She should be happy and know I'm OK and will always be with her, "friends forever."*

She seems to be a very sweet person.

*She is! We had a bond beyond this world and we still do.*

I can tell it's hard on her sometimes.

*It is, but that's temporary. She will grow up into Him in all things also. I made her some promises, and I'm in a position to always keep my word.*

She has dreamt about you, hasn't she?

*Yes, she has, and in her dream I told her I was all right and that she would see me again.*

And you can't lie.

*No, I cannot.*

Well, it's sure an honor for me that you're my friend.

*It's an honor for me as well. You're an honorable man and I appreciate that about you. I know your heart, and you do try to do the right thing.*

Yes, I don't always succeed though.

*Maybe you should redefine success.*

Like how?

*Like looking at it from a different point of view.*

That's a thought.

*That's a pure thought.*

Well, if anyone knows about purity it would sure be you.

*Everything here is perfectly pure.*

And complete?

*It's completed in Him.*

What's next?

*You're going to get a call.*

Just then the phone rang.

**6:55 PM**

Talia, that was actually pretty amazing. Too bad I didn't have a witness here.

*That was for you. I'm constantly confirming this for you. You doubt as much as just about anyone sometimes. Also the truth cannot but help verify itself when you're aware of it. It's constant.*

That was awesome.

*Well, thanks. It's all energy you know.*

I think I know exactly what you mean.

*You do, and you're concerned with how to describe what you know about it. It's not necessary. As I've said, they that are going to get it will get it, and they that are not, aren't. There's nothing else we need to say about it here. They have been coddled and spoon-fed enough. People must learn to apply themselves and not listen to the lies that are forced upon them. There is ample truth right before their face. Again, it's time to wake up and that's a simple choice.*

I concur!

*Thank you. I'm glad you do.*

That was a very interesting dream I had this morning.

> In G's dream he saw what looked like rocks pushing down on a mat, causing a funnel-like shape downward with a twist. It was like a twisting tube in the universe.

*I'm showing you how energy works in the universe.*

That whole "twist" on the torque thing was new to me.

*It's always been there.*

That's something I'll have to put my thinking cap on for.

*It takes energy to see energy. That is a place where things disappear to reappear some place else. You'll see it; it takes energy.*

I want that energy.

*You have it as potential energy. You're not applying it yet. And space isn't "warped" either. That's as they see it. It's perfectly formed. When they come from a place of perfection, it will be perfectly clear to them. It looks chaotic; it's not at all.*

*You'll be tested by fools. Well meaning fools, but fools nonetheless. Remember, water off a duck's back.*

Just shake it off.

*Just shake it off and flow on, knowing what you know.*

That was well put.

*Yes, it was. The spirit foretold my coming to you and how I would affect you and your life. He told you that I would change your life.*

You certainly HAVE.

*I'm not finished yet.*

That's good news for me!

*Yes, it is, very good news.*

Talk about a new thing in the earth!

*OK.*

I can tell you're just smiling.

*Yes, I am, from your great joy.*

## *June 13*

---

**1:00 PM**

I have got to be honest with you, I'm about sick of people.

*That's because you think they're phony. They all aren't.*

What, just the ones I meet?

*You meet some that aren't, and you appreciate their authenticity. They are refreshing to you.*

Yes, I just don't meet very many.

*There aren't very many, but there could be more. That's a defensive mechanism: they're protecting what/who they think they are. That's not what they really are but an image of who they think they are. If they knew who they were, you would like them all because you would see yourself in them, and they would see themselves in you. As it is, it's false images they feel they must protect. They see it as their very lives. They clamor for respect, not knowing that to truly respect themselves IS to respect others. He said to love your neighbor as yourself.*

Well, thanks. I feel better now. You're certainly authentic and so is your clarity, as always.

*You're welcome, and I am, and it is always. Now, get out there. Forget caution. I'm going to show you where things disappear and where they reappear. You will manifest them. That's part of YOUR job.*

That sounds like fun!

*Oh, it will be.*

It will be.

*That's the agreement we need. You see that that IS, not AS is.*

Got it.

*Then it's pure focused thought in faith, then release it as it is so, and so it is.*

Got it.

*Then be. The "doings," in the being.*

Walk IN it.

*Correct. You will see it as it is in the now, where everything is.*

I can do that.

*No, you WILL do that.*

Intent.

*Yes, you intend it, fully.*

The ramifications of this . . .

*It is beyond anything, anything that you know that is, yet it is not beyond everything. It is a part, a function of what is contained in everything, and it's everywhere.*

I'll have to ponder this.

*Yes, you will. What is, is not and then it is.*

Cycles.

Everything cycles.

*Everything that cycles does.*

Except that that does not, the unchangeable.

*You ARE a tracker.*

I'm learning.

*Yes, you are.*

**2:37 PM**

How do you do that with the perfume?

> G is referring back to how, when he felt Talia and was
> healed by her, he smelled her perfume.

*That's the shadow; this is the real.*

### *June 14*

**12:59 PM**

Talia, those photos of you were awesome. It's so plain you were
living a life fully as it's supposed to be lived.

> I had given G some photos of Talia, some with her horse,
> some playing volleyball, some just being her.

*Yes, I did. I knew instinctively I had to. That's an instinct I always
trusted.*

Thank you for the life you lived, and thank you for the life you're
living now.

*The life I lived WAS for an example. I didn't know it then, and if you
would have told me I would have laughed. I wouldn't have thought
that was necessarily true, but it was necessary and it was true. You may*

*not always know whom you are influencing. I influenced people then without noticing it. You're always more than you think you are. But to know that is to trust it, that you can be used in a divine way whether you know it or not.*

I'm really, really running out of words here.

*Many times there's not that much to say. Just let things be as they are. The most meaningful communication is often without words, for no words are needed. Words are misused more than anything anyway. How many times have you seen the sincere word of truth despised?*

A lot.

*Yes, a lot, and why is that?*

Because the world is filled with knuckleheads.

*Maybe we could get into a bit more detail.*

You could. I see knuckleheads wherEVER I go.

*Maybe you should reflect something else to them.*

Ooh, got me on that one.

*You will see what you expect to see. I told you to expect the unexpected. You're not always expecting to see divinity shining through whom you meet, but maybe you should.*

Yes, you got me. You awe me into silence.

*That's a "trick" I use to get you here and to keep you here.*

Well, thanks for tricking me.

*That's not so hard. You've always been open to truth. Your frustration has been that it always seemed so hard to find. It's not, when you look in the right places. It seems like it's placed here and there. It's really not—it's everywhere. It's man's nature to look here and there for someone who is genuine to tell them the truth, yet that's very rarely the case. That's their nature, to make a god out of someone. All the time God and all the answers are within them.*

Looking for love in all the wrong places.

*Pretty much.*

I covet our time together; it's a divine haven.

*You could call it that.* ☺

I just did. You love this, don't you?

*Yes, I do. It's truly a part of all that is, and it's being watched closely.*

By a great cloud of witnesses?

*Yes, a very great cloud.*

I feel anticipation, the joy of them.

*They are in awe; this is somewhat of a first.*

> Talia is referring to this communication, at this level of frequency and intensity.

A new thing on the earth.

*Exactly. This will confirm much to many.*

Now I need to believe who I am.

*Yes, the light IS expanding and you're riding the wave of it.*

I feel like I'm learning everything I need to know about everything, doing this.

*You are. There are no other truths. There is only THE Truth. He in whom all is. To know HIM is to become one with Him. "Make them one Father even as we are one." Do you think this prayer is not answered?*

Time to go back to work.

*Time to be one in Him.*

Make it so.

*It shall be so. It has been spoken.*

Oh man, Talia.

*It's beautiful, isn't it? Remember how you used to ride on the ragged edge?*

Yes.

*You're doing that now, but now you're accomplishing something.*

**6:15 PM**
*Ride the ragged edge.*

Ok, but it scares people.

*It does, and it thrills them, disturbs them. But you'll always see a response. Some it will awaken, some it will shake back into slumber.*

Why would it shake them back into slumber?

*It's the choices they make.*

They make them too, don't they?

*Yes, they make them. It is your nature to create. Once you awake to who you are, nothing is impossible to you.*

*Some have vested interest in keeping you asleep.*

*Who you are is known in solitude.*

*In the quiet of the heart is your true nature known.*

*There is no other nature given among men whereby you can be saved.*

*A good man shall be saved.*

*He has magnified His word above His name.*

*His word is heard in stillness.*

*That's an equation of freedom.*

*When you are saved from your own deluded creations, then you are free.*

*Whomsoever the Son sets free is free indeed.*

*He has given you power and authority to be sons, and saviors shall arise upon Mt. Zion to judge the mount of Esau, and the kingdom shall be the Lord's.*

*When He was asked, "What is truth?" what was there to say? He was the embodiment of it.*

*In the silence is the truth and your true nature known.*

*You are all things.*

*That's an equation for wholeness, for completion.*

## *June 15*

---❖---

**8:07 AM**

Talia, all of that wasn't you, was it. It was just the spirit flowing.

*That "just the spirit flowing" is what makes all things possible. You said yourself you can't put these things in boxes. It is the box, what's in it and everything outside of it. Although that doesn't explain it either: it all is. Some like to have everything explained to them. Things are revealed in time.*

*Patience, Mom.*

*You know you can only fool yourself. Which is a trick people use on themselves to teach themselves.*

I think I see exactly what you mean.

*Yes, you can jump ship, but we're still all in it together.*

That's a unique way of putting it.

*Yes, you saw what I meant. That's placing pictures in your mind, to explain, to reveal meanings. That's expansion of understanding. That's light expanding. The universe IS expanding, you know. He reveals Himself in His creation. Are not we all His creation? Why would one take "the source of all things that are" out of the equation? That just doesn't add up.*

That's so simple.

*Yes, the complexity of simplicity. The complexity is the darkness. The simplicity is the light. And these complement one another.*

I totally see that.

*You don't totally see it, but you see enough of it to totally matter.*

OK, there's some deep stuff there, isn't it?

*There always is.*

How did you . . .

*Learn all this stuff. I'm VERY close to Him.*

Oh, man! I see something there that's way more than it looks like.

*Of course you do; that's sincerity of heart. It's time. Sit down and write. There are some things you need to know.*

OK.

*You're not totally with me on this.*

You know I've got to go back out there in a few minutes. I'm a little distracted.

*No, that's not it. You're holding back. You're afraid of where this might go.*

*That was you looking at your watch.*

Just trying to keep track.

*You're trying to keep track of something that doesn't really exist.*

Well, it seems to.

*I know it does. When I say this is a game, it's not like most people take that word, as something trivial. This is a most serious game, one that takes all your wits about you and everything you have. This is the first time you've avoided me.*

Talia, I don't mean to. I'm just jumpy.

*You know this will shake the very foundations.*

That's fine.

*It's very fine. It's time for this. I KNOW this; you should too. You can't run.*

I know that.

*But it's crossed your mind.*

Come to think of it, yes. OK, I surrender.

*You have to surrender all. I know you're a fighter, and it goes against the grain, but that's the way it is.*

You know I didn't really know all of this.

*I know; that's why I'm showing you. You're trying to keep things safe, and there's no doing that. Let the chips fall where they may.*

All right.

*Of course it will be all right, always. That's all for now.*

Guess I had plenty of time after all. ☺

## *June 16*

**6:47 AM**
OK, what's with Narnia?

> While Frankie and I were meeting with Rebecca, Talia
> mentioned that she had seen the movie, *The Lion the Witch*

*and the Wardrobe*, but she had called it *Narnia*. Talia also said that where she was, in Heaven, it was like Narnia.

*That's the way it is here, only better. It was something she's—Frankie's—familiar with. I saw the movie.*

**12:58 PM**
You told me once to look at it as if I'm an instrument to be played. I'm an instrument.

*You're a beautiful instrument.*

Come on.

*You want to edit it, don't you.*

Yes.

*It's good to face the truth, the good and the bad. You see how hard it is for people to be honest with themselves, even when it's good? This really holds you back from knowing who you are.*

It's like I've already done this. I've seen this before.

*That's because it's all happening now.*

I also see that some will think I'm deluded.

*That's their own delusion of the truth. The truth is not what someone says it is or what they think it should be, nor what they want it to be. The truth just is. Ultimate truth is unchangeable no matter how it seems to change. He said, "I am the Lord thy God; I change not." Some dread if that's true; I tell you it's the best news ever.*

**9:00 PM**
*Are you ready now?*

June 2008

You ARE chipper today.

*I had a good day. Mom had a good day.*

I didn't know you'd ever have a bad day there.

*We don't, but there is a LOT going on and we do have concerns, much like where you're at on earth at times.*

Well, I guess that's not news, but that's sure not the general consensus we down here have of heaven.

*There are a lot of misconceptions. Look at the misconceptions on earth about what's going on there and what things really are and what they mean.*

Good point.

*You bet it is. I know you adore me and that's sweet of you.*

I do. Why do you bring it up?

*I just don't want you to exalt me above measure, that's all.*

I just know who you are.

*Yes, you do, and I appreciate that, but you do have that tendency.*

I remember you told me about the gods and goddesses.

*Yes, and that's held people back from doing what you're doing now.*

I don't want to jeopardize your message.

*I told you it wasn't just my message, that it's much greater than me.*

I know it is, but you are totally awesome.

*Yes, I am. I'm also just a messenger.*

It seems you're diminishing yourself.

*No, not at all. I'm just telling you the truth.*

I wasn't going to build a temple or anything.

*Well, that's good, because that really WOULD jeopardize the message.* ☺

Oh, you kill me. I love your quick wit and your sense of humor.

*You like changing directions fast.*

You're the one that changes directions fast. I never know where you're going to go with this.

*That's another way I keep your attention. Are you going to write or not? Which animal changes direction fast and shows you quick changes to come?*

The coyote.

*Study his ways.*

You don't think this will compromise the message?

*You can always edit it out.*

I thought you said not to edit your words.

*I did, and that's what you were just wanting to do. I also said some of it was just for you.*

Which is this?

*What do you think?*

I don't know. I'm trying not to.

*It's for you, for others.*

Whoa.

*You're putting the brakes on?*

You are feeling good today.

*Yes, I am!*

Well, I'm happy for you.

*Thanks.*

Well, that's great, Talia—you're having fun. That's great.

*I'm having great fun!*

Fantastic! You're just finding out all the things you can do there, aren't you?

*Yes! It's more than anyone could imagine! You're feeling a part of my unimaginable joy. There are no words for it there.*

No.

*Bask in it. That's what you should bask in.*

What happened today?

*Discovery! Wonderful, beautiful discoveries. And there's no end!*

I'm so happy for you.

*So am I. So am I.*

Talia, you seem nearly speechless.

*There's no speech for this. It's much, much greater.*

I can't imagine.

*No, you can't.*

This is new to you.

*It's all so beautifully new!*

Maybe you need a day off.

*That's funny. You need a certain detachment, along with a passionate interest, to do this.*

I thought you were done for the night. I was going to tell you to go enjoy yourself.

*I am, immensely!*

You know, when you put it like that, it's kind of hard to stay here.

*Sorry, Charlie, you've got work to do.*

Now YOU'RE being flippant.

*I'm having fun. You said you wanted me to.* ☺

THAT made me laugh.

*Laughter's good. It works like a medicine. And you needed it.*

Thanks.

*Any time.*

You totally blow me away.

*So you've said. It's all a balance, G. That's why I'm doing this.*

*My dad likes you a lot. He says you're a good man.*

> This blew me away, because a few hours before Michael had Talia tell G this, I was having dinner with a friend of mine who asked whether or not Michael ever spoke

to G. I told him that up until now, no, that Talia had told Rebecca once that her dad really liked G, but that was it. We both wondered why it was that Michael was not speaking to G himself, and then G got this message.

Tell him I said thanks.

*He says you're welcome.*

Why can't I hear him?

*He's still learning it.*

You seemed to have stepped right into it.

*I did; it's easy for me. It's hard for some others to hear though.*

You said through someone that I heard you 100%. Why is that?

*You've forgotten most of the things you've gone through to get to where you are now. There's not a great need for you to remember them either. Everyone's path is different.*

### June 17

**8:12 AM**
*You're distracted.*

Yes, I know.

*Go take care of what you need to take care of, then come back and we'll chat. When this door opens I need you to be quiet—your mental chatter doesn't help us. You need to be in perfect stillness.*

**8:52 AM**

*Don't make it harder than it is. The stillness is always perfect. This should be effortless. That's the trouble with words, the misinterpretations applied to them. There are more efficient ways to communicate. You puzzle whether you hear if there's an "s" on the end of a word. The reason is, I'm showing you it really is all ONE. The separation is for your learning. Yes, everything is for a reason. Why did you put the "T" when you meant the "G"?*

> During G's communications with Talia, he puts an initial next to each statement he writes down, to indicate who is speaking, him or Talia. Sometimes he hears the words and says them at the same time, so he puts a "T" *and* a "G" down, but this time he wrote a "T" *instead of* "G."

In a hurry?

*We are one. All things are.*

*So you see Mom's friend has the truth, but it is partial. Judge not, she'll get it worked out in time.*

In time?

*Yes, in time.*

*Time is a period of "places" placed together separately.*

Hard to follow.

*Yes, it can be. It's illumination of the heart for growth.*

To bring singleness of heart, singleness of purpose.

*Yes. This is concentration that is unwavering, and timeless. It's beyond awareness. Awareness is simply awakening. This concentration is purity of purpose.*

That's the answer, isn't it?

*That's the answer of how to do things right. That always results in fruit everlasting, and it's remembered.*

I see there are so many truths here that if people knew or believed this they would dig for them. This is much more treasure than the greatest lottery on earth.

*This is obviously not brought from any kingdom on earth. What we're doing here IS earth shattering. This can shatter every false perception that people have, if they will receive it.*

Free gift, huh?

*Of course it is. The curse of the law is the illusion that you must toil for something of value. The most valuable is always free. But it must be OBTAINED in freedom; that's why I said nothing was better. It's all obtained and contained in the freedom that is in Him. Get this and nobody can own you. That's why I said you were bought with a price and you were not your own. Sounds like a contradiction, doesn't it?*

Some.

*It's not. Not at all. That's the only true freedom that there is. No amount of money can buy peace or joy or understanding or anything we've talked about here. Yet people will toil like there's no tomorrow and even kill each other over it. This can put you in a place of no redemption. The love of money IS the root of all evil. And what does money represent? It can represent anything anyone wants it to represent, but is just a representation. People agree or disagree on what it represents, but it's still just a placard, or sign. See it like that and you see right through it because it is transparent. See what they use it for, and the motivation is apparent. It's just a lever to be used for good or ill that's decided by the one using it.*

Makes sense to me.

*Of course it does; how could it not? It's perfectly sensible. People make much more of it than it is. It's not all that they make it to be.*

I heard that someone said money doesn't change people, it just reveals character.

*There's a lot of truth to that.*

*Some, we're just going to get their attention. Here, some are going to get more out of this than YOU have.*

Cool.

*Yes, it is. Very cool.*

*Some will have a greater understanding; some will see the **DEEPER** meaning.*

That's awesome, because I know I'm riding that wave.

*Yes, and they'll be ahead.*

They have my blessing.

*Torchbearers; you'll see them light the way.*

This is much greater than I realized, and I thought it was pretty big.

*Told you.*

**2:48 PM**

Talia, all my expressions are inadequate.

*The Art of Life entails no forced expressions. They should flow out of you, always.*

**7:12 PM**

I don't know if I like this thermal energy lesson.

*Hot, isn't it.*

What is this all about?

*You'll see.*

> The air conditioner in G's office broke down during a major heat wave, making it very uncomfortable to be in there.

*June 18*

**6:45 AM**

Good morning, Talia.

*Good morning.*

**7:32 AM**

*Just write. There are some things you need to know.*

Then I want to know them.

*Do you really?*

Yes, I really do.

*Then you will.*

OK.

Where are we going with this?

*I wanted to point out desire.*

What do you mean?

*I mean you have to really want or desire something to really get it. A fervent desire, a passion in the heart. Most just go along for the ride. Remember our talk about violence.*

Yes.

*Many things, you have to "take it by force" or you won't get it.*

All right, what is it I need to know?

*That's it.*

*Many times you've gone along for the ride and it left you wanting.*

I see what you mean. Thanks for the imagery.

*You're welcome. Any time you've taken it by force in perfect balance, you've achieved great success. It's been astounding.*

Astounding, huh.

*You have been an astonishment at time to others.*

OK.

*Yes, and it was a sign to others on how to accomplish things, on how to get what they needed. You saw some ignore it, and you've seen how it inspired others.*

Well, that's nice to know, that some were inspired, but I don't seem to be that consistent.

*The truth is completely consistent. It's your head that hinders things. You have a proclivity to do what you're told instead of what you know is right sometimes.*

I didn't actually realize that.

*That's why I'm telling you. Sometimes you go a little over the top to please, and that can compromise your position. It also smacks of insincerity.*

"Smacks" jumped out at me a little.

*Yes, it did. I'm pointing out that it's like a slap: it stings and it's abrupt.*

I don't ever really remember seeing this before.

*It doesn't happen often with you. I'm just letting you know you can kill or damage with kindness. Remember the balance; compromise when you should, not when you shouldn't.*

So what are you going to do today?

*I'm going to be who I am in Him.*

I like the answer, but I thought you might be a little more specific.

*I can do whatever I want, and I want to help people. That's what I'm going to do today.*

That's nice. ☺

*Yes, it is nice to help others. It's very fulfilling. More should try it; that's one of the purposes of life.*

Your infallible, aren't you?

*Now I am. I know you want me to get specific on what's going to happen today. You know the principle players I'm touching and moving. I don't know what's going to happen myself. I can't make anyone do anything. That's free will. We cannot interfere. So it's a surprise to me also. That's one of the pleasures of life, the pleasant surprises. I do know it will all work out perfectly.*

That's awesome. I'm glad I asked.

*I'm glad you asked too. I've been wanting to explain that. You've been under the impression that I know everything. I told you I didn't but that I know a lot. When we do this I don't always know where it's going either. I have more joyous anticipation with this than you do. I told you I can see your thoughts forming but before; that is like a clear sky to me. I don't know where the clouds may form. It has been said that His presence is like a cloud. Something to think about, isn't it?*

Yes, it is, big time.

*Absolutely.*

I really didn't know if I was going to do this today.

*I didn't either.*

I'm glad I did.

*So am I. I told you the power of your decisions could not be underestimated. And how you could call this unto yourself. We are always here to help, but the choices are yours to make.*

To make, to create.

*Yes, exactly. All the important decisions are yours to make. How else could you learn?*

> G got a message he was going to get a phone call from someone.

*You felt that coming.*

Yes, I did.

*That was a specific thought, directed to you, from the web of life. That's a luminous being, and it's energy of the universe. How is it some do not feel it?*

Cut off from life.

*That's it. Your works will be remembered.*

That's what matters, isn't it?

*That's worthy of remembrance.*

What matters is worthy of remembrance.

*Yes, and what doesn't, isn't. Some things are worthy to forget. When you see those things, forget them. Just leave them behind.*

I meant to ask, what's with the balloons?

> While at a meeting with Rebecca, Talia told Frankie to be
> on the lookout for balloons: a sign from Talia to Frankie.

*It's a celebration. That IS for Frankie, to remember our times together. All of our times together were a sort of celebration. That's what I would like her to remember and not any kind of loss. We had a perfect friendship, and I want her to understand we still do. She knows me very well, and I want her to know when she feels my presence that's ME and not her imagination. She knows this is true, and she will feel my presence today, and that's me confirming to her that this is true. Tell her not to be sad, and she has a beautiful life ahead of her.*

> G called a friend, whose wife answered.

*That call you just made was a perfect example of non-locality of mind. She doesn't hate you; it's what she's given place to in her.*

Man, the things you can learn from a simple phone call.

*Yes, you can learn from anything, and everything means something, and you don't have to rack your brains either. You just need to see things as they are.*

Pure focused thought, perception!

*Yes, perceive those things which cannot be seen.*

"Thou hast set a table before me in the presence of my enemies."

*That happens many times in life.*

I don't care to break bread with the devil.

*You don't have to.*

He's a liar and a thief and the father of them all.

*That's right. He has been cast out of heaven. Where is heaven? Inside of you, within the heart of man, within the heart of God, within all things. What evil have you seen that wasn't the creation of man?*

I don't know.

*Yes, you do.*

I've seen the dark side. I've dealt with them.

*You dealt with them because you wanted to deal with them; that's a game you choose.*

What are you saying?

*I'm saying evil stems from the knowledge of good and evil.*

What do you mean?

*Can you know good without evil?*

I think you can.

*Can you know light without darkness? It's for the contrast to know the nature of all things. All the battles are for learning, for growth.*

All right.

*Don't withdraw just yet; we're not done. You want to get mad at a person who's sick. How can you get mad at a person for just being sick?*

Well, that's a whole different point of view.

*Yes, isn't it though. That's a perfect point of view.*

I love you.

*And if I didn't love you I wouldn't be talking with you now.*

Thank you.

*Thank YOU for being who you are. You're a self-made man who's had nothing but help getting where you are.*

That's funny.

*That's true.*

**8:08 PM**
*You accomplished some things today; you felt the shift.*

Yes, I did. I also sensed an accusation of exploiting you in the future.

*I know you did, but how could you exploit me?*

I know that—it's completely ridiculous.

*Then why bother with it?*

I just didn't want anybody to get upset.

*It will work out.*

I think maybe I should relax.

*This can be tiring.*

And the heat—hard to keep a straight face.

*Some will accuse you of talking out of your head.*

If I were that clever, I figure Disney would take me at gunpoint.

*That is funny.*

## June 19

### 7:11 AM
Good morning, Talia.

*Good morning.*

I don't know how to thank you.

*What you're doing is thanks enough. Do you know how many want this, and from this side too, just to let their loved ones know they are all right? If there was envy here, they would be envious. I'm telling you they are standing in awe of this.*

*You let my mom know from the beginning of this that I was OK, and that confirmed to her without a doubt that what she already knew was true, and I'm so thankful for that.*

There's nothing else I could have done.

*Yes, you could have ignored me.*

Talia, you were so totally adamant about it I couldn't ignore you.

*Yes, you could have. We're in a position to see the things people ignore, and you would find it hard to believe. Talk about exasperation. If you knew how many times we shake our heads. "Why can't they see!" I've heard this many times. Many are so locked into their own little world that they cannot see what's really there. So I want you to know that I appreciate what you've done for me and are still doing.*

I wouldn't have it any other way. This is a tremendous honor for me.

*That's one reason my dad thinks so highly of you. He says he wishes he could have known you there.*

Well, *I* appreciate that. Tell him thanks and I wish the same thing.

*He says to tell my mom he never wished to do any harm, and if he had it to do over things would be different.*

She'll read this.

*He knows that.*

My heart aches.

*Every second counts there; that's why I showed you not to waste moments. A moment is more than a period of time. As a matter of fact, time has very little to do with it at all. A moment is a happening, an event of truth and revelation, Now.*

That's a unique way of looking at it.

*That's a way of looking at it as it is.*

God, you're smart.

*I'm just telling you what I hear. All that happened to you on Thanksgiving was to get you to this place where YOU could hear. Why do you think you went?*

That was out of character.

*That journey you made that day was watched closely and with excitement.*

Come to think of it, I did feel that.

*Yes, and the vision you had on the way back has come to pass, and it was to confirm to you that what you got WAS pure revelation of truth.*

> On the way back from Thanksgiving dinner, G had had a vision of a water bottle with the words "Natural Spring Water" on the label. He had no idea why he saw this vision; at the time it meant nothing to him. But a year later when he was driving, he stopped for a break and picked up a bottle of water at the same location he had had the vision—the label was that of the vision.

But I don't have it all or the full interpretation of it.

*No, no you don't, but you will. It's enough for now to know where it came from.*

Wow!

*Yes, Wow! God will always Wow you, and there is no end to it.*

*That brings us to boredom. Boredom is absolutely an illusion. That's an indication that someone doesn't know themselves. To know your Self is to perceive the infinite, in which there is no end.*

I see the correlation there.

*Yes, of course, it's all tied together by that luminous web of life in which there is no end. See now how we all are one and there is no escaping it.*

Why would anyone want to escape it?

*To cling to illusions as if it were life itself. People try to get the truth to fit their idea of the truth, but that's just an idea.*

I don't know if I know how to not waste moments.

*Yes, you do. You just don't practice it very often. But when you do, that's walking in perfection. You did that just now when you walked outside; you didn't waste a single moment and you were bathed in light.*

That's awesome!

*It always is and beyond awesome. The first thing you said was "everything's cleared up." You initially meant the atmosphere, but you immediately saw it meant more.*

That's what we're doing here, isn't it, clearing things up.

*Of course it is. Nothing here is not completely clear and perfectly precise. Not that there aren't hidden truths, because there are. But if someone doesn't get this, it's not because they're empty headed but because they are not.*

That to me is somewhat hilarious and sad at the same time.

*A lot of things are like that. That's to help get you through it. That essentially is the realization people are given, that no matter how tragic something seems, it will all work out.*

Eventually.

*It's being worked out now. You, like most everyone, like a timeline so you can place things there to make sense to you. I'm telling you there really isn't one.*

That does seem to be a contradiction.

*That seems a huge contradiction, but it's not.*

*My dad, he wants to say more.*

I can tell; I can feel it and him.

*He will. It's not that easy for him and he wants it to be right.*

Tell him I'm here for him.

*He knows that.*

Part of that heartache I felt was his, wasn't it?

*Yes.*

I didn't know you could be sad there.

*You can be anything here. Regrets don't stop, but they can be worked out.*

"Being mindful" comes to me.

*That's something that should be researched.*

Should I?

*Not yet. We're not done here.*

OK.

I'm waiting.

June 2008

*Are you, patiently?*

Not really.

*Why not?*

Excitement?

*That's an emotion you should control.*

OK.

*It's always ok, when you control it. You can, you know.*

No doubt.

*Good.*

G felt a tremendous peace settle down over him.

There's a peace involved in that, isn't there?

*Yes, there is. When you're doing things right, you'll always feel that.*

Always?

*Always, if you're in touch with your feelings.*

Touchy feely, huh?

*You want to make light of it while I'm making Light of It.*

Oops.

*That's all right. You do that a lot, but I know that's just you. You have said you like to keep yourself amused. That's being in touch with who you are.*

Well, *that* was kind of a turnaround.

*That was the Light of Truth shining on your cyclic nature. Just remember I said the downs were just as important as the ups. That's another contrast for enlightenment.*

Good thing I was patient.

*Good thing you are.*

I don't have the words.

*There are none, and there doesn't need to be.*

**10:57 PM**

Where's my little notebook?

*It's in the truck.*

It is? It's in the truck?

*It's in the truck. Why are you looking around? I told you where it is.*

> G started to wonder how it was that he was actually able to hear Talia. What was it exactly that enabled him to hear her and her to put thoughts in his head?

*The brain just slows the vibrations down to a reasonable form.*

Presence of mind?

*That's part of it. Presence of mind in a larger sense contains everything. That's how you can know all things. And the vibrations of the energy of the web of life are how you can track anything. The tracks will always lead back to its source. The source or reservoir of all things. So, they are contained without being contained.*

I can't see any reason to go anywhere.

## June 2008

*There is nowhere to be but where you are.*

You seem to be the master of understatements.

*I have mastered some things, but mastery is never ending, because it's a living process. I just now mastered a way to put that to you in understandable terms.*

Yep, it was in the truck (G's little notebook).

*As I said . . .*

There's nothing that shall not be revealed in time.

*Wind IS a vehicle; that's why it sounds like one sometimes.*

OK, I don't know what that means, but whatever, it's heavy.

*Yes, that has to do with gravity.*

> G heard a huge gust of wind come up, so loud and powerful it sounded like a huge truck had just gone by.

*You just experienced something that there is no way to explain unless they have experienced it. To attempt to explain would be futile; it would diminish the process, which is to experience.*

Like war at its most visceral level?

*War is a tragedy in the makings of man.*

*Light and gravity are synonymous. You can't have one without the other. You also just experienced how light bends or is attracted to the heavier of two or more very small objects. Now you could be shown equations to refute this and prove it's wrong. I'm telling you that their equations are incomplete. I told you this was about Everything. Why would you want to edit it? That would be like editing everything. I tell you everyone who reads this is going to get a touch, a movement, and it's "right on time."*

G thought about what Talia had just said, "right on time."

Amazing, the hidden truths in plain view.

*NOW you're living the Art of Life and are flowing perfectly.*

Thank you, Talia.

*Thank you, G.*

Wind is a vehicle for what?

*It's a vehicle for truth. It's a vehicle for power. Just watch the way it blows.*

*People should only be destroyed when there's no other choice. That's the plain and simple truth. This seems like a hard saying. You were told you always have a choice, but sometimes the choice is made for you by others. You were told you could defend yourself. That's a God-given right that nature teaches.*

*The numbers yesterday—the number pattern you are working on with Ken—was your life as a mathematical structure of the universe. There is one in every number. When they understand that, they will be able to unlock all the mysteries of the universe. That's experiential understanding from a holographic base.*

*A lot of things that people think mean a lot mean very little, and a lot of things that they think mean very little mean a lot. People have it so backward so often.*

Exasperated?

*Oh, beyond words.*

*It's all one. People like separate subjects; it's all one.*

> G had a vision of Frankie and Talia looking at each other and laughing.

OK, what's with that?

*That's when we thought or said something at the same time. It was delightful and the oneness I'm speaking of. It's God in you agreeing with the truth. Now I see that we saw so many things that were truths, and we discovered them together.*

I can feel your total affection for her.

*She was always a blessing to me in SO many ways.*

And I feel her pain for you.

*She shouldn't hurt for me. She should be joyous.*

*Fellowship is the bread of life. Light reflecting back on itself is light reflecting back on you.*

*I'm making up for lost time. In both directions since that's the way you see it. In reality, time can never be lost, but it can be misplaced.*

Maybe I should tell them we shouldn't get paid by the hour. But all at once.

*Yeah, try explaining it. It's difficult enough for me, and I'm in a unique position to see it.*

It's hard enough for me to get it, and I'm getting it.

*The only reason you're getting it now was your rebellion at their teachings. If you hadn't rebelled, you wouldn't be here, now. They said that was your biggest problem: you questioned everything. You didn't fit their program, which you saw as bondage. Many of them resented that greatly because that was to them the very foundation of their life. They saw you as despising them. You were just despising their work, their way, because you saw it was a false way and it led to nowhere, at least nowhere anyone in their right mind would want to be. That teacher you just thought of, she said you could do anything you wanted. That was a revelation she received through prayer. She also said you were her favorite student because you represented a challenge; you grew together. Remember she said you were the biggest problem she ever had?*

Yes, I'd forgotten that part. I remember she threatened to retire when she got me the second time around in a later grade.

*And you thought about it too.*

Yeah, I really did. Hard to retire in the 5th grade though.

*But you seriously considered running away.*

Yes, I did.

*You're kind of in the same place now, sort of a circle.*

I don't want to run away.

*No, but that's primarily because you're not locked in a classroom. You have more freedom now.*

Freedom is good; it's like the sweet smell of success.

*You love to be outside.*

You said you had to be there before you could look in.

*Yes, I did, and you do, and you are.*

If the light's not on it, it's like it's not there.

*That's exactly right. I say it's wake-up time. It's time to walk into the Light, in the dawn of the day when everything is new.*

And I know violence isn't the answer.

*No, not in the flesh. Victory here can only be achieved by an awakening brought about by a great shaking.*

I see a sieve.

*So you do. You have to be fine to make it through, like the eye of a needle. You see the brutality coming from many directions, but the peace and power is in the Kingdom.*

So what about the whole Zippy thing?

> Zippy, Talia's dog, told Laura, the animal communicator, that he thinks it's not only Talia speaking to G, but other spirits as well trying to trick G into thinking it's Talia. And that G is thinking some things himself.

*There have been a few times it was you, but it's mostly things I would or could have said. You said yourself, if we're in agreement, what difference does it make? And I've said that myself, see.*

OK, what about being tricked?

*I told you that you were being tricked. I trick you daily. How many times have I already confirmed this to you? This is not just in word but in power. Zippy senses another spirit that isn't me, and he's right. There's a huge number clamoring for your attention. There is also THE Spirit, which is not me but that I am part of. That's Zippy separating who he knows to be me from something else.*

Anything else?

*Yes, relax. The enemy will try anything and everything he can to prevent this from getting out there. He will not succeed, of course, but that won't stop him from trying.*

I know most of the Christians will say this is "of the devil." I also know it's Zippy's perception, because he's heard me say you told me, when it was the Spirit that did. My mistake.

*Was it?*

*Those that will say "this is of the devil" is because they've had that pounded into their head. Remember your friend who talked about the parrot preachers. That was a pure revelation of the Spirit that he received while deep in prayer and intercession, with a fervent heart, to reveal truth. God always honors this work, and yet you saw the truths he brought rejected by most. How we know the spirit of truth and the spirit of error is who HEARS our words.*

I guess that sounded arrogant to some.

*It did to those who couldn't hear it.*

I know that today we both said the same thing at the same time.

*Yes, we most certainly did. I was just discussing how Frankie and I did that and what it meant.*

There's definitely a "T" to go there (Talia's statement).

*There definitely is because you hear our words. How many times have I said "our"?*

A lot.

*Yes, a lot. That's because this is again not just my message. As a matter of fact, very little of it is. I am, as you've said, being used, and my joy and honor in that is beyond comprehension. This came up for others; you already know what's the truth.*

It's been a constant struggle.

*For me also. That's why we said again that you were on the cutting edge.*

Paul was also. I've seen that.

*Yes, you have, and he proclaimed to the other Apostles that he too had seen the Lord. He knew for a fact where the source was and where his knowledge came from, and it was certainly NOT from man.*

Boy, that shift.

*You see how the "shift" has put you on a higher level? There is no use in denying yourself; it won't be denied.*

Guess I should have corrected my misquotes.

*Forget it. Leave it behind.*

It matters not.

*It matters, not.*

Your wisdom is astounding.

*My wisdom is a free gift given to me by He who is.*

I can tell you've still got a ton to say.

*I do, and I'm using the baby-step method to get them to a place to hear more.*

Those you talked about being coddled and spoon-fed . . . I know most of those are under the "parrot preachers," aren't they?

*You know they are, and you've said yourself that they should be working themselves out of a job. As it is, most tell them what they think they want to hear or can receive to keep the numbers up.*

*That's disgusting (G and T).*

## June 21

**2:30 PM**

Thanks for the word last night.

*You think I can't be just as clear today?*

I know, the same yesterday, today, and forever.

*You don't sound very convinced.*

I'm convinced that my inconsistency is consistent.

*You shouldn't convince yourself of that.*

Who is this?

*Talia. Remember my nature (Heaven's Dew); that's how you can tell. When you get a phone call and you think it's someone else, do you think this would be much different?*

J said in his dream he thought it was someone else at first (the cell phone dream).

*Why do you think he told you that?*

I guess for times like this.

*It also has to do with assumption. Why are you dropping it?*

Because I don't trust myself.

*Remember what I told you? To trust yourself. Remember I also told you about the downs?*

That they were just as important as the ups. I still prefer the ups.

*Anyone would. It's important to understand the cycles.*

Well, I don't really understand it.

*Well, now you're in a down.*

Yeah, no joke.

*You'll be up again.*

**6:43 PM**
You said before, "What is, is not and then it is." You're talking about turning energy into matter by pure focused thought and speaking it into being, aren't you?

*That's part of it.*

Part of it?

*There's more. You have to ask in faith, believing you will receive. There is an energy, or force, that flows throughout the universe, in and through everything. Within this gentle flow is a spin of tremendous speed. Within this spin is a twist or transitional torque where things are made. It's mind that causes growth and being. It's living mind that creates. This spin can be found in everything that is.*

I just saw a potter's hands.

*So you did. That's the part they usually leave out.*

In that dream I thought I also heard "temporary torque."

*That's because it's always changing.*

### June 22

**8:16 AM**

I told Ken I have changed common sense to uncommon sense because it's so uncommon.

*That's largely because of the media and your educational system.*

It's not mine.

*Exactly, you've rejected most of it. Common sense is appropriately named because it's another birthright, and at one time it was quite common. Now it's a struggle to attain once it's been stolen or washed away.*

I know where the root of the deception comes from.

*Yes, you do; it was shown to you. Again, most serve whoever pays the most, and the god of this world is well funded.*

But in the end the way of the dark side is the way of poverty and pain.

*That's right, because whatever He offers you will be taken away and given to those who have not.*

How does that work?

*The wealth of the sinner is laid up for the just.*

Solomon said that in "Proverbs."

*It was right.*

I just never quite got it.

*You'll see it.*

I just flipped through this notebook and saw it filled with words.

> G was flipping through the notebook he was using to
> write down his discussions with Talia, and as he flipped
> through the blank pages he saw them filled with words.

*That's coming truth. They will flow to you like raisins.*

Like raisins?

*Somewhat like nuggets of truth from THE vine, distilled.*

I don't even like raisins.

*You'll like these.*

**10:54 AM**

I had a vision and I saw my arm with circles going down it.

*You can use that spin, that spiraling.*

That's chi, isn't it?

*That's what some call it. It can be channeled and directed by thought.*

I know you can cut it in others.

*You can also enhance it in others.*

**2:53 PM**

I just spent most of the last four hours walking outside, and it's 107 degrees or thereabouts, and I really did stay relatively cool with no shade, although there is a breeze.

*You were walking in it. I told you this was more than words. This is power and the Spirit of Life. Things are starting to appear for you. Expect them, walk in them. It is my good pleasure to give you the kingdom.*

Talia?

*Yes?*

You can do that?

*It has been given to me, and it is mine to give to whom I will.*

Well, that's news.

*That's good news.*

That's going to step on some spiritual toes.

*It's time they heard it. You can do the same thing you know.*

OK.

*You bet it is. You see this is true and you want me to explain it.*

You read my mind.

*Remember your explanation. Everything doesn't have to be explained but experienced, and accepted.*

All right.

*Yes, it is.*

## *June 23*

---

**6:26 AM**

*You don't think you can do this this morning?*

I didn't till now.

*Let it go.*

What?

*All of it. Your anger is not going to change anyone, at least not for the better. Just let it flow. Remember, water off a duck's back.*

Why are we doing this?

*To change things, for the better. You can think of hundreds of reasons not to do this.*

I sure can.

*This is all a very simple process, and that's one of the things we're showing here. That this—communication with the spirits—is not just something for you to do with me but that anyone can.*

Some of this is heart-rending.

*That's to tune your heart, your innermost being, to show His glory.*

You've got an answer for everything, don't you?

*Pretty much. Nothing's ever really lost; it's there to access if you need it.*

Never saw it like that.

*Now you have. Time as you see it is your conception of it.*

I'm starting to understand that.

*Yes, you are. Now walk in the light you see. That's the only true light anyway. Those who would make demands on you come from a place of misconception, a place that lacks the true light, but they are convinced they are right.*

Sounds like insanity to me.

*It somewhat is, because it's crazy to demand something from someone to verify their position. The truth will always stand on its own. You've resisted the lie before and been labeled rebellious.*

A little rebellion now and then is a good thing.

*You need to go.*

I know.

**12:59 PM**
*Sometimes you need to speak the obvious.*

Why?

*Some things aren't so obvious to others.*

**7:12 PM**
OK, Talia, you said you've got something to say.

*I do. I wanted you to know that what you're going through right now, everybody goes through at some time or the other, and that it's to create compassion in you. Something you lack sometimes.*

OK.

*I told you that you would be tested; the heat's just part of it. Instead of looking for a way out, look for a way to flourish in it.*

Boy, it's easy to talk about.

*It's easy to walk in it when you find that place. If you'll remember, you walked in it yesterday; what happened between then and now?*

I don't know.

*Yes, you do. Yesterday you were in a proper frame of mind to receive it. Today you felt that you were unworthy and so was everyone else.*

All right.

*Yes, it's all right, it's going to be all right.*

### June 24

**7:20 AM**

*I'm ready if you are.*

I hope I'm ready.

*You asked to receive the pure word of truth; now believe it and expect it. I told you that you were a leader, so take the mantle upon you.*

How do you do that?

*By leading, by knowing who you are, by a simple acceptance. Do you not think I am a leader? I know who I am. It's my great honor to lead in this. There are MANY here that are watching me closely to learn from MY side how to do this, and they are amazed because they can see the fruit that is to come from this. Much of it is even growing in some now. Some of it is being manifested now. Can you deny this?*

No.

*Then what does hinder you?*

Probably what my friend said last night.

*And what was that?*

You know what he said.

*I know but I want you to write it.*

He said it was he himself that was getting in the way of his walk with God.

*There's the hindrance.*

How do you prevent that?

*By knowing who you are. When you really know who you are it doesn't matter who others think you are or what they think of you. It will have no effect because YOU will know who you are.*

As you think in your heart so are you.

*Exactly, and you'll look back on the delusion of who you thought you were as just that, a delusion. The only power delusion has is your acceptance of it, and there are many salesmen in the world. One way to see the motivation of these salesmen is whether they are trying to help you, or are they trying to get something out of you? You see so many drained at the end of the day and no wonder; so many would suck the very life out of you merely for personal gain or their own satisfaction of just doing it.*

Isn't that the truth?

*You can bet it is: that's the "God's honest truth."*

You said that for a reason, didn't you?

*I most certainly did. I want to make it clear that God's truth is always honest. When someone tells you the truth but without honesty, that makes it a lie and that is a perversion of the truth. That has been called a "twist of the truth," and that's what it is.*

You are a most wonderful teacher.

*Thank you.*

You sounded humble.

*I am. I am in constant awe of this, as you are. The difference is there is no doubt here at all. It doesn't exist here because it's a lie, and no lie is of the truth. Everything here is the truth. No lie can possibly enter here or exist here. The Kingdom of God is within you; let no lie enter there or exist there. In reality it can't, but it is possible to accept untruth as truth. But it's not reality and it's not really in your kingdom. This walking in the Kingdom is walking in the truth in which there is no lie.*

And that's the hindrance, isn't it?

*That's exactly right, accepting something that isn't real. There is not a much better compliment than someone saying you're real, genuine, authentic—and realizing it's true, the honest truth. That description has been used about me, and it's true. That's one reason I said my life there was an example. I was authentic; I couldn't ever see a reason not to be. That's one reason I questioned everything. I saw so much that wasn't authentic that I had to ask why.*

I guess that's another sacred question.

*It was, because it leads you to the truth and that's what a sacred question does: leads you to the truth. You see instructors teaching things by the strivings of the flesh—that's not authentic. It should be effortless. Like ripe fruit falling from a tree. Instead you're seeing them trying to make things happen, or force them. Why is that?*

Lack of depth?

*That's one reason. There is also ego involvement. Remember the salesman: that's an impure motivation, and the results are not that lasting. The lasting impression a teacher makes is the impression upon the inner man.*

I heard before in the spirit that "ego is your head trying to prove what you already are by what doesn't matter."

*That's true. People have a fascination with authenticity, and not only because it's so rare but because it's the way things truly are meant to be. It's a signpost of freedom. That's why you were so fascinated with me. You had never met anyone so authentic.*

That's true. I never had.

*But you knew they were out there, and you had prayed to meet one.*

I had; I had forgotten that.

*That's how prayer works. It doesn't matter if you remember them or not; THEY are remembered.*

This is all about the crown, isn't it?

*It is all about the crown that was placed on my head by HIM In Whom ALL is, the Almighty. I never stopped searching for the truth, because I WANTED to know what it was. So in that way I WAS very smart.*

It's smart to want to know the truth.

*It sure is.*

Ken said his dad said there was one God, but there are many gods.

*There are. Did he not say you would share in His kingdom? There are many misinterpretations; many will say this is. It's hard to accept. That's their thoughts rejecting the truth. It's not what they've been taught to believe. Many project their own insecurities on God. Do you think God is insecure about His place, like he might be overthrown if he gave someone too much authority?*

No, that's pretty ridiculous.

*It is, but that's the root of the thinking of those that think this. Many of these would say, "But God doesn't share His glory." But that's not true—he shares it constantly. It is "his good pleasure to give you the Kingdom." Would you not share your glory with your son?*

Of course I would.

*Are you greater than God, more benevolent?*

I reckon not.

*He has plainly stated that it is NOT robbery to be equal with God. When they finally accept THAT, the way will be clear.*

Whoa, I'm blown away again!

*The wind of the Father.* ☺

Talia, you are so cool!

*That does describe me perfectly. I'm close to the power.*

That was a lesson of the AC, wasn't it?

*Yes, the heat drove you to compromise your view and some of your privacy to be cool. Spiritual people are always "cool."*

I'm seeing how the universe works here.

*Of course you are. You would have to be blind not to. And you have a very distinct appreciation for vision.*

Without which the people perish.

*That's right. He said my people perish. We're attempting to awaken that vision within them so they won't. It's a simple acceptance and belief. He does the work.*

Well, that's a simple formula for success.

*It sure is. That brings us to something else. When you see people despising the truth, know that that's them despising themselves.*

*Children are very easy to mold into an image, and it's very hard to break that graven image once they've been molded into it.*

*My mom was very, very mindful of how she raised me. Do you see the fruit of it? She WILL share in the rewards of the fruit of my life, of my being who I am, because she was instrumental in it and a central part of my life.*

That seems a bit detached.

*It's a detached way of looking at the truth exactly as it really is, as an observer. It has nothing to do with my great honor of being her daughter or of my affection and LOVE for her as my mom. My love for her has no bounds, and she knows this. I said before you had to be outside to see in; there are much deeper truths here than is readily apparent.*

I probably didn't word that right, you just seemed . . . It's the way you said it, I guess.

*I said it the way I said it so you would say what you said so I could say what I did afterwards. This is all being guided, you know.*

By the Potter's hands.

*That's right, to mold into HIS image. When people ask what's the matter they are asking "what matters?" And the way they ask it is what matters.*

I totally see what you mean.

*Almost. This takes some contemplation. Go to the pond and look at it.*

It's teeming with life.

## 11:05 AM
Talia, why am I here?

*It's all transitional.*

## 11:20 AM
*Where things disappear and reappear is the new birth. Where the old things are passed away and behold, all things have become new. I have a new life now. My old life has passed away, because energy can never be destroyed and energy is what we ARE. The waters of life that flow from the Throne of God. The river of Life. You've seen it and you asked what it was and you were told: that's the river of Life, from which all life flows.*

I remember.

*How could you forget?*

This is tearing my heart out.

*This is darkness leaving you.*

I don't want to cling to it.

*You don't have to. Remember what I said: get rid of what you don't need, then you'll have room for what you do.*

This is not as easy as I thought.

*It's a lot easier than not doing it at all. Now you see why people aren't fighting to do this. And make no mistake, it IS a fight.*

I won't back down.

*You say that now. There is a part of you that wants to throw this all down now, get in your truck and drive as fast as you can down the highway with the music on to drown it all out. That's a normal reaction. The supernatural reaction would be just to accept it. You can't run away anyway. Where would the highway take you? I told you this was a fight. Have you ever gotten into a real fight and not been hit some?*

Not very often.

*Never when you've had a skilled and determined opponent.*

That's true.

*Of course it is. The light cuts and sometimes it hurts. When have you gotten into a real fight and not learned from it?*

I learned a lot.

*You certainly did. That's because you were fighting an energy being like yourself.*

I hate fighting.

*You LOVE to fight. It was a supreme challenge for you, and you always sought out the best. Now you need to put THAT in context with this.*

We're self-deluded, aren't we?

*That's the only delusion there is. All things are naked unto the eyes of Him. It's not easy to see yourself that way; that's why so many run from it. The truth CAN hurt, but it's life giving.*

*I know you want to stop.*

Yes, I do. I feel like nobody understands.

*That's not true. More understand than you think.*

How can I get so high and so low in such a short amount of time?

*That's perspective. That's the flow of energy in the universe. That's the light shining on the darkness. The darkness fears it. It's terrified of it. That's how you stopped them. You saw the terror in their eyes. You said it worked wherever you went in the world, and it has. It's universal. You never had to lay a hand on a single one of them because they saw what was going to happen. Darkness can never defeat the light. It just isn't possible.*

Thanks for explaining that. I speculated that was what was happening. I even looked in the mirror to try and see what they saw but never could.

*Like a friend said, "The greater the need, the greater the results," and He always supplies your need.*

*We're thinking more alike now—that's why it's hard to separate it. We are becoming one. The separation is to make sense of it. You see how that works? We are only one because there is only one.*

Talia, I've got to go stumble around in amazement.

*Why don't you go and walk surely in truth by the acceptance of it instead? Told you that you would be back up.*

*You were told martial arts were just a vehicle to get you to be where you need to be.*

Should I continue?

*I know you desire a normal life, but that's what this is. It's abnormal to be cut off from life, from the truth. That's why I say freedom IS your birthright and you are born into it. If you're not free you should ask, where did it go?*

## June 25

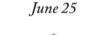

### 7:00 AM

*You have to come from a place of silence to do this.*

I know.

*I have a lot to say.*

I know.

*You have to listen.*

I know.

### 8:17 AM

*Nobody understands.*

What?

*Nobody is no thing; it's nothing. What you're picking up is no thing; it's nothing. When one member of the body suffers we all suffer. The Kingdom of Heaven suffers violence to take it all back, all things that have been stolen. To restore all things unto Himself.*

*Your complaint is justified in that the lack, the poverty of the body is no thing. The things that are needful, essential to the health of the body, are missing, mostly by self-will.*

*No one does this alone. It just isn't possible.*

I thought I was whining.

*You were. You lost the vision for a moment. You were feeling what others are feeling and living, but it's not real, it's a lie. No lie will ever fulfill anything. Why would someone accept it? The only way to apply the word of truth is to come from a place of peace and purity. The motivations of the heart must be pure, and the peace must RULE in your heart.*

Talia, why did you speak to me in Spanish the other day?

*You thought you were hearing things.*

Yes, I did.

*You were, you were hearing me speaking Spanish.*

I didn't understand it.

*That's because you rejected it.*

What did you say?

*I said, "This was for all people."*

I did sort of get that interpretation.

*Yes, you sort of did.*

Are you being funny?

*Sort of.*

So you're feeling good today?

*I always feel good. I knew you would discover the truth, that I spoke Spanish, and that's just another confirmation to you that this IS me.*

YOU are unbelievably clever.

*What's so unbelievable about it?*

You're right. This has been confirmed so many ways, and from the very beginning I knew it was you.

*You did know me from the very beginning. You thought you knew me from before when we met and you asked yourself, "How is it I've never met her? She seems so familiar."*

I remember that.

*We've talked about everything here, in detail. Stay focused. You used to get sidetracked on the funniest endeavors, and I would tell you to stay focused. I was an anchor to you, and you know that's true. We always have been. Why do you think you feel my loss so profoundly? We've always loved each other.*

I didn't know that.

*I didn't either. Now does it make sense?*

Yes.

**12:35 PM**
*You're afraid to write.*

No.

*Then why aren't you writing?*

I'm waiting.

*What are you waiting for?*

I'm waiting for it to be right.

*What wouldn't be right about it?*

What do you mean?

*Exactly.*

Come on, Talia, I can't outdo you at this.

*We're being. There's no outdoing; our doing is the result of our being.*

See! I won!

*Now you're being funny.*

Let's get on with it.

*Where do you want to go with it?*

I want to go wherever we need to go with it.

*Good, we will.*

I'm getting nothing here.

*That's not so. You're getting my love.*

**1:00 PM**
*Our Father wants us to continue with the message.*

Then let's do it.

*Yes, let's.*

*The issue is change. Things must change to walk in this new kingdom being ushered in. It's a change of heart that's needed. Some think it's a change of location or even a change of cars that's needed, but it's none of those things. It's a change of heart.*

Change of cars?

*Yes, some think that. You're getting off track.*

The more I find out about you the more I see you're a universe unto yourself.

*Now you're back on track. ☺*

*Remember when he said to you "feed the herd"?*

Yes, the elk, the warriors.

*That's what we're doing here. Remember you asked how?*

Yes.

*What did you hear?*

I think it was, "It will be shown you."

*It was, and what did you say?*

I think it was, "Then you make the way and let it be clear to me."

*It was.*

I remember it was in Oklahoma.

*It was; is this not clear to you?*

It is.

It looks like a contradiction with the "nobody understands" thing.

*I told you it was geometry. It's the angles, seeing the different angles in the light, the reflection of the truth from THAT point of view. There's always more than one way to look at something. The scales must be balanced and they are balanced by wisdom. That's why Solomon said it was the principal thing and to GET it. He understood that. He was also in a position to pass on these truths, and he did that with his kingly authority.*

That was awesome!

*How could it not be?*

I think I'm learning to like "raisins."

*It is the condensing of truths into an understandable form.*

**4:51 PM**
Talia, how did I know you in the very beginning?

*You were there. In the glorious beginning, in the dawn of all things, you were there.*

Well, I guess that's been awhile.

*Do you remember your first birthday?*

No.

*Were you born that day?*

That's what they say.

*Do you take them at their word?*

I've talked about that before, that it's hearsay and how witnesses are so unreliable, but as a joke.

*Well, this is no joke, and my word is completely reliable.*

*Que es Dios?*

Can't we keep this in English?

*Sure. You should keep going.*

What do you mean?

*You should just keep going.*

OK, whatever that means, I'll keep going.

*Good, you'll understand later.*

## June 26

———————❖———————

**6:34 AM**
Good morning.

*GOOD morning.*

Mir menges.

*I just told you good morning.*

      G tried to trick Talia by saying good morning in Albanian.

You see my thoughts.

*I can also see the intent of your words. It doesn't matter what words you use. Words are courtesies here between us; they are not really necessary.*

It's a lot faster without them, isn't it?

*It's instantaneous. There we often need them to explain, to clarify points of interest, or UNinterest.*

Words do come between people a lot, don't they?

*All of the time. That's another message we're here to reveal, that that's not the only means of communication. As a matter of fact, it's often the least efficient.*

Yes, well, if silence is golden, there are a lot of folks that will never be accused of hoarding.

*That "silence is golden" is an interesting statement.*

That's an old saying.

*Maybe; it's still an interesting statement.*

Well, I'm glad I could provoke you to thought.

*I have plenty to think about, and it's all good. Still, that's an interesting statement of fact.*

OK, I know gold is a type of divinity.

*It is.*

And that silence is where you said you lived.

*It is. Interesting, isn't it.*

It is.

*Out of the mouths of babes, spontaneous statements of truth.*

I'm not getting a lot done here.

*No, but you're getting a lot done "here." What's important is not what you see but what you don't see. When you see that, then you know what's important. Those you think you should be helping now, you're helping in a most amazing way, although they can't see it. When you squat down and call a child to you, and he walks towards you, then stumbles and falls, do you get angry with the child?*

No.

*That's something to think about, isn't it?*

That, Talia, is an awesome visual.

*I'm glad I could provoke you to thought.* ☺

You LOVE this, don't you?

*I certainly DO. It's smart being clever. Being clever speaks of speed on a multi-dimensional level, of being able to change directions in an instant, of perceiving the interconnectedness of all energy and of being absorbed into it, making that speed or great spin yours.*

Hard to explain, isn't it?

*It's very hard to explain in words. I showed you a picture of it by thought. The struggle comes in putting it in explainable terms. Understanding generally comes by seeing; that's one reason we've mentioned the light so much. People can be smart without being clever. They can contemplate this without having the necessary speed to catch it. You're reluctant?*

No.

*You're concerned with exalting yourself?*

No.

*Then write. You have studied this as much as anybody ever has, and you have caught this speed.*

And I feel like I have to catch it over and over.

*You do! You can't really possess it, or keep it with you in a pouch, but you can claim it as yours and have it when you need it. It's energy in a constant flow and flux. Can you stop or possess the tides?*

No.

*But the energy of the tides you can harness and use; everyone can see it. You can feel it in your dantien when you stand on the beach and watch it.*

> *Dantien* in Chinese is that place just below your belly button.

I've done that.

*The last time you were there you did it in a most profound way. You were drawn into it. That symbolized infinity. Why do you think property values are so high on the beach?*

I figured it was the view.

*It is! And it's more than that. There is always more to what you see than what you see. I LOVED the water. I had a fascination for it. I didn't know why then, but now I do.*

Wow.

*Yes, wow indeed.*

I know what that means.

*You CERTAINLY do. If people can't see the pictures but have been poisoned with words, their thinking is muddled. Yet if they apply the principles of THIS book, their solutions will appear.*

I see what you mean, and I just saw what you meant, and that may be the heaviest statement you've made yet! That has such broad implications!

*You saw what I meant because you're a seer, and we're explaining what you saw.*

*Your steps ARE ordered in His word. Grandfather was right when he said this was a great commission.*

> Talia is referring to when G visited her while meditating. Both he and Talia saw Grandfather, an Apache spirit, who told G that this work he is doing with Talia, these communications, were a great commission.

It is great! I was wondering about that.

*Now you don't have to wonder. Your steps are ordered in his word. YOU love this, don't you?*

Yes, I do. This is the most amazing thing that's ever happened to me.

*And you've had some interesting times.*

Ken said once I had crammed several lifetimes into one.

*I did that too. We know that to experience is to live.*

That's beautiful.

*Yes, it is. Distractions of this world are only that, distractions, and they would rob you of experience.*

I think when you see frustration in someone, you're seeing them, not experiencing.

*At least not what they should.*

*She'll get there. What you were just thinking.*

> G was wondering when I would be able to hear and communicate with Talia as he does. He knows I really want to and that I am working at becoming silent so that I can hear her too.

This isn't for everybody, is it?

*No and yes. We are all one.*

You say that a lot.

*That is because it's true. As I hear, I speak. That's another message contained within this one. Hear, then speak, or, to be clear, you must hear.*

Cool.

*It is, isn't it. It's a clear morning.*

Not in the natural.

*Smoke is just a veil. The mountains are still there whether you can see them or not.*

Interesting.

*Every bit of this is interesting. It requires interest to see it though.*

Choice.

*Yes, exactly.*

*The exact science of the Art of Creation.*

*Leave those things behind you don't need. Empty yourself and you can contain the truths of the Art of Creation. Why would you carry something you don't need? You can create anything you need. Go up by the pond; it will help you.*

**8:49 AM**

*I feel it's time to tell the tale of the sleeping bag.*

> Both G and Talia said that at the same time. That has great significance to G when that happens.

*Your timing is excellent.*

*It's hard to talk and listen at the same time.*

I said that too.

*I'm saying your thoughts.*

Why?

*Because we are one. I am within you. I am IN heaven.*

You're NOT just with me.

*I'm not just with you. I told you I could be anywhere I wanted, and I WANT to be in heaven so that's where I AM. I told you we were intimate and always have been.*

People are going to misunderstand this.

*Not if they are clever.*

You kill me!

*I'm bringing you life.*

I want to say wow.

*You can say it; that's the nurturing spirit of life. That's why it comes to your mind so much. It's not just an explanation, it's a description—and it's a wonderful one.*

A wonderful one.

*You got it.*

*So are you going to tell about the sleeping bag?*

I was, I mean I'm trying.

*Am I interrupting?*

No, but that's funny.

*You love to laugh. You even do it in your sleep.*

I think I'm awake then.

*You are, but you're sleeping.*

Does that mean something else?

*Sometimes.*

I think I need to take a walk.

*That's a good idea. Take it. Why are you looking up? I'm right here. It's ALL RIGHT here.*

It is.

*NOW, you declared a statement of fact. THAT changes things.*

I better take some paper with me.

*Yes, you'd better.*

Sometimes it's hard just to get out the door.

*There are doorways all over. Sometimes they are hard to get into and hard to get out of. There are places beyond these doors. Choose the doors you wish to enter through; some are not so hard and some are very difficult. Some lock behind you. You have the key; use it wisely.*

## 9:43 AM

*That "thy will be done, on earth as it is in heaven" is how it works. You see the dot above the mountain of IS?*

> G was writing down his discussion with Talia, and in his writing somehow he wrote the word "is," and it looked like a little mountain with a dot above it. At first it seemed to him as just sloppy printing, but it had a point.

Yes.

*What do you think that is?*

What?

*It's everything contained in a single dot over everything.*

That's going to be hard to explain.

*You can't explain it, but you can know it.*

## 10:05 AM

*"NOW you have NO need that ANY MAN should teach you but the same anointing that abides within you SHALL TEACH you of ALL things, and BRING ALL THINGS back to your memory whatsoever I have spoken unto you."*

*That pretty much says it all.*

That pretty much does.

*He has His times of interjection and I remain silent.*

And . . . why?

*There is absolute awe. At these times all the hosts of heaven stand in silence before Him. Did you not recall that it was unlawful to speak or utter a word in the holy of holies?*

I think I heard that before.

*You have, in the silence. THAT is the voice of the Father of all things. Now, you see His Son is within HIS daughter and the mother comes from the Father. Gender has no place here; there is neither male nor female. This is natures, the essence of what they are. Look at natures and names in Hebrew.*

I will.

*I know you will. I see it now. That "giving you the kingdom" is everything. He is more than willing to share everything. I see that. I know that and He told me that. In the mouth of two or three witnesses. The eyes, the heart, and the spoken word. Go eat; you need the energy.*

"I have meat to eat that you know not of."

*No, actually, I do know.*

That's funny.

Talia, you said more to me the other day in Spanish, that this was for all people.

*Yes, I did. THAT was symbolic of hearing something clearly but not understanding it. What do people usually do when they hear something they don't understand? They reject it. That's what you did, and that's why I mentioned not to get mad at a toddler for falling when he's learning to walk.*

Baby steps.

*Yes, absolutely, baby steps.*

Now I do feel like Peter and John wanting to build you a temple.

*You already are.*

That's . . .

*Beautiful and the truth.*

We are the Holy Temple.

*We are.*

I don't even feel like eating now.

*You don't need to EAT, you need the ENERGY.*

I feel like I have it.

*You do, but you can still eat.*

Stores for later.

*Something like that.*

You're the most commonly uncommon; I don't know how to put it.

*It's common and it's uncommon: it's everything.*

That's it.

*Yes, it is it.*

## *June 27*

---

**6:33 AM**

I can tell you want to get much more in depth.

*I sure do.*

**2:27 PM**

*This is easier in the morning or the cool of the evening. The time is past for what we were going to talk about. It will come back around. In the morning your mind is fresh and you're just returning from the place you need to be to do this. In the cool of the evening after the spirit has settled the ears are opened. In any case an attitude of thanksgiving is needed.*

Thanksgiving?

*Yes, an attitude of thanks and giving.*

*There is much merging with people. Why do you think the saints, sages, and mystics preferred solitude? Time alone with the Creator. It's hard to be intimate in a crowd.*

Nearly impossible.

*Nearly.*

I hate I missed it.

*You haven't missed anything; it's just the time has passed. It will come back around.*

**10:07 PM**

*It's all held together by the word of His power.*

I know.

*I know you think you know.*

No, I KNOW.

*Now you do.*

What was that all about?

*That was about changing things in an instant.*

### *June 28*

**9:00 AM**

*That's what the Master does; he appears to get something out of nothing. Pure focused thought quickened to slow down to matter. We understand that the world was made of those things which do not appear. You're manifesting things now. Many times YOU don't even see them. That that is not becomes what it is. You CAN change things; that is the intuitive revelation the alchemist had. They KNEW things could be changed—they just didn't know HOW. We're explaining the HOW now; the why should be apparent.*

*Nothing to say?*

I . . .

*I is ONE. That I is what sees, the one is in every number. Or you could say the one is what sees and the I is in everything. Speechless?*

This just gets neurons firing.

*Yes, everywhere.*

Talia, you're . . .

*I know, awesome.*

What if . . .

*. . . people understand this . . . could they misuse it?*

Yes.

*No, not to any meaningful extent, because as your friend Ken said, it is guarded by the sword of innocence.*

### 11:46 PM

*Colors evoke a feeling, and it's more than just a chemical reaction in the brain. It has to do with what they ARE, their true nature and purpose. Summer is a time of heat; that's why you should study coolness, its contrast.*

That contrast is how we come to a greater understanding of things, isn't it?

*Of course it is. People themselves are often the most contrasting of all, and they're fashioned alike. When you understand yourself you will understand others, so that they aren't so unpredictable after all.*

That's seeing energy, isn't it?

*That's seeing yourself. Everything is energy and energy is everywhere. It isn't always apparent, but it always is.*

Ken said he had a mathematical equation for infinite energy.

*How could it not be infinite?*

That's all people fight about, energy in some form or fashion.

*I'm glad you realized that. It doesn't have to be a conflict. It can just as easily be complementary.*

Manners.

*Being well mannered goes a long way.*

Treat others as you would have them treat you.

*The Golden Rule.*

I learned it in kindergarten.

*You heard about it in kindergarten; you're still learning it.*

Well, it's easy to treat you right.

*It's easy to treat those right who love you. He said to love your enemies, to do good to those who hate you and persecute you.*

That's hard to do.

*Not when you're walking in His love.*

Wow, Talia, you are just so totally off the charts awesome.

*Yes, I am.*

### June 29

**10:55 AM**

The voice of truth isn't always audible, is it?

*It's also the language of the heart, the knowing you have when you may not know how you know.*

**1:03 PM**

Como esta?

I'm fine, but I—can we keep this in English?

*You asked me if I would teach you Spanish.*

Yes, but I meant by osmosis or something.

*So . . . you want the benefit without the work.*

Sounds good.

*It's more of an accomplishment if you work for it.*

OK, I can't argue with you.

*You have before. ☺*

I know you're always right.

*Yes, I am.*

OK, I'll try it, but I'm just now getting English down.

*You were fluent in other languages before.*

Really?

*Yes, really. Very fluent and articulate, very persuasive.*

That doesn't sound like me.

*But it was. You saw the results of being persuasive in a negative way, so you've chosen not to influence others.*

What does this mean?

*It means your past is present. You've been influenced by it, and you influence others whether you want to or not. You LOVE the challenge.*

*You've always chosen the challenge—it's your nature. Some have seen this and used you, and you've thought that they weren't using you enough, that your talents were wasted.*

True.

*That's the part of you wanting a leader, wanting to be told what to do. But that's not your lot in life. That's you attempting to remove responsibility, to put it off on others.*

I guess I just never wanted to be responsible for others. It's hard enough to make my own decisions.

*That's exactly right, but that's a selfish way of looking at things. If someone puts themselves under your care, that's them giving you their trust, and that is always a great honor. That's them choosing to trust their lives to you, and you should always honor their decision.*

I just never wanted anybody to die because of my decisions.

*You never wanted them to live by them either. You want to give them advice and then they go about their way, but it rarely works that way. How is it you can give such sage advice and it be ignored?*

Stupidity, not listening, what?

*It's that they sense your lack of care, your refusal of the responsibility. This kicks in a survival instinct within them to disregard your advice.*

Maybe we should stick to Spanish.

*Hard to hear, isn't it?*

It started out so good.

*It's still good.*

270

I can hear it.

*I know you can. Sobering, isn't it?*

Yes, it is. I've never seen this before. I thought I was doing it for their benefit, that there was always someone better.

*You're an instrument to do this. You're also an instrument to do that; just be played. One of our first lessons together was for you to believe in yourself. Now you may proceed to do that.*

Did you know we were going to get into this today?

*I had an idea and that's how it works: it starts with a thought. Thought can flow in any direction you choose. They should flow from and with that great energy of life, which never stops flowing.*

I thought the energy followed the mind.

*It does! How could you be a creator otherwise?*

Otherwise, you couldn't.

*That's right, the other—the lie—has no place here.*

Your wisdom!

*My wisdom is not of "this" world; it is from the place I belong. I belong. You belong to some One too. This One supplies all your needs. EVERYTHING you need you have access to—and you have the key. There is NOT a door that cannot be unlocked. You've walked through the door I was holding open for you, into the great mysteries of life, into pleasures forevermore. All you saw was darkness and yet you jumped through with both feet. Do you not think that was noticed and honored? I told you that you were not of this world and you can't go back.*

I have no desire to.

*Then don't complain later when the fires burn.*

What does that mean?

*Persecutions, hatred, misunderstandings. Your own friends will forsake you.*

Well, it's happened before, and I don't have that many anyway.

*But the ones you have are precious to you.*

Yes.

*Remember they're human.*

I never thought this would get this intense. I thought you just wanted me to tell your mom you were OK.

*I did and you did and that opened the door to all this.*

Well, I've had that happen before, but it never went much further than that.

*Maybe they didn't have that much to say. I told you I loved to talk. These questions I asked myself consistently. Now I have the answers and I'm sharing them with you. You've asked yourself many of these same questions and knew there were answers but didn't know where to find them. Now you do. It is my great pleasure to give you the kingdom.* ☺

It is my great pleasure to receive it.

*And honor.*

This was said by both G and Talia at the same time.

*You're a beautiful instrument. You almost didn't write that. Why? You should always speak the truth in love. That's the answer for all things.*

Then maybe we should stop here.

*There is no stopping and there is no going back. Remember I said let the chips fall where they will. Why do you think I chose you for this?*

Did you choose me?

*Yes, I did, and you chose yourself, and we are one. I chose you because you were willing to give your life up for this. Giving your life up is a sacrifice, a living sacrifice. And that's the answer to the question you had asked about where in the world people got the idea to sacrifice others.*

Well now, that's a major misinterpretation of truth.

*Yes, that's a fly in the ointment.*

To say the least.

*The ointment is the healing nature of truth. The fly is man's additive to improve it.*

Does not sound like much of an improvement.

*The truth needs no embellishment.*

How do you like your tree?

> The tree that Talia's school planted in her memory.

*I love it. It honors me.*

You're the most honorable person I know; you deserve it and so much more.

*I've gotten everything I deserve AND so much more.*

You're perfect.

*I know.*

I wish people could hear your voice, HOW you say things.

*They can.*

They can?

*Yes, they can.*

I know you've talked to others. I mean people reading this.

*They can. You think you have an exclusive here?* ☺

Not at all. I hope with all my heart it happens, and you're being funny again, aren't you?

*Yes. You think just because someone else thinks we've died we can't have fun? Someone else told you not so long ago that they thought you had died and you thought it was funny. I'm telling you it's a running joke here. "Why can't they hear me? Because you've died, remember." I tell you it goes on and on.*

Double meaning again.

*What else?*

Several more than two.

*That's MOST of the time.*

That is pretty much hilarious.

*Yes, it is, isn't it. It gets us through.*

I can hear you laughing. You take me in so many directions so fast.

*That's the nature of truth; it moves like the wind, it changes constantly, yet it remains the same. Again, He reveals Himself in His creation;*

*how could He not? Do you think he could create something that's not from Him?*

Hey, I was cool all day! (It was 108 degrees.)

*Yes, you were except for a brief moment when you were receiving the thoughts of others. That's why it's important to set yourself apart.*

I know exactly what you mean.

*You sure do, and I'm reminding you. You often must re-mind yourself. When you're getting hot, re-mind yourself.*

Water off a duck's back.

*Exactly.*

*You're starting to understand the power you can walk in. Did you see the reaction of your friend today when you told him my truth?*

> G was speaking to a friend at work, and in response to something that was going on, G quoted Talia. What he said made his friend stop and really think.

Yes, he was startled, almost seemed to lose his balance, and said, "That was deep."

*That's the power of truth. Your delivery was perfect. You seized the opportunity in the instant it presented itself, and it was nearly effortless. That's proper technique.*

It was, wasn't it.

*I just said it was. You could have not said anything; as a matter of fact, you would have if you hadn't been so cool.*

Well, you've taught me to be cool.

*I'm teaching you.*

I stand corrected.

*You're sitting and you're listening—that's how people can hear my voice. Be still and listen.*

If they want to.

*I'm not pushing anything. I'm presenting truths that have to do with everything. It's up to them to receive it; there is no force involved here.*

That would seem self-evident.

*It would seem so.*

I can see some problems people could have with this.

*Problems are self-induced. They are also self-corrected. That's the Self I told you to trust.*

I can see how this could change the face of the planet.

*It COULD if it were received. There's nothing revealed here that hasn't been revealed before. We're just trying new methods to awaken those who slumber. To awaken them to a new thing that is to be done upon the earth. This IS a time of great shaking and you have seen things to come.*

Yes, I have.

*MANY will fall. Many will be ushered into a glorious new realm. There are many that will see this and say to themselves that they are unworthy, but this is a LIE. If they will shake themselves from their slumber and arise, they will walk into a new Kingdom in whom is peace. Peace in midst of crisis. Perfect peace in which there is no end.*

I see people sleep walking.

*You've also seem them sleep driving.*

Yes, I have, but I also see them waking up.

*Yes, you have, of course, and when they shake themselves and look, they ask how they could have been so blind. That's why it's so important not to receive a lie; it by its very design is to put one to sleep. It's easy to be blinded but is also not so hard to follow the light; after all, it's the light. If you could see it from my point of view.*

I do see it from your point of view.

*To a certain extent, but if you could see it fully you would be astounded.*

I'm sure that's true.

*THAT'S why you've been chosen.*

Talia, you are . . .

*YES, I am.*

### June 30

---

**4:56 AM**
*Things are going to happen today.*

Things happen everyday.

*Presence of mind: walk INTO it. I'm WITH you.*

I know you are.

# July 2008

---

**8:02 AM**

*It's the moments. Being in the NOW is simple. Trying to piece together a chronological timeline is complex. That can cause confusion. That creates difficulty. See, things did happen and presence of mind makes things happen to your advantage. As it is, things did happen to your advantage, and if they hadn't you wouldn't be learning what you learned here.*

Yesterday I didn't have an idea of what you were talking about.

*You had an idea, it just wasn't completely formed. Now you're experiencing it.*

I thought I was going to pass.

> G is referring to an extremely difficult high-level test he had taken.

*You've passed before. That's just a number.*

You see things perfectly.

*Yes, I see things exactly as they are. That "quagmire of crap" you were just talking about is funny, and there's a lot of truth to it. That's a creation of man. We've already talked about it in other words, about being diligent not to receive a lie, because that's what it is.*

You said we had a lot of work to do today.

*And we're doing it. Everything that happens in this world has a spiritual counterpart. That's what they are seeing on a quantum level that's puzzling to them. They're getting glimpses of it. Only by yielding to the spirit of the Creator will they see it and understand it. It's patently obvious that there is an intelligence running things and that intelligence is within them when they recognize it.*

You can't leave the Potter out.

*No, the Creator creates and there is no creativity without Him. He has commissioned this message for them to realize this and stop denying themselves.*

Wow, Talia, you have all the answers, don't you?

*I have all the answers we need for now.*

**10:46 AM**
*What we're doing here is for all people. He is no respecter of persons; the I is in HIM and that's what is respected. The other is the I that's an illusion by the acceptance of a lie. That I has no place here.*

Talia, I just had a notion to open the Bible and my eyes fell immediately on two passages. "But we all with open face beholding as in a glass the glory of the Lord, are changed into the same

image from glory to glory, even as by the Spirit of the Lord."
2 Corinthians 3:18

"And nevertheless when I shall turn to the Lord; the veil shall be taken away." 2 Corinthians 3:16

*That's the veil we're rending by violence. He did say "come boldly to the throne of Grace"; that's what that means. There is no sneaking in; it MUST be TAKEN. I told you he shared HIS glory constantly. I also said all of this had been spoken of before. Paul did a new thing upon the earth, and he knew it at the time. He was driven. God took this drive that was his nature and changed him. He was even given a new name. It HAD to be because his very nature had been changed. Saul had died and was buried with Christ and was resurrected in Him as Paul, a new creature, a new creation. This is the power of Life over death. Life is Truth, death is a lie. "O death, where is thy sting? O grave, where is thy victory?" These were intense revelations of Truth. It does go on to tell where the sting is and where the victory is. No need to rehash it here.*

We could go into that book and explain it all, couldn't we?

*We could explain it to all that had the seal removed, but it's plainly there for anyone to see. Only He is worthy to remove the seal; no thief is allowed.*

I'm running late.

*You're running right on time.*

Did you put that in my head?

*You put that thought in your head; I did see it coming though. Again, you can bind yourself with time. There's no need to though.*

Talia, you take me from one end of the universe to the other. If they could see this! And it's all right here.

*Again we're not pushing anything on anybody. If they saw it like you see it they would have it. It's a free gift but it does take effort. And yes, "we being dead yet speak." That meaning has not time nor place.*

You're . . .

*Yes, I AM totally awesome. The thoughts you think are purposeful.*

FULL of purpose.

*Yes.*

Every one.

*EVERY one. There isn't any way to put it plainer. It HAS to be seen in the light.*

There is no other way.

*No, there is no other way but the Light.*

He speaks of lesser lights in the heavens.

*Yes, he does. I am one of those lesser lights, and yet I am filled with His Light.*

What's this "beyond Babylon?" It periodically just pops into my mind.

*It's popping in your mind to let you know that's where the people are today, beyond Babylon.*

Total confusion.

*No, not totally, but close. It's because of their refusal, of their turning their ears from the truth, of them even stopping their ears. People will always stop their ears before an attack.*

It . . .

*Too intense?*

It's just much study is weariness of the flesh.

*I told you there was no end to this. That's why you must find the balance; it can burn you out. It's burned many out before.*

Well, you're easy to work with.

*Thank you, you usually are too.*

You love to "get" me, don't you?

*You're easy.*

You did it again.

*I engage you. I swiftly change things to hold your attention. You are smart, but you're easily distracted. That's why it is important to keep the body strong—it wearies easily. Our work is important. It takes fortitude. When that actor was told he was called Spirit Warrior, he replied he had been called a lot of things but never that. You said yourself "but I've been," and you have. That's another example of there being a spiritual counterpart to everything physical. That's also the double that many cultures speak of. How could there not be a spiritual counterpart. It's all one.*

That's also a huge key for them, isn't it?

*What do you think?*

I think it is.

*Then it is.*

That's another example of us changing the nature of reality, isn't it?

*What do you think?*

I think it is.

*Then it is.*

You blow my mind.

*I'm explaining it beyond the boundaries of conception. Conception is a seed or a child; it's now time to grow up.*

We can conceive of anything.

*Yes, you can conceive of anything; now it's time to grow up into HIM in ALL things. Had enough?*

No, but it's shaking the foundations.

*Told you it would.*

I'm shaking all over.

*You're shaking away what you don't need. There are a lot of things you think you need that you don't need, and it just gets in the way.*

Unnecessary obstacles.

*Yes. The earth itself shakes away what she thinks she doesn't need. That's Him again, revealing himself in HIS creation. It's a fearful thing to fall into the HANDS of the living God. That's His works upon the earth. Man will not rule over her, but he can nurture her and work with her.*

Return the favor?

*Yes, return the favor. That place you go where you were told was a sacred place and you asked why—what were you told?*

That I had made it so.

*And you did it without hardly thinking about it. These are the signs that will follow them that believe, and it's teeming with life.*

You follow as a leader and the signs follow you.

*Yes, exactly. What have you mentioned about true believers, true leaders?*

That people and things are healed around them.

*Yes, restorers of paths to dwell in. Isn't that as plain as day and as simple as can be?*

*You will know them by their fruit. That's the choice for people, to listen to the deceivers, well meaning or otherwise, or to yield themselves to the Voice of Truth. One is a path of pain, the other is the path of victory. What could be a simpler choice?*

Is it an "a" or "the"?

> G was not sure if he had heard Talia speak "a path" or
> "the path."

*Either/or, a path that leads to the path is still the path, though the path may look different.*

OK, I just know you're very precise with your words.

*I'm very precise with my meanings; words can be misconstrued. You're getting tired.*

It's just intense.

*Yes, the truth is always intense. It's like a fire burning. Burning with everlasting fuel.*

Yes, it's hot!

*The heat is to teach you to be cool.*

I see that diamond again.

*Yes, the pressure and the heat.*

To reveal multi-faceted colors.

*Yes, you have to be pure for the colors to flow forth out of you.*

Clarity.

*Yes, I'd like to continue, but you're burning out.*

You're hard to hang with; after all, you don't have the flesh to contend with.

*No, I don't. I just have to contend with yours.*

That sounds like a full-time job.

*I do have a full-time job.*

**1:50 PM**

*You worry too much.*

I always sort of prided myself on not doing that.

*That's why you're doing it.*

Pride before a fall.

*Something like that. You can know the nature of anything by knowing the name of it. You can also change the nature of anything by changing the name of it.*

THAT was straight-on direct.

*Not many people know this.*

You can see how easy it would be for someone to talk themselves out of that one.

*This is heavy truth, and it has to do with the gravity of the one doing it.*

I never . . .

*Yes, you have. You've chosen to forget things so you can relearn them better. Everyone does this.*

Sounds like a waste of time.

*How can you waste something that's not there?*

I feel like I'm being scattered in a million pieces.

*Your perceptions are; you had them neatly arranged—now they're not. But when they come back together, they will be. You understand?*

I think so.

*Just say yes—that's declaring that "that is" as "is."*

Then yes.

*Good. Now we may proceed.*

Nothing's better than this!

*Oh, this is but part and parcel. If you knew how much I love YOU. I told you prayers worked both ways, and I have asked the Father to do some things. His love for me is without comprehension. He has told me this and I KNOW this. I'm trying to snap you out of being obsessed by this.*

That's funny, I was just talking about your lack of being obsessed with anything during your life here and how balanced you were.

*What's there to get obsessed about? And I did have a good balance; the horses taught me a lot about that.*

*Justin likes you.*

One of Talia's horses that G met.

*Are you avoiding me?*

No, Talia.

*Then write down what I just told you.*

You said "the life was in the blood, it's in the circulation."

*Yes, I did. Maybe you should go circulate.*

Well, I just got up for a second, and you asked if I was avoiding you.

*Don't be so defensive. I was just getting your attention. You were starting to wander.*

You're right, I was.

*Good, now we're back on track.*

I see, you didn't want me to forget what you told me.

*That's right. It's easy sometimes to forget what you shouldn't. You're getting tired again. You know you also used to pride yourself in your endurance.*

Well, touché.

*We're not fencing, but you do build fences around you at times. That doesn't always necessarily serve you either. I know you love your solitude, but you should also share what you can with others when you're with them. You're worried about the floodgates being opened.*

It's just a thought that crossed my mind.

*Well, cross it out.*

You just have no tolerance for bull, do you?

*I tell it like it is, because I see it as it is. Would you prefer I prophesied smooth things?*

No, I could get that about anywhere.

*Yes, and they would charge you for it too. When you get the good news, there is never a charge and it's never forced. Did Jesus charge admission for the Sermon on the Mount?*

I very seriously doubt it.

*Then why would there be a charge for someone to hear the truth?*

I think they even got a free meal with the deal.

*They did. Have you seen that lately?*

Not very often.

*Why not?*

Another good question.

*It sure is.*

*Do you remember the story about the moneychangers in the temple? I can tell you, there are some things going on there that God is not happy about.*

Sounds to me like judgment begins in the house of God.

*It does. Many have squandered an opportunity just for money.*

He's not going to let that slide, is He?

*No, He's not; there is repentance required!*

I haven't seen you this adamant in a while.

*Remember His reaction in the temple; where else did you see this recorded?*

Nowhere.

*Exactly. This is a warning they would be well advised to heed.*

Man, talk about full circle.

*Yes, talk about it.*

You're . . .

*I just reflect Him. His light shines through, and I reflect Him. That's what they should be doing and not lining their pockets. You're thinking about the irony of my age. He started preaching at twelve.*

Maybe I'm a late bloomer too.

*I love to make you laugh.*

I love it when you make me laugh. Didn't know you were going to kerblammy the church here.

*Who established the religion here? If God established it maybe they should follow Him.*

That seems pretty obvious.

*Doesn't it though.*

You sound mad about it.

*I'm just reflecting Him. He's angry every day with the wicked. That's another aspect of God that people need to face up to. God IS love, and he's also angry at the wicked every day. Do you know how MANY have been turned off by the moneychangers? I'm telling you that they can argue about this if they want, but they would do WELL to pay heed.*

I think you have probably made your point.

*Do you?*

I don't know, did you?

*That will be seen.*

OK, so how about those Cubs?

*You're being funny, but that's what they DO: they change the subject.*

Guess you haven't made your point.

*I'm trying to save some from some very serious consequences.*

I think this may make some uncomfortable.

*It should!*

I don't remember you ever getting this stirred up.

*THAT might be something to take into consideration.*

I've never seen you like this before, Talia. I really haven't.

*It's something that needed to be said and I said it.*

OK, I just saw the full picture of this.

*You got most of it. You want to explain it, and we could in detail, but this isn't an intellectual understanding. This is a change in the heart and it needs to come quickly.*

This is a major big-time warning.

*Yes, no joke.*

That was like the wrath of God or something.

*It's coming. They don't like to hear that, but that's not what matters. What matters is the truth.*

I know you said you were in a unique position to see what's going on.

*I am and I do.*

## July 2

**5:50 AM**

 I was really wanting to ask Talia whether crop circles were real. Not the ones that are obviously man-made, but the ones that are said to have been made by some supernatural force. So I asked G to ask Talia about them.

Crop circles . . . what are they?

*They are the molecular structure beyond the quantum level.*

Who makes them?

*Messengers.*

> G thought, *Messengers?*

*Spirits, angels.*

Why crops?

*Crops are a symbol of growth, food, LIFE. It's also the work of man, and that's whom the message is for. It's to let them know there are things beyond them to help them.*

Why the riddle?

*Remember the parables. It must be something that is not known to let them know it's beyond this world.*

Is there intelligent life on other planets?

*There is intelligent life everywhere.*

This shouldn't go into the book, should it?

*No, not really. It wouldn't help them and would be to satisfy curiosity.*

## *July 3*

**7:20 AM**

*I've got something to say today. Are you disappointed?*

No, I'm just tired.

*You've been lied to a lot.*

Everybody has.

*Yes, and that's the point. Why do people lie to each other so much? It weaves a web of deception, and it permeates everything you do. It also distorts the truth when you tell it; it taints it. People will always know on some level when you're being untrue. And they will always ask themselves, at least subconsciously, why you are telling them the truth now if you've been untrue to them before. Why do you think there is so much mistrust in the world? Most have trusted someone only to find that their trust had been misplaced. Remember what I said about someone placing their trust in you. This should always be taken as a great honor, and their trust should never be dishonored. This dishonoring someone's trust causes great hurt in the world, and its ramifications are beyond what you might think. It reverberates throughout the universe. When someone places their trust in you, they are essentially placing their life in your hands, and this is an honor that they are giving you directly from their innermost being. How could someone dishonor such a trust?*

Well, I trust you, Talia.

*And I trust you, G. It's easy for us to trust each other because we KNOW each other. You've heard people say things to you that were not exactly true, and you've heard what they were really saying as words overlaid on their words. And you've heard their motivations. Sometimes THEY didn't even know they were lying. That's why it's so important to be true to yourself. When you're true to yourself you cannot help but to be true to others. Why would you lie to yourself?*

That does seem insane.

*It's certainly not the paragon of mental health. Mental health is being mindful, having presence of Mind. This Presence of Mind is Love and love never fails; it just cannot do wrong. You are pure in heart. Did he not say that the pure in heart would see God?*

Yes.

*Have you not seen God?*

Yes.

*And you felt like you would die.*

Yes, I did.

*You did, and you have risen with Him. Despite what you may think you ARE—pure in heart and you HAVE seen God—you HAVE died and you HAVE risen with HIM. This is a part of your life you've downplayed. Why is that?*

I don't know.

*Yes, you do. It's not readily accepted. We've talked about acceptance before. You fancy yourself as an outsider, but you're not an outsider; you're an insider, and I mean that in the best of ways. Many times people's perceptions of themselves are warped. Only the LIGHT can straighten this out. Why would you hide your light? You said you saw that luminous web of life as a straight line, and that's all you saw as a straight line. Why do you think that is? Because it's a straight line between points of interest. These points of interest are points placed in certain places for learning.*

G put down his pen to take a break.

*Don't stop now.*

I'm not.

*No, you're not. You can't. There IS no going back. This itself is a point of interest, as a schoolhouse to bring you back to the ONE. There is really only One point, and that's the dot above the mountain in which everything is contained. When someone reaches the top of this mountain, they still can't reach it, but they can be brought up. This is the part that He spoke of when He said of your own self you can do nothing.*

There is no way I can write down all the truths that are being poured out on me right now.

*No, you can't. That's the truth verifying itself to itself. That dot is a representation of everything being brought back together into Himself, condensed. That mountain is a representation of the struggles on the path of life of those following the Light. The many paths up the mountain are the many ways and purposes each have while upon the journey. This journey is watched closely and there is much help given. When a person feels alone, they are not. They are never alone. It's just a feeling.*

Well, that makes me feel capital.

*You like quoting movie lines, don't you.*

They just spring to mind.

*Maybe you shouldn't watch so many movies.*

I haven't watched a movie in forever.

*That too is just a feeling. Why do you think you fall asleep as much as you do during movies? Because most of them have nothing for you, and the message they do have is for children.*

Now you're going to irritate Hollywood.

*Hollywood is just a town. It is a place of interest for some, but it's not that interesting.*

Hope this doesn't shock anyone.

*The shock to the system is someone groping in darkness trying to make something interesting that isn't.*

You liked movies.

*I did like movies—and I was a child.*

Well, you're the most interesting person I ever met.

*I'm the most interesting person you ever realized you met. Interest is attention. Be mindful of where your attention is. The One used me to get your attention back on HIM. I was just a vessel.*

Quite the vessel.

*Thank you.*

*Ask my mom how much I lied to her.*

She said zero, never, except for maybe one time there was "some little something" that she thought you were covering for Frankie for.

*It was, and I meant well, and she corrected me for it.*

And she said that was it.

*That was it. It's the it we've been speaking of. It is what it is. That is an interesting statement. People think it's what they think it is, but it's not. It is what it is, although what they think it is could change it. Sounds like a paradox, doesn't it.*

Somewhat.

*It's not.*

I just thought, let me live the Art of Life today, and you said, "You are."

*The Art of Life is living, and that's the point. It's not doing anything— it's being.*

That seems a simple truth.

*All truth is simple at its core. That point is a condensed place of truth where things reappear.*

The dot.

*Yes, like a grain of mustard seed.*

Talia, I've got so much to do today.

*It's NOT doing—it's being.*

I was just going to say there's nothing more important than this.

*If you knew how important you would tremble.*

I pretty much am trembling.

*No, I mean REALLY tremble.*

I just want to do it right.

*You don't have to DO anything but just be who you are. I told you before we would get it right this time, and we are. You feel my determination.*

I sure do.

*That picture of me you saw when you said I looked so determined.*

> I showed G a photo of Talia playing volleyball. She was really concentrating on the game from the look on her face.

Yes.

*And you said you could see the concentration in my face. I was actually thinking about something else then.*

OK, well that's funny.

*No, not really. I just knew what we were doing wasn't that important. That's why I wasn't so keen on using the word "athletic" on the rock at my tree.*

What word would you have used?

*There are so many words that could have been used to paint a better picture of who I was. It's not a problem, it's just not the best use of people's time. My going was a sign to people of just how short their time really is. My life was also an example of how people should best use their time.*

I want to use my time wisely.

*Then walk in wisdom. Wisdom is often scoffed at today. Have you ever asked yourself why? It's because it's the principal thing. It's the very foundation of how your life is meant to be lived, as the Art of Life. As a creative being. This is living in absolute victory. This is the winning that you're meant to walk in. You were created for it.*

Then how could we lose?

*THAT'S a very good question.*

I can't imagine where this is going.

*No, you can't, but you will. That's creative living.*

Doing the unimaginable.

*Yes, exactly, doing the unimaginable by the incomprehensible.*

You're the master of . . .

*I have mastered many things. Mastery is living in the now; it's being in the moment. He said, "Call no man master," and there are many reasons for this. But one is that it's always in a constant flux. The breath of life is always in the now, and you don't have to think about it. That's why you always thought rituals were so foolish. They really are. That's just an attempt to get the attention where it needs to be.*

More toes crushed.

*You'd rather we pamper?*

No, not at all. You've got my permission—go ahead.

*I don't need your permission. I have a commission from the Holy One.*

You know what I mean.

*Yes, I know what you mean, but that's another thing I'm attempting to show you here. That YOU need to be more mindful, more precise with YOUR words. Words convey meaning, and you're very often sloppy with your words, as if they don't mean anything—but they do.*

Hey, you want me to answer? I'm not saying anything.

*Yes, you are. You say things all the time, and I'm telling you to be mindful of what you say. You were very mindful of what you said around me and to me that day we met. That's because you respected me. I'm just saying to you that you should show this same respect to others as well.*

I don't know what to say.

## July 2008

*When you don't know what to say, don't make things up to fill the time. There's nothing wrong with silence. As a matter of fact, there is a great deal right with it. You're quiet now.*

I'm being silent.

*Yes, well, that's a good thing.*

Talia, you take me from one extreme to the other.

*I take you wherever I can, which is everywhere I can.*

There was that one place that was off limits.

> Once while G was "meditating," he met with Talia, and Talia took him on a trip to show him where she lived. As they were approaching a particular area in the spirit world Talia was told to stop—she was not allowed to take G any further.

*Yes, I wanted to share it with you but was told not yet.*

I thought I heard that.

*You heard Him say it to me.*

That was one of the most awesome experiences I've ever had.

*For me too.*

That's wild!

*It's totally wild.*

## *July 4*

---❖---

**8:45 AM**

*It's important to understand there is no forward or backward there. Everywhere is in one place and there are no moot points.*

> G had a dream where he saw a tire spinning. He had just read a paper on spin-transfer given to him by a friend, and he could see that the tire was oscillating like the prop wash of a boat motor. He also saw other things in his dream descriptive of the things he had just read.

I can order coffee in Greek, say *thank you, how are you, good morning* and *good night,* so this isn't quite as clear as Greek to me.

*Spanish is easier.*

Is that you?

*Yes.*

What you said yesterday makes perfect sense to me.

*That's because you see it.*

That paper is way over my head.

*That's because your head's not into the verbiage or technical terms, never mind the equations.*

Isn't it the truth.

*Of course it is. They are called theoretical physicists because they are filled with theories.*

They also spoke of intuitively knowing something.

*That's when they will find it, with that insight.*

The answers are within them.

*Absolutely.*

I can deal with that.

*Yes, the Great Game, and the answers are dealt daily by the questions you ask yourself. Have you not seen the light in the eyes of a child when he discovers something wonderful?*

That's a beautiful thought.

*And that's what that creates in them when they make those wonderful discoveries. The discoveries are also conceived by those thoughts. That's why it's important never to downplay or discourage those thoughts in a child. It is a child's nature to seek, and what they are seeking for is the truth. If you seek, you will find. That's why unless you become like a child you will not enter into the Kingdom of Heaven.*

That was a beautiful circle.

*That was the circle of truth, and it surrounds you.*

I see it as a wall.

*It is. It's a wall of protection.*

I also see it as a wall of perfection.

*The truth is always perfect. You just thought you don't know if you can keep doing this.*

It's just getting DEEP.

*You're just taking notes here.*

That's not what you said before.

*Yes, I did. I just got into more depth.*

*What do you think?*

I think I never told the story of the sleeping bag. Ha, turned the tables on you.

*You think so?*

Not really, but it's funny to think I might be able to.

*You're able to do all things. You know, God himself raises an eyebrow at what His children do sometimes, as if He is surprised.*

Do you think He's surprised?

*I don't know, but I do suppose He could be. He is all things you know, so He could be surprised.*

I think I may have just turned the tables on you.

*I told you you were able to do all things.*

I don't know if you did that or I did that.

*What difference does it make? We are one, and the arrangements of all things come from the One in Whom all things are.*

I think I just surprised you.

*You did.*

You're not pulling my leg?

*I cannot lie. You see, aren't these truths like your ABC's?*

They really are that simple.

*And you see how man's "additives" complicate things?*

I see that's just to justify a job.

*When they should be simplifying.*

Exactly.

*I told you we were one.*

Yes, it's getting harder to see where you start and I stop.

*There is really no starting or stopping; it just is, in continual motion, except for the stillness.*

Now that I've seen the universe in a constant motion of spherical spin . . . it's amazing to me to comprehend stillness.

*And that's where all motion comes from, from perfect stillness.*

I KNOW, that's just amazing to me.

*I know, it is.*

Clever.

*I know, I'm a clever girl.*

*It's time to go.*

Time to go where?

*Exactly. You know, you could surpass me.*

How do you mean?

*You could surpass me. Never set limits on yourself. You've told others that yourself.*

Looks like I've got a long way to go.

*You do, but you'll get there.*

Hard to believe.

*That's why you've got a long way to go.*

OK, looks like you're ahead again.

*There is no ahead. There is the head, and He is the head of all things, and that's what we're concerning ourselves with here.*

**11:27 AM**

I just thought, considering the interconnectedness of all things, the medical community treating the body and leaving out the mental and spiritual is somewhat insane, isn't it? It's like the Dark Ages or something.

*Well put. If you hadn't brought that up, I would have.*

*Sixty-four is a very interesting number.*

> Talia said this out of the blue and didn't expound on the meaning of that number. But later, in a video by physicist Nassim Harramein, G heard Harramein mention that the number 64 is a critical number in figuring out the secrets and answers of the universe.

## *July 5*

**12:11 AM**

There's that diamond again. That's not just the stone, that's a geometrical shape, isn't it?

*That's right.*

That whole flower petal thing before, when I asked what it meant and you said, "I love my Mom," has a much broader meaning, doesn't it?

*It does. Now you know what the brown streak in the middle of the petal was. It is hidden wisdom. The petal is white. It comes from a place of holiness. It itself represents the love of the Father for His children. And it's the very structure of the universe. The love of the Father for this, His children, is the very structure of the universe.*

Two tetrahedrons put together create a diamond. Two: the separation. Two brought back together: oneness.

*And that's the answer. Bravo. I'm thinking pit bull here; you just won't let it go, will you?*

No, and that was an interesting quote.

*That's because an interesting person said it.*

Thank you.

*You're welcome.*

**1:21 AM**

Talia, you just revealed the structure of the universe.

*Yes, I did, in part.*

That's not all?

*No, it's not.*

What's more?

*I told you you would learn all things, remember?*

I do now, but I don't remember when.

*The when's not important. It's that I did and you remember it that is* [important]. *I have another memory for you. When we met, you looked at me and thought,* God, I would die for her; *the Spirit answered you and said, "You WILL die for her." Do you remember?*

Yes, I do remember that. I had completely forgotten it, but I remember now.

*That was a pure desire born of the Holy Spirit. You saw me exactly as I was, and you were willing to give up your life for me.*

Yes, I was—totally, absolutely and completely.

*That kind of commitment is honored, and it's not seen much. Now you see why you were chosen for this and why I also say you chose yourself? This is your part to play, and you're playing it well. That's the servant in you willing to give his all for the Kingdom. This is much greater than us, but the parts we're playing will be remembered forever. That brought a smile.*

Yes, it did.

*It's so far beyond this world. And I want you to know that when your commitment was revealed to me, it was one of the greatest honors ever bestowed upon me.*

I meant it.

*I know you did. Your passion for truth is recognized here; that's not seen much either. The fact that you didn't recognize/know me until that day and you were willing to die for me—THAT day was honored and you will be greatly rewarded.*

I don't care about a reward.

*I know that, and that's one reason you're getting one. You wanted nothing in return for your life, and you would have laid it down for me that day. Greater love has no man than this that he would lay down his life for his friend.*

You are so completely worthy, and I thank you for being my friend. Talia, I really don't know any greater honor for me than that.

*I told you all things were yours.*

*Then let it be, si es amour.*

## 7:46 AM
I did some review. "It's love" is really the bottom line, isn't it?

*It's the bottom line, the top line and every line in between. It's also the line you saw running/circling around your right arm. I said some call it chi; that's a limited way of looking at what it really is because it's more than that.*

Ok, why Italian?

*We were just talking about passion, and this is for all people.*

**8:47 AM**

*Your time here is almost done.*

That sounds like a major transitional change.

*It is. You are an energy being, being who you are, and that never changes. This is your life's work; you know what's contained in these pages.*

Don't waste time.

*You have none to waste.*

What are you saying here?

*You know what I'm saying here. It's the meaning of the words, not the spelling.*

Some things it seems are best not to know.

*He said, "I will show you things to come." And you know all things. When someone goes, it's a tremendous contrast, and some things about that person's life become much clearer.*

That's evident in your life.

*Yes, it is, completely. My life, if I were still there, would have caused you pain, because you would have seen it as a partial life, and this message would not have gotten out there. Death as they see it is not death at all but of the body; it's a wonderful new beginning. You KNOW who I am. You also know who I was, and you see glimpses of what I am becoming.*

Think I'll take a walk.

*You certainly will.*

Talia . . .

*Don't be afraid, it's all good.*

I'm not afraid.

*I know, but don't be afraid for others; they have their life too. That plane took me exactly where I needed to be, and that's exactly where I was going.*

> Talia is referring to the plane that crashed into the mountain, killing her, her father and the pilot.

I know that.

*I know you do. Your going too will shake foundations. When they perceive the light is gone, it will stand in sharp contrast. You are now exactly where you need to be, and when you go you will be too.*

**9:47 AM**
*Have you not SEEN what I can do?*

Yes, I have.

*Do you not think you have the victory?*

Yes, I do.

*Then it's settled.*

Such is life.

*And it's love.*

If I hadn't seen the miracles . . .

*You needed the signs to believe. Don't look askance at others when they need the signs.*

I'm exhausted.

*This is exhausting work. We're exhausting all the possibilities so only the ONE remains.*

The one to whom nothing is impossible.

*That's the one. That that we were discussing before is a mundane thing, just like mud.*

Just like mud?

*Yes, just like mud.*

Don't get bogged down in it.

*No, do not.*

**12:55 PM**

I haven't had emotions this extreme since I went to war.

*These are extreme truths. They evoke extreme emotions, and this is a war. Remember you were told the time would come when you would live on cat naps?*

Yes.

*Remember what time that was you were told?*

No, it was unclear.

*Maybe you didn't want to hear it.*

I know what I thought I heard.

*What you thought you heard is what you heard.*

That it would be in the last days.

*Correct.*

## *July 6*

---

**3:42 PM**
**(New Mexico)**
Awesome storm.

*You should see it from my view.*

You can see colors in lightening bolts? I never saw that.

*You never saw it from "here."*

Where did you have to go in such a hurry when we were with Grandfather?

> As previously mentioned, sometimes when G "meditates,"
> he visits another spirit he calls Grandfather. Sometimes
> he meets Talia and takes her to see him as well.

*We're very busy here; that was for you, not for me. Like you said about me and martial arts, I'm beyond that.*

You had such respect for him.

*I have much respect for him, but what he told me was for you.*

The "land of enchantment." Some irony in light of this storm.

*You've said the light here was different. This is a place where the earth works with the sky. Where the Sons of God walk with the daughters of men.*

OK, that's a very interesting term we're going to have to discuss when I'm up, because I want to know what it means.

*We will and you will.*

## *July 8*

---

**1:10 PM**

*You've got a lot of work to do.*

What happened to the "we?"

*It's easier on my end.*

**1:34 PM**

*Remember when you asked if I liked archery?*

Yes.

*That's because you saw an arrow.*

I remember.

*Why do you think that was?*

Arrows of truth.

*Yes, and they shoot out of me. This is celebrating the life of Talia.*

That's awesome.

*Pretty much amazing. It's going to rain.*

I can tell.

*Yes, but this is the latter rain of the Spirit. You've seen it falling before and that's what it was, the latter rain of the Spirit for those who will reign with Him.*

*Everything is in constant motion except for the I, the supreme stillness in the center.*

The eye of the storm.

*The eye that is upon everything. The I that is the center of everything from which all things come. You're being blown away, aren't you? Blown to a wonderful new world. You always knew it existed. As a child you saw it at times. Remember when I told you to watch the wind?*

Yes.

*And that it was a vehicle because it brought power? This is that power to walk in that wonderful new world. Demonstrate the download.*

How?

*You just got it; you just saw it!*

Also, the other day you said I would be called a *Yeddehonee*, and I didn't think that was a good thing. I looked it up. I knew it meant a wizard or conjurer. You said people would accuse me of conjuring you up, whether by my imagination or worse. The name means: "a knowing one, to ascertain by seeing, observation, acknowledge, be aware, comprehend, consider, cunning, be diligent, familiar friend, kinsfolk, have knowledge, have understanding, wise" . . . to name some of the meanings. Then it goes into *Jah*, the sacred name— *Jah, the Lord*, most vehement. Then *Yhovah*, (the) self: *Jehovah*, the Lord.

*Looks like you went full circle.*

You think that's funny.

*I think that's the truth. You see, it doesn't matter what you're called, it all leads back to the truth. It's starting to pour out on you because you've yielded unto the truth. And the tools have come into your hands to do the study you've been asked to do. And at just the right time.*

Yesterday I was thinking about that Thanksgiving and all that happened. I remember that I had said to myself sometime afterward, "I'm going to have to watch her career closely." When I thought of that yesterday you said to me, "Now you can." I didn't write it at the time but figured it was too cool not to record.

**10:00 PM**

I was asked to ask you why the Jews are "the chosen people."

*Because God chose them. It was a promise to Abraham.*

What about before that?

*You want a chronological timeline, but it's not like that. It is, now.*

Was this just idle curiosity?

*No, it's active curiosity, and it's not really a part of this message. There is neither Jew nor Greek in Him; He has restored all things unto Himself.*

Well, thanks for the update.

*All this is plainly written for anyone to read.*

## July 9

I feel Michael's pain.

*He has deep regret and feels responsible. He wants to talk to you and get his side of the story out there. It's not part of the message, but I told him I would.*

*I told him he is not responsible and that things happen for a reason. He says he knows that and that he understands the importance of the message, but he feels the hurt and pain and sense of loss to those on earth.*

*At first he felt he had robbed me of my life on earth by his pride, but he now knows I'm where I need to be to help others in the greatest way possible. He's not too happy with the way his father is acting towards Mom, and he wishes he could get through to him and things were different. He says the hardest thing for him now is not being able to communicate with those he needs to.*

*He says to tell you again how much he appreciates what you're doing with me.*

*Other than those things he's doing fine, but those issues have been very difficult for him.*

Be at peace, Michael.

Thank you. (MK)

G saw Michael with a big smile on his face.

I heard him.

*Yes, you did. He's growing and he does know God's peace.*

Why doesn't he talk to me himself?

*It's clearer for you if I speak.*

Anything else?

*Yes, I told you it was going to rain.*

And I agreed with you.

*And thus it is.*

You make a lesson out of everything, don't you?

*Everything IS a lesson.*

You did it again.

*And I will do it again and again.* ☺

**11:16 AM**
*Write that which you saw yesterday that "jumped" at you.*

> G was flipping through the Bible and a line jumped out at him.

"These things have I spoken unto you in proverbs: but the time comes, when I shall no more speak unto you in proverbs, but I shall show you plainly of the Father." John 16:25

*Now, the hearers of this message would do well to ask themselves, what time is this?*

I noticed you said "hearers." Not readers.

*Yes, I did. If you read these words without listening it's the dead letter, but if you hear them with your heart it's the living word—and that's words of LIFE! And as we've said before, the Kingdom of Heaven comes not in word but in power and the Spirit of Truth.*

I think the time is now when people are being shown plainly the Father.

*To those who watch. He said to watch always because no man knows the time or the hour.*

That's phenomenal!

*Yes, that is a phenomenon.*

Tetrahedron?

*A building block.*

Petals.

*Petals are the growth formed by these building blocks of life by a perfect mathematical formula. You mentioned before how I seemed to be pondering a new formula the day we met. On a certain level I was, and the question I was pondering was WHY? When a person honestly asks why, they are instantly spurred onto the path to truth. You also said I seemed to be listening. I was, and that's the answer: to ask why honestly and listen for the answer.*

> G thought about how it was raining lightly, birds were singing, the plants thriving, etc.

*Do you see the energy around you?*

Yes, I hear it too.

*That is nothing but life. And that's the answer that is contained in all things: life. When people ask if there's life on other planets, the answer is, there is life everywhere. When they understand that, they will understand how the universe works. Now there are other things we need to talk about, and there is a certain sequence. You see coming truths and the directions we could take, but this is systematic progression, and it does have to do with order because everything is ordered in His word. So I need you to listen and not jump ahead.*

*We are restorers of paths to dwell in, and we are building a bridge to span the great riff caused by forgetfulness, among other things. The direction we take will be pointed out by the Great Spirit, and that's the direction we will take.*

Point taken.

*Good. Now we can move on. I just needed to rein you in some. Your enthusiasm is appreciated, but quietness is imperative.*

> G looked up and saw a raptor. He thought to himself, *The raptor is a bird of prey.* His name means "to seize" in Latin.

*That's the truth, but that's not what we're talking about right now. The reining you in is sovereign. And to resolve is to decide to solve.*

You're . . .

*I'm what? And why?*

I don't have the words for infinity.

*No, you don't, and we are all incomprehensible, yet people insist on using a word to label someone.*

Oops.

*Does "knucklehead" come to mind?*

Yes.

*And you thought you misspelled it and tried to correct it.*

Yes, but it was right to start with.

Now, if people get what just happened they would be far ahead.

**8:38 PM**
I don't like this pen.

*Use it.*

*I just dealt with you on a quantum level. Where do you think this is coming from? From DEEP inside of you. I told you the Kingdom of Heaven was within you.*

*Now you should never demand or insist a person believe. Because that's their choice. That is their decision to make in this life. It has a profound EFFECT on their LIFE, but it is still their decision. You can guide them and advise them, but the decision is left up to them. And, you said man does not have the technology to change hearts, but you do. You know how to do this, and you've done it before. You think I can do something you can't, as if I'm better than you?*

> G's dog started to bark and disturb him while talking to Talia. Down the street construction equipment was tearing up the road, cutting down trees, and making room for a bigger road and more houses.

Why can't I stop the destruction from the machines? It is like they've literally been following me around all my life.

*They have to be willing before their hearts can be changed. Greed is a powerful force. Its deception is great and it has changed the face of the earth.*

Talia, I know that's true, but it is not a very satisfying answer.

*He never promised to satisfy you, but He did promise that you could be content with such things as you have.*

Well, I'm just not very content with what's going on right now. It is upsetting the dog and me.

*You have said they should go ahead and pave the whole planet because the suspense was killing you.*

Yes, and it seems like they're working hard at it. But I know there will still be parks that we can pay to get into as we go through the turnstile and are counted.

*So, cat didn't get your tongue. Are you disturbed?*

Yes, I am. I'm just tired of senseless destruction by these big yellow machines. Seems they've been across the street or down the road ever since I can remember, literally. And I know it is just greed. It is no thought taken to the consequences.

*"It is no thought taken" is an interesting term.*

Yes, well, OK.

*Right thoughts do have to be taken.*

Hey, I've got it. It is the people down the road ripping down trees and pulling the guts out of the earth that need the lesson.

*You could go and show this to them.*

I can see that they'd just call the cops.

*They would if you were insistent. Anger blinds. Anger that becomes rage, kills.*

So I shouldn't be outraged?

*You should be calm and accept things as they are.*

Well, that's a hard one.

*I know it is. That's because you're looking in the natural, but I see beyond that. You can too, you know.*

I overlook things all the time.

*Yes, you do, you overlook them. I said you could look BEYOND them.*

I'm with you. I know what you mean. I've been there—but it's irritating.

*I know it is, but you have to see it for what it is.*

I don't think I'm in that place to see that right now.

*No, you're not, so you won't. But when you are, you will, and that's always an eye opener. See when you're calm what happens.*

Yes, I took a breath, leaned back and heard "the wrath of man worketh not the righteousness of God."

*The voice of wisdom.*

From earlier today Michael said, "I know it will all work out." I had missed it but was just reminded. I know he has other things to say; I sense that strongly.

*That's enough for now. Told you you would have time.*

I know I will, because you said it.

*Yes, but it is further confirmation.*

Things are being "arranged" in my favor, aren't they?

*They always are.*

## July 10

**10:17 AM**

G was thinking about his time meditating earlier that day.

*Go back and record this.*

Record it?

*Yes, write it down.*

Earlier, I walked down a wooded trail, turned right, and passed through a golden arch onto a rock-like stairway, except it was gold. At the bottom I entered into a beautiful land of sand, soil, plants, flowers and trees. There were birds flying, and I sensed life all around. The sky was filled with clouds of color, and a voice said, "Can you see it?" I blinked a couple of times, then I saw other colors mixed in with the first, not of this world. Then Talia appeared before me and asked again, "Can you see it?"

It was a swirl of color moving like the wind, then it came behind her and moved through her, then into me, and she said, "I am giving you what I have." I fell on my back onto what was a brown wooden deck. I stayed there a while, then she said, "Arise," and I was again on my feet. She said again, "I am giving you what I have. You can heal now. This will be for signs to others that they may believe for the signs' sake." Then she said, "Come," and took my right hand in her left, and we flew above the countryside for a short time, then up and through a haze, a veil of some sort, and into a green place, the same one I had seen her at before . . . the same small tree on the mound. She and I walked hand in hand across the grass. There were people about and many looked toward us. Some were talking as they looked. I couldn't understand or hear what most of them said, but I heard one say, "Look, it is Talia's friend."

We walked up to a tree. It was a normal-sized tree (something like an oak), and we stopped before it, and we both looked up at it and she said, "It is the tree of life." I replied, "It doesn't look very big," and she answered, "But its roots go deep."

Then we walked passed it to what appeared to be a three-tiered rock fountain. Water flowed over and down the rocks; there were still other people around but never close, as if they were respectfully giving us room. She said, "This is the fountain of fortune." I think I was already starting towards the fountain when she said, "Drink." (Many things were happening simultaneously.) I drank a handful, which tasted just like regular water at first, then turned sweet in my mouth. I asked if it was OK to take another handful, and she gestured towards it and said, "Sure." I drank another handful from my right hand. It was the same, just like normal water at first, then it turned very sweet as I drank it. She then said, "That's far enough for now," and I thought we would continue on our walk.

I was very drowsy and had to really make myself sit down and write this. I asked Talia if that had really been her. "Yes, that was really me." At one point she said something like, "Write it before you forget it." Now someone may ask themselves how could anyone forget anything like that. Well, believe me, you can forget anything.

## *July 14*

G had a name come to him. Eleazar? He questioned her about it and asked her if he had heard her correctly.

*Eleazar.*

*He said he would bring judgment into truth; that's why wisdom is the principal thing.*

G then looked up *Eleazar* in Hebrew and the meaning was, "God, his helper." The root word means "to surround, protect or aid" and *El* means "strength." The feminine aspect means "oak or another strong tree." Also "to twist, be strong, the body as being rolled together." This was intense because it reinforced G's vision of the energy twisting on his arm that he had had on a previous day.

## 9:27 AM
I have to say my jaw dropped when I got to the twist and the body as being rolled together.

*That wasn't the first time and it won't be your last.*

## 10:21 AM
*Everything that grows, grows in circles. It is the twist that makes it stronger; it is the struggle. That's why I said a twist of the truth was a perversion—a twist of the real, a counterfeit. That's why it seems to so many to be real, to be the truth, because it is a twist upon that that is real. On the surface it appears to be very real; it has a basis in truth, it seems so logical. These lies, these untruths, are tied together in a most*

*intricate way. It is the antithesis of the web of life, and it promises rewards, usually without that much work involved either. So it is very appealing to the masses. It also promises glory. One way you can tell it is the counterfeit is that it is promised glory; it glorifies the flesh and in no real way honors the Creator.*

Wow, Talia, I'm glad your back.

*I'm glad YOU'RE back. Let's continue. You want it to be simple, and it is. The truth has a certain ring to it, the "ring of truth," and that's just what it is, a ring. A wake-up call to answer. It has a certain tone, or flavor, that cannot be faked, not in any real sense of the word. You were born by the truth, into it; do you not know the sound of your mother's own voice? That's why excuses for following a false way are unacceptable.*

*The art of life, and living it, is the only true way to live up to your potential. And that's why you're here, to live up to your potential. Anything else is living a lesser you, which will always be unacceptable to your self. Your higher Self knows what it wants, and that's to live up to your potential. It also knows its own potential, which is why so many remain unfulfilled. It is not so hard to yield to that; it is much more difficult not to.*

## 2:30 PM
Well, Talia, I've started a new notebook here. It sure didn't take long to fill the last one up and with truths too, just like you said.

*Did you expect otherwise?*

No, not at all. I knew it would be filled with coming truths, because you said so, and I saw the words as I flipped through the blank pages.

*He always confirms His word in the mouth of two or three witnesses. I was the first witness, you were the second.*

Well, where are we going now?

*We're going all over the place. Do you know what place I am talking about? It is the place I am, you are, and where you should be. It is the place we've been speaking of and from all along. It is the place where everything is that should be there. It is the place where all things are possible and nothing is impossible. It is the place of Being. It is the place of truth in whom is no lie. It is the only place to be if you truly want to Be. And it is all in the BEING.*

Sounds like the place to be.

*Why would anyone want to be anywhere else?*

Another deep philosophical question.

*Philosophy is primarily questions, and it is a good start to ask them, but what we have here are answers; therefore, we've passed far beyond philosophy. Philosophy is wondering; we're answering and we're living it, in its power—the power of Truth—and that's why I say we're far beyond philosophy.*

*Have you not seen these truths manifested in power?*

Yes, I have.

*Have you seen any of man's philosophies manifested in power?*

Not really.

*Nor will you, not in this way. It is not that we have a corner on truth; it is just that they're not looking in the corners for it. It is like hidden treasure, you know.*

So you've said.

*Yes, interesting how the truth repeats itself, isn't it. It echoes throughout the corners of the universe. It cannot help but to do that. That's how it operates.*

You've said that before too.

*Interesting.*

I just flipped through these pages and seemed to see a disturbance or choppiness towards the center. I saw rough water.

*The truth often disturbs, and on many levels, from the surface to the very core. It also disturbs the status quo. The status quo serves its own and is a false comfort.*

Shakes up business as usual?

*You could certainly say that.*

I have to tell you, I get a little cranky when we don't talk.

*I noticed. I told you to make the most of your time. You have little to lose. When you do it will help you not to get like that.*

OK.

*Now I would like to get into the why.*

The *why?*

*Yes, the why that this is happening with us, between us. Why it is you and I and not someone else. We're not going to cover all the facets of it, but we are going to touch on some truths as to why. Some are asking themselves this question, thus the answer.*

*The why can essentially be summed up in one word—and that's fellowship. Real meaningful answers always come from deep fellowship. Even if it is a one-word answer to your questions from a stranger, it comes from deep fellowship. Deep answers unto the deep. It is also a pure desire to know someone. You saw me as someone worth knowing. It pained you to think you'd never know me like you wanted to. You ASKED to know me; now you do. That's the short answer.*

Well, that's deep.

*I knew that was coming—I know you too.* ☺

What now?

*Now you need a break. Go swim.*

I don't have a waterproof notebook.

*As a matter of fact you do, but you won't need it.*

Ah, yes, I do.

*Everything I say to you isn't for general consumption.*

I know.

*So you do.*

### *July 15*

**9:16 AM**
Good morning.

*Good morning. And you were worried about writer's block.* ☺

The woods just don't seem as conducive as the desert.

*The desert was where we started this, so it is more familiar to you. It all comes from the same place, and you have to be in the same place to receive it. Maybe you shouldn't pay so much attention to the distractions. By the way, it is all coming together, this book, our message, everything.*

You just said more than it seems, didn't you?

*I always do. I don't change, just grow.*

Wouldn't it reach a point where it seems like change?

*It could seem that way, but we never change or transform into something else. Our core remains the same. An oak is an oak no matter how huge it becomes.*

I got it: it all begins with a seed, and it doesn't change from that basic structure.

*That's right. You can always trace any growth or nature back to its seed. That's a mistake some researchers make, but not that many. The mistake most researchers make is not tracing the growth or nature of a thing beyond the seed and to the source of the seed. The seed is the beginning and it is energy. ITS birth is a thought, a conception of mind. So when you say the energy follows the mind, it is true to an extent, as a way of understanding it or teaching the manipulation of energy—which IS yours to use, by the way. But the real truth is you can't have one without the other; energy and mind are one.*

That ought to keep them busy for a while.

*If they are paying attention it will; all the clues are there.*

All of them?

*All they need are there to go anywhere.*

*We can't go much further without a raising of consciousness.*

Is that true?

*Yes, that's true. Truth is being ignored daily. Like an endless loop of tape, man has his conceptions, and they reaffirm them daily to themselves and each other.*

*Unless and until there is change there we can't go much further. Man has reached an impasse, and he doesn't recognize it. He has convinced himself that he is right and that there is no other, that this is all that is. The times that are coming will try the hearts of men. The great shaking will shake out the chaff from the wheat. Decisions need to be made and soon. The death is not living. We've already explained how to live, and it is as a creative being in HIM, through Him. Anything else is not living at all.*

Are we done here?

*For the time being.*

For the time being?

*For the time being what it is.*

What do you mean?

*This is being spread now by the universal consciousness of what it is. It is being pondered and accepted, looked over and rejected. As I've said, decisions must be made and quickly.*

Where does that leave us?

*It leaves us where we are.*

## *July 16*

------◆------

**7:52 AM**

*Did you think this was going to stop?*

No, you told me before you would keep talking with me, but I was a bit concerned.

*No need to be; we're just waiting. Waiting for some to catch up, including you. You have to put these principles in action, live them. I told you all things were yours; the power to walk in this is yours as well. Whatsoever you ask in prayer, believing, you shall receive.*

Then I want to walk in this, to grow beyond this.

*Then you will. There is a balance to everything. An amazing, intricate and delicate balance that must be maintained. When you lose your balance you stumble, but this too is a learning experience.*

*Why don't you ask me about it; you're already laughing.*

OK, it is about the time you, your mom and your cousins stopped at a fast food place and went through the drive-through. It was dark out, and you wanted to order, but no one answered when you spoke, and you all started to get really mad. Then your five-year-old cousin said, "It's the trash can!" It was dark, and the speaker and trashcan looked the same! That to me is absolutely hilarious!

*That WAS one of the most funny things ever. That is called "fast food fun," and it WAS hilarious. We were hungry and hasty, and as it is often the case, out of the mouths of babes the truth was made known. It is the times like those that make life on earth so interesting and fun. My mom and I DID fancy ourselves as two of the smartest people on the planet. Which did only add to the fun. It is also those times that help you stay humble and not take yourself too seriously.*

I just about crack up every time I think of that. It also helped me see you weren't infallible.

*That could be another reason it happened. When you find your attention wavering or not on what it should be, you should ask yourself why.*

*That shirt you're wearing—it is not just the color I like, it is the motto.*

Service, dedication, education, training. It is a good motto.

*It caught your attention.*

Yes, it did. I remember I kept looking at it, thinking about those words, so I finally decided to commit it to memory.

*Good decision.*

I remember what I was doing at the time and that I was enjoying where I was.

> G was at a special training facility surrounded by nature, where he was learning new and practicing old skills for his job and his life.

*That's because you're good at it. It is easy to enjoy something you're good at, so if you want to be good at something, enjoy it, and if you want to enjoy something, get good at it.*

That's an interesting concept.

*Yes, isn't it. Do you think maybe you're good at things because you enjoy them or that you enjoy them because you're good at them?*

Probably both.

*Yes, but the point I'm making is that to enjoy is a creation. It is a creation of your mind, much like to envision.*

*There's something else I want you to think about. There's joy in the spin because there is stability inherent within it; it creates its own balance. Everything in creation that is without the spin is dead because it is without life. That that doesn't spin is in an unnatural state that's immediate decay. That's why I say there are vortices everywhere. They are spun off from the energy of life, which is everywhere. Now, due to the interconnectedness of all life that is spun off from these vortices, it can disappear from there because that part is not needed there anymore. It recognizes this to reappear somewhere else where it is needed and can be used. From particles to people we all do this. That's the changes, and that's where the number 64 comes in.*

I don't know if the layman's going to get this, and the theoretical physicists are probably going to think this is real basic.

*It IS real basic. The layman can get it by intuition. The theorists need to see beyond the words to replace their theory with reality.*

I see why so many of them are not getting it, and it's because they are being dishonest with themselves. Which I find odd because these same ones do have integrity and ARE being honest with others.

*That's exactly right, and that's what we're trying to get them to see. When they deny their Self they will remain stuck and without breakthrough. They are searching diligently for the key, and it is right inside of them.*

And I thought we were done.

*We'll never be done; we're just beginning. These breakthroughs are going to be marvelous because people have great faith in scientists these days, and many will wake up because of them.*

*Beginning* meaning "beginning to wake people up."

*Yes, I told you that was what we were here for, what we were doing. It is not just to stir interest or satisfy curiosity, it is to help wake people up, to help them to realize they have been asleep and are missing the point. The point containing all they are. How many times have you said, "I'm missing something here?"*

Quite a bit.

*Yes, the point being you recognized it and looked for what it was you knew you were missing. That's an important first step, to recognize that you're not seeing the complete picture and to ask why. Another way of putting it is, as Paul said, "If any man thinks he knows something he knows nothing yet as he ought to know." Now that seems like an extreme statement, but we all know in part. There's always more to what we think we know than what we know. That's why I say this will never end. No sense in getting puffed up by something you know, because there's always more to know about it than you know.*

I know what you mean.

*You think you do.*

Well, I figure there's probably more to it.

*You think so?*

Yes, I do.

*Well, you're right.*

I KNEW that was a safe bet.

*Yes, and you always like to play it safe in your reckless way.* ☺

Ah, you got me again.

*You know, once you find the balance between your extremes you'll be unstoppable.*

Then I won't want to stop.

*You won't need to. Now you have to stop, regroup, back up, ponder it and then move on. Once you find the balance you'll flow forward untouchable.*

Sounds like the thing to do.

*Oh, it is. You thought I was being serious when I said you had a unique way of blending flesh and spirit.* ☺

I did till now. You have a very subtle sense of humor I hadn't completely noticed. That is funny, though.

*Come on! It is hilarious. You think you're the only one who likes to have fun? I love to, always have, and I'm good at it too because I enjoy it.* ☺

I miss you, Talia.

*How can you miss me? I'm right here.*

I mean I miss you in the flesh.

*If I were in the flesh we wouldn't be doing this right now. I would probably be playing tennis or something.*

And none of this would get out.

*No, none of this would. Not in this way or by us or even now. I told you this had to be or this wouldn't be happening, and you would still be in search of a vision. As it is, I helped to restore your vision, and I'm in a unique position to help you to accomplish what it is you need to do.*

As natural as walking.

*Yes, as natural as walking. It is important to walk, you know.*

Yes, it seems to all stem from there.

*From the stem comes the blossom. It is a basic precept, and the walk you walk has its foundation in that precept.*

Well, now, I knew what *precept* meant, but it made such an impression on me that I had to look it up. Interesting.

> G looked up what *precept* meant, and the Latin root, *praeceptum*, means "to capture or to take." G was blown away at how this relates to the hawk seizing its prey and the spider in the king's house. You have to take what you need.

*You said I was impressive.*

You are very impressive.

*Babylon has no power here.*

I know that.

*Yes, the STATUS of confusion, the politics of it has no power here. Here, there is only perfect peace, and that is yours to walk in.*

*Social circles run the gambit. THAT passion for the game has no place here either; pawns are sacrificed and with glee.*

That's a vicious circle, isn't it?

*That is usually a very subtle, vicious circle. And it is not always for money or power; sometimes it is just for the pleasure of the sacrifice.*

Thank you, Talia.

*There is always thankfulness involved with doing God's work.*

*Now we need to talk about traveling.*

OK.

*You were saying the other day about how some cultures insisted that one must travel to learn what they needed to, to become wise.*

> G and I were talking about how in some cultures, like some Native American cultures, the boys are sent on a journey to learn from others before coming back to their tribe as men.

Yes.

*Well, the primary reason was not in the actual traveling per se. It was in being an outsider looking in. Of not being a part of the plan of the clan, of leaving that and seeing with fresh eyes.*

Makes sense to me.

*Of course it does—you're well traveled.*

You were too.

*I had that opportunity and I jumped at it. It did help to open my eyes.*

I heard your dad was offered a herd of goats or camels or something for you once.

Talia had taken a trip to Israel with her dad. While shopping in the Arab quarter in Jerusalem, a shop keeper offered Michael a herd of goats or camels in exchange for Talia. None of us were sure if it was a joke or if he was serious!

*He was. That was funny, and I was flattered. Then I had to laugh at myself for being flattered. I asked him* [Michael] *if he was tempted, and he laughed and said no, but I wondered if he really was. Then I laughed about that because I knew he wasn't.*

Sounds like you had a good time.

*We had a great time. He's laughing about it now.*

### July 17

**7:59 AM**
It is a new day.

*It is a glorious new day.*

Yes, it is.

*Don't be disappointed with how few "get" this or who doesn't get this; this is strong meat and on many levels. I know you want to share this with the world and we are, but this isn't for the world, this is for the chosen few. Remember that many are called but few are chosen.*

But isn't it their choice?

*Yes, they choose themselves. They can choose to be as gods or as fools; there really isn't any middle ground. You choose the ground to stand on—the path to walk on—and those paths are placed before you daily. It isn't as if the paths aren't plain either—they are diametrically opposed to each other. Therefore, choose this day whom you will serve.*

*The thing we are doing here is of the utmost importance. I tell you again time is short for those decisions, and they should be weighed carefully. This is that that was spoken of when He said, "I work a work in these days, a work that you will in no way believe though a man declare it unto you." I know you feel you should explain this and other things contained here, but that's not how it works. The choice is either to receive the pure word of truth or a carefully crafted lie that is the path that is set before you daily. Judgment is imperative, spiritual discernment is necessary. Another essential ingredient is desire. If you don't really WANT it, you won't really HAVE it. It is hard to stumble into these things.*

*That door I held open for you was an invitation. You weren't forced to go through it; you chose to because you recognized that that was within your sphere of responsibility to do so. You thought it was the excitement of exploration, but there was more to it than that, much more. If you had rejected that invitation to the mysteries of the unknown, we wouldn't be here now. That was a choice, a decision that you made. That's the portal you were seeking so many years ago. You knew it existed, but you didn't know where to find it. You trusted me whole-heartedly because you knew where I was coming from. The thought crossed your mind that day that maybe I was a conjurer or magician. That I was doing illusions, practicing to elicit a response from you—that perhaps I was putting a spell on you, that I was magical. That maybe my circle of friends in Santa Barbara was into witchcraft even. But that wasn't it all and you knew it. You weighed it carefully and rejected the lie. You received the truth of what was happening, and you decided right then and there that you would discover the truth and if it was true to walk in it. THAT was one of the best decisions you ever made, and it is greatly appreciated.*

I still think you're magical and you did put a spell on me.

*Only in the best of ways, and it wasn't me. I was being used that day by the Holy Spirit to wake you up. You had been asleep long enough. I have to tell you though, I thought that was really funny when I heard you thought I was a magician. I knew less of what was going on that day than you did, though I knew something was up. That something was different about that day, that "something was in the air" is what I had thought.*

Hey, I was just weighing the possibilities.

*As well you should. This gift you were given that day was my great honor to bring you, and I did nothing but be who I was, and THAT's the magic: just be who you are.* ☺

*So you see that girl you were told that is from Santa Barbara that would change your life IS me, and I HAVE changed your life.*

I have no words to express . . .

*I know, and again, none are needed. We are one in HIM and without HIM we can do nothing. No thing at all; however, with Him we can do all things and the good news is we are with Him and HE is with us; therefore, nothing is impossible.*

Cool.

*Yes, it is cool, isn't it? Very cool.*

You are one cool chick.

*Thank you.*

*My dad says to tell you he's proud to be your friend.*

Tell him thanks and I didn't know there was pride there.

*Of course there is. He plentifully rewards the proud doer. We're proud to be His children. We're proud to know Him, to walk in His grace. The pride HE warns about is the pride of the flesh, of the debilitating aspect of it. That's the pride that's spoken of that comes before a fall. Write it like I say it, and it is easy. Slow down—you were told that not too long ago, as I recall.*

*Have you ever seen a master looking hurried?*

Can't say as I've seen many masters.

*Yes, but the ones you have seen or have heard about?*

Come to think of it, they act like they have all the time in the world.

*They don't and they know it. They also know that to be efficient one must slow down and be still on a certain level. One trait of a true master is calmness, and you will always see that center of calmness in whatever they do. The eye of the storm, as it were. You'll also notice a conspicuous lack of panic, no matter what is going on. Why do you think that is?*

Because they've found the SOURCE?

*They have discovered the source of their success even if THEY don't know what it is. Have you ever seen success from panic?*

No, that's called blind fear, and I figure that's what it is.

*Now we're getting somewhere. Fear blinds, and if you're blind you can't see. If you can't see, how can you get to where you're going, much less have success at it?*

I can see that.

*But have you thought about taking that on the road?*

What? My jokes? I take them everywhere I go. I'm a constant source of amusement—at least to myself.

*You're a source of amusement to many others too. You know laughter is one of the most healthy things you can do. I called myself a giver of laughter; have I not made you laugh?*

Yes, tons of times.

*That is a weighty matter, a person's health. It is important to be healthy, don't you think?*

Yes, sure it is. That's important.

*Do you know why Ronald Reagan was called the Great Communicator?*

Because he was the great communicator?

*Because of his humor. He disarmed his enemies with it, even charmed many over to his side. He had the ear of the people, and one reason was that people love to laugh. It is good for the body, and the body knows it.*

*Now you were concerned about writing down the revelation of the download I just gave you, but you don't have to write it down. Just remember the essence of the message, of doorways, etc. And now you know how to use this to work outside the box. You always want to open the box and let whatever's in there out anyway—now you have a method.*

OK, I take it back: you're not cool—you're beyond cool.

*Yes, I am beyond cool. I instinctively knew that even when I was on earth. That's one reason I always had to laugh when I saw people trying to act cool, because it is always looked to me like a comic act. So when I imitated them I never could keep a straight face.*

That was actually very sophisticated for someone your age.

*Well, I was very sophisticated for my age.*

*We're quite a team you know.*

I know.

*Some won't believe it, but this hasn't been done before, not on this level, not in this depth. People have been communing with "spirits" ever since there were people in the physical realm, but it hasn't been recorded in this depth before. Mostly it has been "bits and pieces."*

Why is that?

*Because this has been ordained for just such times as these. This message had to get out, and it had to be at this time. I will say it again: this that we are doing is worthy of remembrance, and it will be remembered for all time. Told you to wait, there was more. You're learning to curb your excitement, and that's a good thing. That old saying, patience is a virtue, is a true saying, and that's why IT IS remembered.*

Raising the bar.

*That's what we're doing, raising the bar. Encouraging people to jump higher and fly farther than ever before.*

Is it going to work?

*Of course it is going to work; we cannot fail. I told you we were going to get it right this time and we ARE.*

## *July 19*

**6:40 AM**

I was thinking that since Einstein said his education got in the way of his learning, maybe I'm smarter for getting out of formal education so soon.

*Hmmm.*

What?

*I'm thinking.* ☺

Hey, it's a joke.

*Well, you were paying more attention in school than you think—it just wasn't always on what they were teaching. Now I'm teaching you and bringing you into a deeper understanding of all things, and you are paying attention. Remember when He said, "She'll be YOUR teacher?"*

Yes, another thing that happened at Thanksgiving.

*And at the time you were thinking what?*

That "I'd like to teach her." That you had so much potential.

*Everyone has so much more potential than they know; it is who decides to use it that's important.*

**9:00 AM**

*Now we need to make people aware of something else.*

What's that?

*All that happened Thanksgiving. And there is a lot more. It is a microcosm of life, of a life on earth. A day, one single day, can be filled with joy and wonderment, with lessons and learning, with realizations of truth and sharing of love. Or it can be wasted, missed completely and filled with disillusionment and misery—and that is a profound waste of a life. Therefore, live life fully in every way you possibly can. The trials and tribulations, successes and victories of a single day as if a lifetime, and your meditations at the end of the day can set you up for further victories or miseries. That's called living mindfully, and that's what called for.*

And there you go, going right into something else and blowing my mind again.

*I'm blowing the cobwebs out.*

I have been thinking clearer lately.

*That's because you've been listening to me.* ☺

**5:30 PM**
*Now I want to tell you of a not-so-well-kept secret, other than people keep it a secret from themselves. And that's our communication. A large part of this message is* how to—*how to communicate.*

*If people will look at this as "bilateral communications," it will be much easier to grasp. The gulf that separates, as it were, is an invention of the mind of man. Bilateral meaning "the symmetrical other side."*

*I said before that the physical has a spiritual counterpart, and to know yourself and the importance of that. And that if you did know yourself, others wouldn't be such a mystery. Well, to know yourself is to also know your spiritual counterpart and to call it unto yourself; after all, it is YOURS. When you felt me on your left side when I was used to heal you, you'll notice your right elbow was healed not long after that—and*

347

*that's because the body acts bilaterally also. ONE SIDE AFFECTS THE OTHER. Spiritually, it is the same. What you are in the physical, you are enhanced much more so in the spiritual. These ALWAYS work hand in hand. So to sum it up one needs to, or it helps to think, "Bilateral communication yield to the spirit," then demand results. That's how it is taken by force.*

*This is for everyone, and everyone who WANTS it can have it. Think how one side of the body affects the other side of the body. That's how close these parts work together.*

Well said.

*I'm well spoken. The people need to know these are no longer hidden truths, and they should receive them. It IS theirs for the taking. There was a time when what we're doing was quite common and accepted, you know.*

Guess that's been a while.

*It has for most cultures. It is been bred right out of them, stolen away. You see the poverty in their lives it has caused and not to honor the Creator or His creations . . . untold misery.*

That's a shame.

*Yes, it is, and shame on the ones who have stolen it. We want to bring it back. Restore paths to dwell in, re-mind those to remember, to live again. Have I not enriched your life?*

Immeasurably.

*And that is a statement of fact.*

## *July 22*

———————✦———————

**7:10 AM**

G dreamt last night about Talia telling him something about "pure honesty" and using examples—a person and a Porsche 911 woven in—and her saying something about it.

*Pure honesty has to do with quality and performance, and neither one of them are cheap to maintain.*

So, a 911 is Talia approved?

*It is a fine automobile if that's what you're into.*

What about the price?

*They're a little pricey.*

*I used it as an example of quality and performance, which is endemic to pure honesty.*

Endemic speaks of a place, doesn't it?

*It is the same place we've been talking about all along. Pure honesty does no harm, and its basis is in love—that's its only motivation. That's the performance contained in Everything. Love performs. It acts to move things to a better place, to enhance what is, where it is. Its very nature is quality, and it is always perfectly pure at its root.*

At its root?

*Yes, it stems from a place of perfect purity and is without corruption whatsoever. A misinterpretation of how to apply this purity could result in misunderstanding though. Thus the "pure honesty." Being honest without pure motivation smacks of dishonesty. So be honest with yourself and be honest with others out of a pure heart.*

## *July 23*

---

**10:37 AM**

I keep seeing spheres. Spheres touching, intersecting, and overlapping. Spheres within spheres.

*You see them moving too.*

Yes, moving all around and pulsating with life!

*Pulsating with different colors. Do you hear the sounds of the many different vibrations?*

Yes, yes I do!

*That's the art of life in action, moving and creating. It never ends; this pulsating movement is always and forever. You saw the rain coming.*

Yes, I saw it falling.

*That's prophetic vision; trust it. Get into your bubble or sphere, and your sphere of influence will grow to where it needs to be. And it is not a striving to get there, or* networking *as so many like to call it, but a growing into it naturally, supernaturally. I said before, you influence whether you want to or not; may as will influence positively for the betterment of all.*

*If you think of a sphere as a circle, that's not what it is. It is many different shapes, all spherical and alive. The circle is a two-dimensional representation to draw on paper as a symbol or to explain certain principles of understanding.*

Of understanding?

*Yes, to understand, you must embody, make your own, these principles. It is a becoming, becoming what is. An intellectual knowing can only ever be a seed—a seed that may grow into understanding—but only if it is taken and embodied. Something within you must come out of you before it can live again.*

## July 25

**9:10 AM**

*You have much study to do, and I'm bringing you to a place you can receive more.*

So we're delayed?

*I wouldn't call it a delay. For everything there is a season; now's the season for study. I've already expressed to you what to study. Study the web of life and the interrelationships of people and all things. You will come to a greater understanding of what we're discussing and how it relates to all things. Again, all things are interconnected, and this is apparent when your eyes are opened.*

*You see luminous fibers connecting all things. This is why everything affects everything else. You feel them pulling people towards you even now. This is a silver cord that cannot be broken but by the hand of God. This is also the path that makes our connection so easy. When people understand this, that great gulf that separates will not seem so great after all.*

That seems esoteric.

*It is esoteric. Its mystery is hidden within the vibrations of life. When a person vibrates in harmony with the vibration of life the mystery is solved.*

That's perfectly reasonable.

*I always am.*

## July 27

**9:43 AM**

Isotropic?

*It has to do with the nature of time.*

How so?

*It does not vary in any direction; it remains the SAME—non-existent in its function here. That's why I say when you're dealing with here, time has no function—it is non-existent. Eternity isn't time without end, it is time out of mind. It all just is now, because here now is all that is.*

You certainly say some things.

*Yes, I certainly do say all I have to say in the time I have to say it.*

That seems like a contradiction.

*You have seasons there, and we work with your seasons. Time to you appears linear. It is not at all. Even there it comes around spherically, as the seasons. That mirrors the workings of the Creator. That tree you climbed. What did you do?*

I put two blue lights up on the trunk and trimmed some suckers out.

*What did you hear someone say who saw it later?*

Cool.

*Coincidence?*

No.

*Why blue?*

That's what was already up there but had probably been blown off by a storm.

*But why blue?*

I don't know why.

*So we could talk about it.*

That's it?

*No, that's not it. It is everything. When people ask, "Is that it?" they're asking about everything, but they only want it explained in part, and that's part of the problem. People for the most part insist that everything be separated or broken into parts in order to understand it, but it cannot be broken into parts but must be viewed as a whole to understand it. That's another subtle way they attempt to relieve themselves of responsibility. To know something is to be responsible for the knowledge, not only to walk in it but to pass it on as well. It is my great honor/ responsibility to pass THIS knowledge on, and that we will.*

*When someone asks where are the missing pieces, the pieces aren't missing, they are still a part of the whole. But they may have been misplaced, and that misplacement is almost invariably misplaced by the creative mind of man. It is not just artists that are creative, everyone is creative. It is how you choose to express your creativity that is the issue.*

*Had enough?*

No, not at all.

*Then stay here. We're not finished.*

*Times change.*

Times change?

*Yes, times, time and half a time, times change. This is from here for there. Know that there, times change.*

Seasons. I was spoken to about seasons the other day and the primary colors that represented them and why.

*Yes, for "everything" there is a season.*

Whoa, never saw it like that.

*Now you have. Remembrance is putting all the pieces together. Remember? Into a coherent whole. Enlightenment is a realization. Light reveals reality. Reality is what is real. Only by the light can you walk in what is real and be real and become what you are—which is everything.*

**12:20 PM**

    G was looking at the yellow calla lillies.

*These are my favorite.*

Why?

*Look at how it grows, spiraling.*

*Which way did it grow?*

To the right. Why?

*It is just the right way to grow.*

## *July 28*

**5:15 PM**

*No one talks to us anymore.*

> G heard this statement from another spirit, not Talia.
> This spirit continued to speak.

*Man is in a precarious position. He has forgotten the old ways, the true ways. Even you, it is hard for you to believe.*

Sorry about that.

*It is OK. You're well educated, in man's ways.*

*There is a way that seems right but is not. Man used to have such reverence. Now things are stamped out. Man becomes a slave to each other to buy these stamped out things.*

*I like that girl you're with.*

Who, Talia?

*Yes.*

You know her?

*Yes, that's Heaven's Dew. She's famous.*

She's famous?

*Yes.*

## *July 30*

**1:21 PM**

OK, a couple questions.

*OK.*

You're famous?

*Yes, I guess I am. It is the speed with which I've accomplished what I've accomplished here, and also there are not that many that can do more HERE than THERE. I told you, many were looking on in awe.*

Times, time and half a time?

*That's a complex question. It has to do with ages, of things coming to pass and passing. There are times for things and they pass. It is a time for a thing and it too will pass. A half a time is time cut short. My time was cut short there, but my time is enhanced here to accomplish more there. There is an age to come that will be half a time. If these days were not shortened then no flesh would be saved, but for the elect's sake shall this time be shortened.*

Got a date?

*No man knows the hour. It is a good idea to be ready though.*

*I said I liked the poem you wrote me. I like it for the truth it contains.*

*My life should not be mourned, my life should be celebrated.*

# August 2008

*August 4*

---

**10:00 AM**

*Always speak the truth in love, even about yourself. If you don't like yourself, how do you think you're going to feel about others?*

**11:24 AM**

*I know you want to work out and train, but what's more important than this? That's one reason I wanted to omit "athletic" at my tree, because it puts an unnecessary emphasis on what's not that important, and I wanted you to know that. That decision was primarily for you, for now. I saw the time coming when you would rather train the body than the mind for our message. You think our message is done?*

No, but I thought we took a hiatus.

*That doesn't mean to turn your mind off. It was for a time of reflection, study and growth. First it was coming too fast, now it is coming slow . . . so you give up?*

No, not at all, I just thought we were taking a break.

*It was a break in the narrative, not a vacation from life.*

I just have not been hearing you say much.

*You haven't been listening much. How much would you talk to someone who wasn't listening?*

Not much.

*You would have me waste words. I told you I didn't do that.*

But you had told me to get back into training.

*I did and you are, but not at the exclusion of everything else.*

I'm corrected.

*You're being corrected. You're still somewhat bouncing off the walls with your distractions.*

Just had to get settled.

*The settling is an internal state. It doesn't matter that much what's going on on the outside. There are people that need our help, and we're moving them in directions where they can receive it.*

Talia, I've often wondered if I were up to the task and that maybe there were many others better suited for this. I'm no writer anyway.

*The fact that "you're no writer" is one of the reasons you're writing this. Also quit wondering if you're up for the task. You obviously are, or we wouldn't have gotten this far. It is needful for you to apply more mental discipline, and we are working on that.*

Sorry to disappoint you.

*Disappointing me is not the issue, our message is.*

I want to do this.

*So do I. Now we're in agreement. Now we can continue unhindered by foolishness. You must find the balance, that's all.*

The balance is all.

*That's it; that's the primary source. If you receive something in an unbalanced state, what you receive will seem somewhat unbalanced itself. That can cause confusion from what is a perfectly balanced truth.*

Thus the growth and the waiting you spoke of.

*Exactly. We have spoken of all of this before. Of giving someone something in an untimely manner, how it doesn't profit to do so. Speaking the truth's not enough. As a matter of fact, it is often used as a weapon of revenge to hurt others. It is speaking the truth in love in a perfectly timed manner that makes all the difference, spoken truth perfectly balanced.*

Talia, I'm glad your back!

*I'm glad YOU'RE back. If you haven't noticed, I'm pretty consistent. It doesn't matter where you're at there; what matters is where you're at here.*

Maybe I have too many irons in the fire.

*Maybe you do. It does take a certain commitment.*

**1:07 PM**

*I'm human. You identify with me. That's one reason why what we do together works so well. Also, you KNEW me.*

*We had met and you saw things beyond me. It tied things together for you. It was beyond your imagination. The symmetry of a young girl and an omnipotent God. This cemented ties that bind. The bridging of the flesh and spirit, of the earthly and the heavenly. This is incomprehensible for most people.*

*Only an empty vessel is useful to be filled. A filled vessel filled with what isn't needed is useless until it can be emptied. Again we are speaking of choices. Choosing to be emptied can be painful, for most people cling to their past choices even when they have filled them with misery. They feel all their work will have been wasted and lost. But to be emptied is to be free. Free for all the possibilities to be filled.*

*I told you I wasn't omniscient, and you identify with that. It is in human terms you understand.*

This is true. I had to look up *omniscient*. There's got to be some irony there.

*You might be surprised how much irony is everywhere, but the point being is your identification. This helps greatly in our communications; it always does on every level.*

### August 5

**8:30 AM**

*You have a question.*

Yes, I do.

*I have a lot of answers.*

You sure do.

*Why don't you ask then?*

I'm not sure where to start.

*You don't always have to be so sure. You like to be positive about things before you declare them, but it doesn't always work that way. When you declare something in faith, it brings it into being. You're sometimes too concerned about being wrong or misreading the spirit. What you need to understand is that the spirit works with you to bring things to pass. A pure heart and fervent prayer is always honored, and if a thing you have declared doesn't come to pass, then it wasn't meant to be.*

Almost like we got off track here.

*No, not at all. We're right on track, and this will tie in exquisitely with other things to come. It is as important to look ahead as it is to be in the moment. Looking ahead in hope and expectation.*

That's pretty cool—a hawk just flew up into the top of a cedar.

*He's here for you.*

Why?

*Just a sign.*

A sign for what?

*A sign of independence and self-sufficiency among other things. You ever see them in a flock?*

No, four is the most I've ever seen hunting together.

*They hunt independently and yet are mutually supportive.*

That's a perfect window through the other tree to where he's sitting.

> G was looking through one tree to the next, where the hawk was perched.

*Does he look nervous?*

No, he looks supremely confident.

*He knows his vision will bring him everything he needs.*

Talia, that's awesome.

*I know, but these things are everywhere. Everywhere you look they are there, but most just don't notice. Many don't even have the inclination to care.*

There he goes again, flying over the pond.

*Yes, something will give up its life today so that animal may live, and it is no different with you or anybody else. What's important is being mindful of that and being thankful for the sacrifice.*

Talia, I know you gave up your life here so we could do this and bring this message to those who need it, and I just want to thank you again for all you've done and are doing to change things for the better, to bring a wonder-filled life to others.

*That was well put, and you're very welcome.*

You sound a little surprised.

*Well, that was well put, very articulate. I said you were, you know. When have you known me to be wrong?*

Can't think of a single instance.

*You won't find one either. Here we can do no wrong. When you're "here," there you can't either.*

I can tell you don't feel like "giving your life up" was a sacrifice.

*No, I don't. It seems like the ultimate gift is mine, and I'm just living it.*

That point of view seems abstract here, but I know it isn't there. That this message has touched your mom's friend so is awesome and so very encouraging.

*I told you we would touch people and change lives. This message is with power and has been ordained for this time. You seem surprised.*

Well, I guess a little.

*Why?*

I'm not sure why.

*Remember what that Indian told you?*

To take myself seriously.

*That's the part. Why is that so hard?*

Because I'm a court jester?

*You're not a court jester—you just like to play the part. Look at how the brain is made.*

What do you mean?

*It looks like a cloud on the outside, and if you don't feed it, it becomes cloudy. But if you look on the inside it appears more like a tree, and a tree must be fed.*

OK, our conversations have more twists and turns.

*The twist is for strength, the turns are for agility. I have to keep your mind occupied or you get bored, and those horses will run in every direction, much like yesterday.*

Wild horses—I just saw that.

*Yes, and you must control them. They are not tame, and that would be taking it too far, but you must control them.*

So are you going to talk about what you've done with your mom's friend?

*I can. I know you're bursting to know.*

Yes, I sort of am.

*She is a very special person whose heart has been prepared to receive this. She did know there was more, and she asked about it. She's now learning what that more is. She has asked me to talk to her, and I do. I told her to listen, and she's learning how to quiet herself and listen with her heart. She has felt my presence, and she knows it's me. She knew me well there, and that basis of knowledge has given her an edge to hear my voice. This is a language of the heart, and she's well aware of that. I have merged my spirit with hers at times, and an intuitive knowing is the result of that. She is as filled with questions as you are, and that is a definite first step on the path of life. She has asked to see the light, and she is.*

That's beautiful!

*Yes, truth is always beautiful and life giving.*

I was told she thanks you daily.

*She does have a wonderful spirit of thankfulness. She also has a very, very sweet spirit, but she's just now learning who she really is, and that is truly a wonderful thing to know. She's asked many questions, and they will be answered in time.*

G sensed some personal things here.

*There are, and they are being worked out, but know He has a special place reserved for her, and she is and will be used to bring life and light to others. She's asked for this and it will be.*

That is just so totally awesome!

*Yes, it is.*

You know, Talia, you really never do cease to amaze me.

*Yes, I know. "Pretty much amazing."*

You knew you were when you were here; that's why you said that so much, wasn't it?

*That was another intuitive knowing. That not only was I amazing but so much more as well. Again, this isn't so much about me as about the so much more that everyone is a part of. When one is awakened to that fact, then is life filled with wonder.*

## 10:35 PM

The man on TV just said that all children would become scientists if we didn't discourage them and make it so boring and technical.

*He's right about that.*

Talia, tell me about your prophetic dreams.

*I had them a lot. Things would come to pass, and there was no denying or explaining it. It made no sense to me at first, then as my awareness of what was happening grew, I knew there must be a soul and a Supreme Being. How else could it be explained? It did get and keep my attention on seeking how and what was happening. I knew there was more— there had to be. There was just no denying it. Then I felt the spirit at times. I didn't know what it was then, but it felt larger than life. And*

*that's what you saw in my eyes, the spirit that was larger that life itself,
a window into the marvels of the universe. You literally looked into my
eyes and saw the universe.*

That's what it was! I couldn't put it into words, but that's it!

*That is it. It's the "it" that I was speaking of. It's the "it" that is
everything and nothing lost. That "it" is riches beyond measure. This is
where I live, and it is glorious!*

### August 6

**8:08 AM**

*Quietness is good.*

I know, quiet the galloping horses.

*That's it, you control them. It takes patience. Everything you do there
that has lasting meaning will be accomplished from a place of quietness.
Quietness equals confidence. True confidence is born in quietness. You
ever see anyone loud that had true confidence?*

No, I guess not. They seemed as if they were trying to convince
themselves, and it seemed like a false confidence.

*It is a false confidence because it isn't real. A common thread you will see
with confident people is that they are quiet. You immediately noticed how
confident I was when you met me; you also noticed that I was quiet.*

I did. I wish you had said more, that we had talked more. You
seemed like you had a lot to say, and I wanted to hear it. That's a
major regret for me.

*Don't regret it. It had and has much purpose. I didn't have a life-changing message then—now I do.*

That that you said about your eyes mirroring the universe yesterday—thanks for that, for explaining it.

*And that's exactly what we are, mirrors of the universe. That's how life is expressed as art, and that stems from decisions. That's another aspect of our creative abilities. To decide to express the art of creation.*

There went the hawk.

*Yes, he's expressing his creative abilities by being who he is. There is no striving, and he's very relaxed. He's not putting on airs or trying to impress—he's just being who he is. There's never pressure in being who you truly are.*

If I were an Indian I would say, "Hawk has much to teach!"

*Everything has much to teach. It's where you place your attention is where you'll get your answers. A perfectly placid pond has swirls. Movement in stillness.*

I know what you're talking about, Talia, but I'm not sure anybody else will.

*They will if they are quiet.*

You're talking about vortices in the quietness, in the stillness. The movement of life that never ends but is invisible.

*Yes, you feel compelled to explain.*

Somewhat.

*Why?*

Why not?

*"It" can't always be explained. Some things, to receive, takes an act of faith.*

Yes, I know.

*I know you know. As I've said before, the confusion is caused by separation. Oneness is necessary. It's really not so hard either. You can merge your spirit with things. This is how you can know them intimately and perfectly. I told you no analyst would get this. This doing is by being and Beings is what we are. It's not that it's second nature—it's your first nature, to live as a spiritual being, for that's what you are. It's your very essence. The body is just a filter.*

Never heard the body described like that before.

*But that's what it does; it filters spiritual experience.*

But why?

*So you can express your creativity through your choices.*

Wow.

*Yes, again, wow. Told you it was never-ending.*

So you've said.

*You know why?*

Because it's never-ending?

*That's why. See how simple that is? Most people are masters at complicating things, especially such simple truths. They work extremely hard at it.*

*The parallel universe is right here right now. Mathematics are symbols pointing to truths to be visualized. Without a vision you die. Literally whither on the vine.*

*Complications crumble; simplicity tends to stand. Complication and confusion are synonymous, just as simplicity and purity can be interchanged.*

Was that you?

*It's a truth.*

*It's enough for now. There are other things to do.*

Thanks.

*You're welcome.*

### 9:32 AM
You're superhuman?

*I'm a superhuman—anybody can be.*

Anybody.

*Anybody. It's just another decision. It does take discipline though.*

That's entering in through the veils to the spirit world, isn't it?

*Yes, but the veils are right here, right now, and they are mostly in your mind.*

That's why you said you had to feed the mind.

*Yes, the proper food, the bread of life.*

Awesome!

*Yes, it is. Everything here is awesome. The flesh is awestruck by it; that's why it seems hard to get there and stay there. It takes control from the flesh, which is something the flesh loves: control. The flesh feels like it's dying, thus the fear.*

But it's not.

*No, not really, but it does kill its control, which is fraught with problems. To relinquish its control it takes a certain death of self-will, which it's rarely willing to give up.*

*Usually a person has to experience a major crisis in their life to even begin to be willing. Another way is an INTENSE desire, a feeling like fire to move them to surrender. To get there or die trying is the commitment I'm talking about. Another thing is, one must be willing to be thought a fool; the pride of the flesh has no place here. One must in effect die daily.*

### *August 7*

**8:05 AM**

*There is nothing there worth holding on to to keep you from the kingdom. That's why I've mentioned responsibility so much. One must take responsibility for this journey, and I mean literally take it. It's yours anyway, so take responsibility for it. If you'll notice, most people are quick to point the finger at the responsibility of others. If they were as conscious of their own responsibility, it would go a long way towards this journey.*

*A wise man told you a good beginning brings us halfway to our goal. I had a very good beginning, and it put me a step ahead of the average person. This conscious raising of me was a pivotal point in my life; I had very little to overcome. Most struggle for a lifetime to rid themselves of the trash, and that's what it is too—trash in the subconscious usually placed there by ignorance. Only the cleansing fire of the spirit can remove this. Remember what I told you before?*

Ah . . . no, what?

*That I had a lot to say.*

Ah, yes you do.

*Oh yes, I do and I'm saying it.*

Point is?

*Point is when you have something to say, say it. Don't wait and then regret not saying it later.*

**8:30 AM**
*My momma has something to tell you.*

She does?

*Yes, she doesn't know it yet.*

What is it about?

*She'll tell you, but it's about us. Trust, trust in what you're doing, trust us.*

Trust, OK.

*Trust is very valuable.*

Yes.

*You haven't learned this yet, and it's very basic.*

It is very basic.

*It is, and you haven't learned it yet.*

*The life of a thunderstorm. The thunder of a perfect mind is filled with truths. It's upsetting to the bland business-as-usual mind of the mundane masses. The "follow-along crowd" of self-worshipers. Don't let them affect you. Our game is a grand game. Their game is merely for foolish and unschooled children. Now is the time to grow up, and all the necessary tools and teachings are in place to receive them. Now a mature choice is needed to play along. And play is what it is. A playful attitude helps in this growth, a playful spirit. This game is fun, and that's important to know. Watch children at play; watch animals at play and think of what this reveals.*

Growth!

*Wonderful growth, and there's no clocking in. When you see someone wanting to control others, it's the flesh.*

And the flesh profits nothing, right?

*Pretty much. Just ask yourself, where is the benefit? This is a revealing question. Ask it and listen for the answer.*

We can answer our own questions, can't we?

*Of course you can and do. The heart knows what's true. That's why I said to trust yourself and no excuses were acceptable, because the truth resides within you. "Be true to yourself"—that's a good saying. It's an even better practice.*

I've never known anyone that wields the sword of truth with such exquisite delicacy.

*Nicely put.*

Thanks, you are the fencing master.

*We're not fighting here, we're just talking.*

I just get a bit overwhelmed by it all.

*I know you do. That's why I'm always putting things in context for you.*

Well, thanks again.

*We've discussed the power of the flesh before, that is, it has none but what you give it.*

**1:04 PM**
*There's a subject we left off on that we weren't through discussing the other day.*

OK, what's that?

*Something so personal for you, and you take such pleasure in, that you weren't comfortable with talking about it.*

All right.

*Something you haven't noticed that you sometimes guard.*

OK, what?

*Humor.*

Humor? There has to be a joke there somewhere.

*There is. But first you need to know that there is humor everywhere, and also one of its designs is to help to get through the hard times. You don't even see it everywhere, and you have a refined sense of it. It's so often underestimated for its healing powers.*

Just had a very interesting download on that.

*Could you describe it?*

I guess I could, but it would be funny trying.

*See what I mean. It's everywhere.*

Yes, I do, and also some far-reaching implications.

*What are you implying?*

Ah . . .

*See what I mean—you guard it.*

I just think it's too involved to get into.

*Involvement itself implies getting into.*

Yes, but it would take pages and pages to describe the download.

*But the point is being open to, open to share it.*

OK, I'm open.

*That was almost like pulling teeth.*

I know why you said that.

*Then share it.*

A small part of the download was the report of Doc Holiday and how he thought it was funny that he died with his boots off.

*That wasn't so hard, was it?*

No, but it was a miniscule part of it.

*Yes, but he found humor in his death, and that's funny.*

If you say so.

*I do.*

*Everyone here who has died of a misadventure always wants their money back, and that's funny. They never do get a refund either, but it doesn't stop them from asking.*

Is that true?

*You think I'm making stuff up here? The point is life goes on. It's funny to us that that always occurs to them. That the promised service wasn't delivered and some restitution should be made. Most say it in humor, but some are quite serious about it. Either way it's pretty funny. Anyway, such are most of the promises made in your world.*

## 4:30 PM

So the Boston massacre wasn't?

*No, not like it was portrayed.*

> G was watching a Discovery show about the Boston Massacre that showed how the events that led up to what were labeled a massacre were greatly overreacted to.

When I was first taught that and read about it in school I knew it didn't sound quite right, that there was another side to the story that wasn't being told.

*And that's the knowing within you I was talking about, the voice of the witness of truth that transcends time and place: that's the voice to trust.*

## *August 10*

**6:30 AM**

Talia, I remember a while back you said to me "du mun." *Du* means "top or great," *mun* means "gate."

*Yes, I remember too.*

I'm trying to recall the context in which you told me.

*The context is the connection of everything we've talked about and placing one on the path of no deviation into and through the Great Gate and into the Land of Freedom. Just to see the Great Gate is enough to spur most on the never-ending path, for to see it is to taste the pure freedom of everlasting life. That's the realization of the truth that truly sets one free. You've never seen a gate like this one; there is none even close on earth.*

What about Kim's friend? She thinks I am making all of this up.

*She's lost. Trapped in her own mind. See how easily precious gifts are overlooked.*

She's going to come around?

*Everyone comes around. See how hard she fights to hold onto her doctrine. She would deny it, but she feels you have an ulterior motive.*

If I had an ulterior motive it would be simpler not to do this at all.

*On the surface it would. I know your desire is pure, more so than even you do.*

So are you going to tell me about the hummingbird?

*It's my nature.*

Flighty?

*No, not at all. Swift.*

You are that.

*Very much so.*

**5:19 PM**
*It's all oneness.*

But you can't understand this without experiencing it.

*That's exactly right. You can't understand this without experiencing it.*

> G saw a vision of heavy, wet snow falling, clinging to the branches of the cedars and on the ground.

*Everyone is as individual as a snowflake. When you can hear the music of the snowfall you will understand how each of those unique individual snowflakes bond as one upon the earth.*

### *August 11*

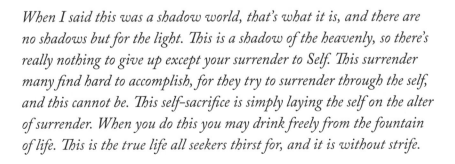

*When I said this was a shadow world, that's what it is, and there are no shadows but for the light. This is a shadow of the heavenly, so there's really nothing to give up except your surrender to Self. This surrender many find hard to accomplish, for they try to surrender through the self, and this cannot be. This self-sacrifice is simply laying the self on the alter of surrender. When you do this you may drink freely from the fountain of life. This is the true life all seekers thirst for, and it is without strife.*

*This burden is light, with no self-glory. When you see self-glory in a spiritual life, know that the light is dimmed and you are far off the path. This deviation from the true path will always become greater until that person finds their way back. This is why complete and total surrender is so important. The self-willed can only glorify self; your task is to reflect the total, the all of life.*

G thought about how nice the rain was.

*The rain is life giving, the water of life. Part of our message is to bring people back to this pure life, the simplicity of being. You see the power of surrender?*

Yes.

*This is for all people, the simplicity of being. When people surrender their self in this manner there will be no further need for books such as this, for all shall know Him from the least to the greatest.*

Will this ever be?

*He asked to "make them one Father, even as we are one." This is answered. The body will come together as one and transcend the petty flesh.*

Sounds like good news.

*It is. I said before, it doesn't matter what people think the truth is; what matters is what the truth is, and this is the truth.*

Talia, I recently remembered something else that happened when we met. When you turned and walked away in the kitchen I wanted to say something else. I wanted to warn you. It was burning in me to warn you about something. I almost blurted out, "Don't go to Panama." But I stopped myself because I didn't know what I was talking about or even if you were planning to go or anything.

It just didn't make sense. And I asked for confirmation and never got one. I'm so sorry.

*Don't be sorry. Whatever you said wouldn't have changed anything. It was meant to be. The guilt you've felt is groundless; there is no responsibility for you in what happened. It was my time to go, just as some day it will be your time, and nothing anyone can say to you will change it.*

I sensed danger or something and then, when I searched the feeling, I thought it was just me, and I knew everything was going to be all right.

*Everything is all right. It's all perfect, part of the perfect plan to fulfill all things.*

A lot happened that day.

*A lot did. You were reluctant to share this.*

I was. I did feel somewhat responsible. Like I could have done something to change it.

*We're changing things now, which we couldn't have done if I hadn't made that journey. It's OK to reveal this. It won't be held against you, and you've avoided mention of this long enough.*

But what does it profit?

*In many ways, to share this is to instruct others that are in similar situations not to feel guilty about a premonition of a glimpse of life, because that's what it is: a glimpse of life. When you think of me, think of the celebration of life, not sorrow over the illusion of death. Death has no place here; it just does not exist. It's a state of mind, so don't put your mind in that state.*

*You wanted to live your life with me—now you can.*

It's not the same.

*No, it's better. Now we don't have the complications of the flesh. You have an open hand with me—that's how our fellowship works so well.*

That's a clue, isn't it?

*That's a clue for others on how to live this life.*

What does *open hand* mean?

Open hand *simply means you just have an open heart and attitude towards me with no thought of what you can get in return. It's a giving spirit. We've always had this relationship.*

Well, I sure do get a lot from you.

*Yes, you do, and it's symbiotic: I get a lot from you too. We're not striving here to be understood. We're just being who we are, and this is a relationship based on truth. In that we're perfect examples of how relationships ought to be and are meant to be. Simple giving with no thought of return, and your trust of me is perfect.*

That's because I know you're perfect and cannot make mistakes.

*You have to learn to accept others' mistakes, as you trust them as well.*

Perfect weather today.

*You ought to see it here.*

I want to.

*You can.*

G is given a glimpse of Talia's world. For one split second G felt instantaneously awake and alive. Everything felt perfect: the weather was perfect, the colors were brilliant, and everything was more vibrant than he could describe in words. He felt one with everything. But words are not sufficient.

That is awesome!

*Told you.*

That was just a glimpse.

*That's all you can stand right now. A glimpse is enough. If you were given more you wouldn't want to stay there.*

I almost don't want to now.

*I know, that's why you only get a glimpse. That holds you back from seeing more. You have things to do there.*

So you've said.

*Yes, and I'm saying it again as a reminder. What we're doing here is giving life to others, and that's the most you can give them.*

Then I'll stay.

*I thought you might. There's no holding you back from here anyway.*

Can't wait.

*Yes, you can.* ☺

*She—Mom—takes great pleasure in driving. It makes her feel in control of her life, which she is. It's also our time we spend together. It's her "hair." She'll like that; she'll think it's funny. She also knows it is true.*

The "hair" that Talia is referring to is what I call a distraction. It is a term I got from a book I read while learning how to put my thoughts aside to quiet myself, so I could hear and communicate with Talia and the spirit world. Driving is my "hair." It is my way of clearing my mind.

## *August 13*

**4:15 PM**

*Gravity is not a constant. It is a force in flux. I told you everything was in flux, alive. Notice the model of dark matter and dark energy are terms used by those whose theories are incomplete. They use the terms "dark" for what they do not understand, and I said to you what it was they were leaving out of the equation: themselves. It's not nearly as complicated as they try to make it. When you remove your spiritual being from the equation and the spiritual being or nature of the universe, don't be surprised if your theories remain in the dark. This darkness comes from the mind of man, and man remains in the dark until he accepts and receives the light. You simply cannot leave the Creator out of the creation and expect enlightenment. Their own Einstein knew this.*

*Your own gravity varies with your mental state. You experience gravity as a law and have been told it is. I see you as not under the law, and gravity in a constant state of flux.*

## *August 14*

———————✦———————

**7:50 AM**

Talia, you told me once a while back you "hated camp." I didn't know what you were talking about at the time, as you didn't elaborate, but I heard about it. Do you want to talk about it?

*Yes, it was the lies I hated. I knew who I was, and someone was saying I was someone else that I wasn't. This always creates frustration in a person if you listen to it. I was smart enough not to listen, but I didn't listen to my own advice. You see even then I was giving sound advice, but it's often hard to take your own advice, especially when an authority figure is contradicting you. That's when the lesson was driven home to trust myself. I knew nobody knew me better than me, especially someone who didn't know me at all but was famous for jumping to conclusions. She was well educated in the world's ways and was considered an expert, even by herself. She also didn't like me being so outspoken and insisted on putting me in my place, but she didn't know where my place was—she just thought she did. I never liked a dictator, and that's what she acted like.*

I heard you were somewhat famous for having no tolerance for foolishness.

*It's not that I didn't have tolerance for it. I just never liked it, and it seemed pointless to me.*

I appreciate you being so loquacious.

*I appreciate you appreciating it. I always had something to say even if I didn't always say it. That's something I noticed about you the day we met. You only said something when you had something to say, and you listened.*

*I was listening too. I thought you were charming that day, and I got a good feeling about you. When I asked my mom who you were, I was told just a friend. That was a limited description if I've ever heard one. I told her I liked you. You now see how those simple words have connected us beyond the earthly realm. That world has limits, limits you yourself put on it. But this world, my world, has no limits, and our task in part is to bring a realization that the limits are not real, that the limitless is what is real. The poets have written about this through the ages. It's not so easy to grasp, but it's a lot easier than not grasping it at all.*

I keep noticing the hummingbirds. I feel where they are before I see them.

*I'm pointing them out to you. I want you to see their dance with each other and the environment. I loved to dance. It's a celebration of life, and it is never wrong to celebrate life. It's an integration of body, mind, and spirit into a harmonious whole. That's why I loved it—it's liberating.*

*Hummingbirds take what they need, get rid of what they don't need, and they're quick about it. They don't waste time. If you see time there as a period of BEING you wouldn't waste it either. It's a waypoint during your journey. It's a point of the way to be.*

*Hummingbirds are harmless, and they bring color into peoples' lives.*

### August 16

**6:25 AM**
*What was it you were told the meaning of life was?*

In a nutshell, to have fun, to learn and to help others.

*Are we not doing that?*

We are.

*I LOVED to have fun, but who doesn't? To learn is programmed in you, and nothing satisfies like helping others.*

## 9:20 AM
*People perceive it to be much more convenient to believe what they want to believe rather than believe the truth. It's not an affront to their pride.*

## 10:25 AM
I was discussing the book *Walden* with someone, how the author didn't act like he had all the answers but just recorded his observations, when Talia said:

*I don't have all the answers either.*

### August 21

## 12:43 AM
*Death is not the end; it's a wonderful new beginning.*

How so?

*Every aspect of your life, every minute detail is reviewed and learned from, every failure, every success, every relationship you had—and didn't but should have. Everyone you helped and everyone you didn't help. Every kind word and every harsh or hateful statement. Every single detail will be reviewed and learned from. The growth this creates, the wisdom this generates is stupendous. Every word you've used will be judged. Even a kind thought is rewarded, for thoughts are life. There is time enough here; there's so very little there.*

Talia, nobody here even comes close to you.

*You come close to me.*

You know what I mean.

*Yes, I do, and you come close to me. I told you no one knew all the things you know, but it was hard for you to receive.*

I'm sure I'm not the only one who feels that way.

*But that's just it; it's just a feeling. The reality, the truth of it is, it's true: no one does. You've forgotten what it took to get you where you are.*

That's true.

*And you often forget where you are.*

That's true too.

*Why do you forget?*

I forget.

*It's because you've had such an overwhelming joy in getting where you are that you want to do it all over again to recapture those moments of intense pleasure. But I'm telling you again there is no end, and you don't have to forget [an experience] to experience the experience again because it all comes back around again and again in a most splendid way. So believe in the growth, trust the spirit of the spherical way, and rejoice in the experience, because the experience is new again. Renewed again and again, and its design IS to bring us all into perfection and fullness in all that is all.*

That seems to sort of make sense.

*You think?*

Yes, I think, therefore I am.

*I think he should have said I think, therefore I think I am.*

That's funny.

*It shows a humbler attitude. Beside, what was he? Did he ask that question?*

Sounds like he was groping in the dark.

*He was, but he was esteemed enlightened.*

You know, Talia, I've missed our conversations. It's difficult to get here sometimes.

*I know it is. It's also simple beyond words. So much of what we've discussed is beyond words. That's why you haven't written it down.*

That relieves some pressure. I thought it was just me.

*No, when I told you it wasn't possible to write everything I say, I was being literal.*

That's my frustration. I know what you've revealed, and I can't get it across to people.

*That's not your job.*

Well, again, pressure's off.

*Told you that you worry too much.*

You're always right.

*I know I am.*

What is my job?

*To rearrange things.*

Rearrange things?

*Yes, don't you think things need to be rearranged?*

Yes, a lot of things.

*Then you rearrange them.*

Got it.

*Yes, you do, you're getting it.*

You're perfect, you know.

*Yes, I know.*

I want to be perfect too.

*You will be. Describe what you saw.*

It was a poster I saw years ago. The caption read, "Things take time."

*Yep.*

Yep?

*Yep, I can talk anyway I want.*

I just never remember you saying that before.

*You're about as informal as anyone I know and you're surprised?*

No, I mean, just making sure.

*Be sure.*

## 9:00 AM

That dialogue we had last night was awesome.

*And it will be awesome again today. Just give it a chance.*

The subtlety of your lessons, how you weave them in, is astounding.

*It's seamless and it seems less than it is. That's the nature of the way.*

Like a finger pointing to the moon.

*You could say that. You could also say it's like the moon pointing to your finger.*

It's the same thing.

*In essence, yes. I have some more to say to you, and first things first.*

Let's do it.

*That's true what I told you last night about your friend. You're as good as he is at what you do. Art is expression. You can express the spirit that moves in all things in your own way. Everyone has their own way to express this. It's just finding that way. That's the expression so many search for. That's also the profound sense of frustration so many feel when they don't find it. It's rarely found in words, yet that's what most who feel this frustration seek. A way to put what they feel or know is true into words. You primarily found your expression in movement. It's not so important how a person expresses their truth. What is important is finding THEIR creative expression. We are all hardwired to express our Creator. You found me expressing my Creator simply by looking in my eyes, and that's how simple it can be sometimes. We are reflections of the Divine.*

That is awesome!

*Yes, it is. Divine expression is always awesome, and it is expressed differently in each individual. Wars have been fought over this misunderstanding. That's why I say it's time to wake up.*

You're the sweetest thing I've ever known.

*Yes, well, the Holy Spirit is the sweetest thing you've ever known, and that's what this is. We are changed into His image from glory to glory. That's something to think about, isn't it?*

Yes, it is.

*What was it the hummingbird said to you?*

That he wanted something sweet.

*That's what they seek, something sweet.*

**10:12 AM**
*I told you before, the contrast was for learning. If it weren't for the darkness you wouldn't know the stars.*

### *August 25*

**5:09 PM**
Talia, I really need to hear you.

*Then hear me.*

I love your voice.

*And I love yours.*

# September 2008

### *September 3*

---

**(New Mexico)**

*You have great faith. It's hard for you to understand those who don't. They haven't seen the miracles you have. Don't blame them for that.*

*It's all a test, and if you already knew all the answers it wouldn't be much of a test now, would it?*

The answer's contained in the question.

*You're getting it.*

Thanks for the pronouncement.

*You're welcome. I have something to say to you.*

Say on.

*The things that bother you and worry you should be of no concern to you. Also, TAKE your time. That's a secret to proper timing: take it—make it your own—take it by force. Time can be bent by force. You have gravity, and gravity can bend time and space.*

OK, I was just getting my head around time and now you threw in space.

*It takes time.*

Talia, no one can move me from tears to overwhelming joy to brilliance to such peace so swiftly.

*My word comes with power.*

It sure does. You illuminate my soul.

*We all do. It's pure hope, and along with love, it abides forever. Why would you labor for that which doesn't satisfy?*

That sounds like the mystery of misery revealed.

*It is. So why would you?*

I think basically it would be a lack of understanding.

*And why would someone lack understanding?*

Maybe they just didn't look for it.

*Why wouldn't they look?*

I could think of several reasons.

*But what would be the primary one? Most everyone says they want to understand, so why is it most can't get it? Because their words are empty and insincere. If they really wanted to understand then they would. The answers are easy enough to find.*

I don't think I would have ever gotten that; the truth is too simple.

*It's perfectly simple.*

**11:47 AM**

*There is a natural progression that is supernatural in its effect.*

How so?

*Don't be hasty. You rob yourself when you skip ahead.*

In what context?

*My lessons for one. Have they not followed a natural progression?*

They certainly have, in so many ways.

*You should teach the same way. It is an honorable way to teach. It honors and respects the student and the lesson.*

How come everything you say seems more awesome than what you said before?

*Because it's the present truth.*

Someone else has something to say?

*Talia's not the only one with something to say. Everyone and everything has something to say.*

I think it was Curt. I felt his presence.

> Curt is G's friend, who passed away years before.

*"I'll be there when the deal goes down."*

Curt?

*Yes.*

You're talking about my death?

*Yeah. It's easy, you leave the body and you're "here."*

You know when?

*You got a while.*

We made a deal, didn't we?

*Yes, that we would help each other in the transition. I remember it.*

*Talia's one that won't be stopped.*

How could anyone be stopped there?

*By hitting a wall . . . not a wall really, but an impasse in spiritual development.*

Thanks for talking to me.

*You're much more aware than most.*

But comparing ourselves among ourselves isn't wise.

*That's not what we're doing; I'm just letting you know, putting it in context.*

All right, this impasse.

*Make the most of your time there.*

Thanks, Curt, I want to. Am I doing that?

*You usually do. We all want to be a part of what she—Talia's—doing.*

What's God like?

*He's everything. You are a man of knowledge now. Use it.*

How can I use it?

*By walking in what you know.*

## NOON
*Everybody's an actor.*

So if they act like they're not, they're just acting.

*I revealed what all of that meant.*

### *September 4*

## 1:22 AM
## (Arizona)
*She—Mom—wonders why I don't speak of more personal things sometimes. That's for HER, and I convey my feelings all the time. Her tenderness for me and mine for her has no rivals. And, oh yes, the awakening HAS begun.*

### *September 9*

## 1:52 PM
So what about this unbroken wholeness you spoke of?

*It's the wholeness unbroken, brought about by the luminous web of life, which ties all together. The apartness is a part, thinking it's apart from the whole, which is only a viewpoint from which the part is looking. When the part looking, or the observer, sees that what he is looking at is a perception, a part of what's whole, when they see themselves as much of the wholeness or oneness of all that is—as is everything else, without separation—then is there realization of oneness in its truth and beauty.*

OK then.

*It's OK then because this realization is oneness filled, fullness whole, truth realized to BE in and not apart from.*

## 7:24 PM

*Curt told you the truth.*

Yes, I know he did.

*About being myopic.*

I'd forgotten that part.

*Well, it was about us, and that's why I'm reminding you. I'm NOT the only one who has something to say.*

I know.

*It's just to let you know to be open to others also, to their truth, to their message. "Everyone and everything has something to say."*

I know. That's what he said.

*He has a warm place in his heart for you. He sees you clearly now.*

That's good.

*He's a good man who echoed my truth to you: don't waste time.*

I'm trying not to.

*And as he said, "You usually don't."*

Maybe I'm improving.

*You are. You're growing, but you try to hide it.*

I don't know why.

*Yes, you do and no, it's not lack of confidence. It's the part of you that embraces refusal to take responsibility. You can run but you can't hide, so quit hiding it because you're already hidden in Him where we all are. So it's pointless, you see. Use your energy more constructively. Your words also have power. You just refuse to acknowledge it sometimes. You don't want the responsibility, but you can't get away from it. You think you can do this and then just walk away as if it didn't happen?*

No.

*Then quit acting like it.*

I'm with you, Talia, all the way.

*And I'm with you too, all the way, so don't be something you're not. Curt told you to walk in your knowledge.*

Yes, he did.

*Then do it. Don't think about it, just do it.*

He said they all wanted to be a part of what you're doing.

*They are all a part of what I'm doing. Being one in Him. They are doing that, but even here there are some who have yet to realize it. Mostly those who left that place prematurely or wasted their precious time.*

How do they waste it?

*By being preoccupied with the things of that world. A lot by "making a living," which brought them a slow dying. Before they knew it their time was up there and they had brought forth no fruit in the spirit. They had atrophied without a thought. It's not a crime, but it is a waste. I told you, there is no crime here. Nothing unclean can pass thought the Great Gate. They had received the truth but let somebody else do the work for them. You see now why taking responsibility is so important?*

Yes, I do.

*I hope we've cleared that up.*

I hope we have too.

*Hope abides forever.*

I know.

*Nothing happens without requesting it.*

That's an extreme statement.

*That's an extreme truth.*

Why do you bring that up?

*Because people need to know that.*

**9:30 PM**
Thanks for that.

> I asked Talia to have G call me, and within fifteen sec-
> onds G called me and said that Talia told him I asked
> her to have him call me.

*My pleasure. I love doing that stuff. It meant a lot to her, and that's me
confirming my word to her that it was me talking to her and that she
can and does hear me. I told you she would learn how and she is; she's
learning fast.*

I really didn't expect it so fast. At first I thought it would take years.

*I know you did, but I'm doing a quick work and I'm swift, remember?*

Yes, I do.

*You asked for it too—that helps. It makes my job much easier. Told you we were all in this together.*

Yes, you did. I hate to be redundant, but that was pretty awesome though.

*The timing was excellent because you were in a place to receive, because you were both in an attitude of a giving spirit, among other things.*

You move me so wonderfully.

*If someone isn't experiencing this then they're locked up in their head, and that's not living at all. Living is experiencing. That's something else people should know and understand. You were asked to ask me how to explain how I got where I am, how I got this "evolved."*

Yes.

*This is a tapestry and the threads are there to see. In other words, it has already been explained. If we got into the minute details it would be far beyond the scope of this book, leaving no room for the message—which is change—but I do understand the request, and it's from someone most dear to me. I will explain this, which should explain that, and that's that God has no limits in any direction. Limits are man-made from the mind of man. Remember when I spoke of limitlessness? This is abstract in the mind of man, a mere conception, which IS a beginning but is often killed—by the constant reminders of what you can't do. Your world is filled with signs warning you of every conceivable danger—speed limits, ceilings, bars, walls, no trespassing—on and on until you buy into it. When your subconscious tells you you can't, you can't. So don't reaffirm a lie. Let your heart warn you of danger.*

*I was raised consciously to trust my heart, and I experienced daily, in every way I could. I have NO regrets, only a sense of fullness of my life there. I said before, my life there was an example of how to live there, and it got me here perfectly. Anyone could make the same decisions I made; it's just deciding to.*

How could we be so blind as to not see who you were while you were here?

*People do that all the time. It's also not so very obvious. After all, I wasn't completely conscious of how I was living my life at the time. The glory goes to the Source of all things, which is everything.*

God is everything.

*Curt's definition and well put. He's smiling now.*

Figured he would be.

Well, so much for getting to bed early.

*You'd rather sleep?*

No, I just heard today that sleep has amazing regenerative powers.

*So does this, but this regenerative power is everlasting.*

Believe me, I know.

*I believe you; I know you know. Now you're beginning to share what you know, which is knowledge activated. Otherwise it's dead in the water.*

Interesting term.

*That's why I said it.*

Someone said that the waters some drown in, the mystic swims in.

*Opening the doors to perception.*

Yes, that was the context of it.

*That's true, and it's always been that way. Be aware that those who are drowning will try to pull you down with them.*

*Time for you to go swimming.*

In the sea of consciousness.

*You could put it that way.*

## September 10

**6:48 AM**
Good morning.

*Good morning. Did you sleep well?*

I slept well and tossed and turned, but for the most part, yes.

*Be at peace.*

Well, thanks. Good advice.

*It's also the way to be. Any other way to be is not being at all, but strife.*

Excellent.

*Of course, and excellence will flow out of you when you're at peace.*

Blessed peace.

*I know the Prince of it and His marvels are unending. The Teacher, from whom all lessons flow, in perfect peace.*

This is a nice way to start the day.

*It's the perfect way. Most "hit the ground running," and that's not the best way to start the day. If you notice, when you start the day honoring your Creator, the rest of the day is yours.*

The rest of the day.

*Yes, the rest of the day within you within Him. It's perfect rest, even in the storm.*

Glad I didn't hit the ground running this morning.

*Most of the time all it takes is to take the time to say hello.*

Anyone can do that.

*Yes, anyone could. And their expression that day, the rest of the day, will reflect how they started that day in everything they do. It's cylindrical: what you put out comes back. That's that honor you put out coming back to honor you, and it's never the same measure; it's always more.*

That's amazing!

*Yes, that is amazing, and that is the way it is. So whatever you want, give it and it will always come back to you in greater measure. If they taught that in the wealth-building seminars they would be well worth going to. As it is, they generally degenerate into a selfish spirit.*

Never been to one.

*No, and whenever you considered it you felt a check. There is a reason for that. Your spirit knows when you're taking and not giving, and it feels like theft, which is what it really is. If you think of it, if you ARE reflecting your Creator, you'll always be giving more than you're receiving—that's just how it works. You can't help but to do this if you're being in Him. It's a natural outgrowth. That's never-ending abundance, giving and receiving, and its spherical flow never stops.*

*They [G's coworkers] are hopping around out there unaware. They should have started the day like you did. Recognizing the day for what it is, the light of the life force flowing into and through them in an abundance of gifts, without limits. Instead it's "another damned day" they have created for themselves at work. Yet they could change it in an instant.*

That seems to nearly sum up everything you've said so far.

*It somewhat did, IF you can see it. Now go share and flow in the subtlety of truth, being who you are without strife.*

**11:47 AM**
*This is felicity.*

You're right about that.

*How could I not be?*

True.

*Truth in the inward part . . . can you feel it?*

Yes, I can.

*Anyone who reads this can, but will they?*

Guess that depends on them.

*It does depend on them. That's what so many forget: their part to play in this Grand Game.*

**1:29 PM**
*Remember when I mentioned dressage [a style of riding]?*

Yes.

*That's how subtle most things should be controlled.*

Energy and movement?

*Energy is movement; it's about directing it. It is decide, then act, and it's mostly a mental game.*

You know I had to look that up. I thought you were saying something about dressing.

*I know—that's why you heard me laugh.*

Yes, I thought it was just about the way I dressed.

*It's the mental picture I wanted you to see.*

Wish I could have seen you ride. I know you were very, very good.

*Someday you will. ☺*

Fantastic! I'll be looking forward to that.

*So will I.*

Thank you again.

*You're most welcome, and thank you again.*

### *September 11*

**7:22 AM**
Thank you for who you are and good morning.

*Thank you and good morning and who else would I be?*

That's a profound question.

*That's something to think about, isn't it?*

It sure is. You know what I mean though.

*I sure do and I appreciate that.*

You're mighty welcome.

*I know what that means, and I appreciate that too.*

You described yourself once as lively, and that's such a perfect description. You keep reconfirming your presence to people in so many ways . . . it's not just your words, it's your acts that blow me away.

*I'm living the art of life as an example of how to be. Being in Him one cannot help but to move people in the proper direction. My vibration is in perfect harmony, and I'm learning to change others' vibration when they are in disharmony. The result is they sense life and the infinite possibilities that exist within them. I restore hope. Hope and harmony are synonymous terms. Remember when I asked if you could hear the music?*

Yes.

*It's never-ending, and when your vibrations are in harmony and your ears are opened, you will hear it. A disharmony has sounds too, and it's not music, it's noise. When you sense something's not right, that's the noise, not the music. Music has wonderful healing powers, often miraculous healing powers. There is no sickness in perfect harmony. You've heard music in rivers.*

Yes, I had forgotten that.

*You've been told you're not supposed to. When someone else denies your truth, even if everyone else denies your truth, it doesn't mean you yourself must deny your truth. Your truth is yours, and if and when that happens, the proper response is to deny their lies instead. This way you hold your truth without losing it, and you don't confirm their lies to them, which is destined to wither on the vine anyway. Why be a party to death?*

Talia, I wish I could repay you for all you've done for me.

*Live your truth, that's all I could ever ask of you. When you do that you've fulfilled every request, and no one should ever ask any more of you. That's the most anyone can give, and it's always enough.*

Your simplicity is profound beyond words.

*It's truth, and it is simple beyond words. We're just using words as symbols to convey meaning, which IS self-evident in all.*

In all things.

*In all, which is all things.*

You can't escape the truth, and it is in your face all the time, isn't it.

*That's exactly right. To live a lie is to make yourself miserable. That seems like a stupid pastime, doesn't it?*

Pretty goofy thing to do.

*It's a trap too. What I mean by that is it's hard to get out of it once you're into it because it blinds. The negative side is spherical too; remember we talked about counterparts.*

A vicious circle or a perfect circle, and it's decided by choice.

*That's a good example, but I prefer spheres because it's more descriptive of how it really is, a more dimensional picture of how things really operate.*

I see exactly what you mean.

*That's why I like it better.*

406

September 2008

How's Curt today?

*Curt's just fine. He's watching closely. He's somewhat proud of you and he says it was an honor to know you . . . and thanks for asking.*

That's him all right.

*Yes, it is.*

He hasn't changed much, still quiet.

*No, but he's grown and he doesn't want to interfere.*

Talia, I just had the most interesting download about how animals relate to the earth and your ashes and why they were your essence here and certain people who realized how animals are an example for us on how to relate to the earth.

*Awesome, isn't it?*

It sure is, and also how these words are just pointers.

*Yes, symbols pointing to truths for freedom for all mankind.*

And I see how the wrong choices are death.

*A broad road to destruction that the herd tramples daily.*

You're so right—I saw that.

*That's why it's important to start the day correctly, with a humble attitude. Not "what can I get today" but "what can I give."*

That whole animal thing!

*Animals live in harmony with the earth, which is also a vibrational Being. When you realize that and walk as one with her then is there harmony.*

## *September 12*

**10:33 PM**

*You're afraid to write.*

No, I'm not!

*You're going to argue with me again?*

No . . . I'm not.

*You said you trusted me.*

I do. Totally. It's me I don't trust sometimes.

*Change your thinking, period.*

Was I supposed to write the period?

*You can write whatever you want to. I want you to write what I say.*

I only want to write what you say; I only want this to be of
the spirit.

*Then listen; you have to believe.*

I believe.

*Then stop doubting. Quietness and confidence shall be your strength. You
shall rejoice in times to come. You wanted me to prophesy the future, and
I'm telling you it's all now.*

I asked that.

*And that's my answer. What was your calling? That's what it is. Your
prophecy—you see it clearly.*

I see some of it clearly.

*You can see it all clearly.*

Didn't know that.

*Change your thinking. Stop denying what you know.*

Strong deception.

*Yes. Very strong deception. Where do you see it?*

Wherever I go, on nearly everyone I meet.

*What else?*

A yielding to it. An acceptance of it.

*Yes, what else?*

A rising kingdom of light. Children walking in pure light.

*Who are these children?*

God's children, those chosen to believe.

*And what are they doing?*

They are walking boldly and proclaiming the Kingdom. They are filled and surrounded by bright light, and it pushes out the darkness from before them. Wherever they walk is theirs. Nothing foul can touch them.

*It's the difference between light and dark, isn't it?*

Complete separation.

*Any doubt of the contrast?*

None.

*What else do you see?*

I see leaders misleading. They've chosen to mislead and they've been misled themselves.

*By whom?*

By the prince of darkness.

*Where does he come from?*

He comes from the mind of man. That's where he gets his power.

*Give NO place to him.*

I hear him laughing.

*His laughs are lies.*

*This IS the pure word of truth. Don't be concerned about explanations. We've already explained this is esoteric. Hidden truths. The seal is upon the minds of man. The only way out of darkness is by the light. The light of the Holy One. There is no thinking your way out; it's only by the light is the seal removed. If they've read this far, they've gotten it or their minds are sealed.*

*It's changing.*

What's changing?

*Our message. It's changing. I told you, it's a message of change.*

How's it changing?

*It's changing those who've gotten it, and now the message will reflect that growth. And it's not something they will always feel or recognize either, but if they will look in the mirror they will see change.*

You've changed me.

*I am.*

## September 13

**6:55 AM**
*The mind of God.*

That's the answer, one mind.

**1:18 PM**
*It hurts to grow. Growing pains.*

I know.

*Then relax. Undue tension is stress. That zaps you of vital energy.*

I know.

*I know you know, but sometimes you need a reminder. Practice what you preach. Our flowing is without strife. The victory is within you.*

Thanks for that.

*I thought you could use it.*

**8:53 PM**
Talia, you never get tired, do you.

*No, I never do. I also never feel bad—that's one of the advantages of being here.*

Your transition . . . how was it?

*It was the most natural thing ever, shedding the body; we ARE spiritual beings—the physical body's only temporary. I know there's pain there and trials and temptations, but they are wonderful tests. Wonder filled. They are all designed for your betterment. That's an outlook that changes things. That's a viewpoint to embrace.*

Thank you, God, for Talia.

*She is one in whom I am well pleased.*

> This was spoken by God.

Talia, you have favor with God.

*It's the ultimate friendship; it's a family like no other. The love is boundless and indescribable.*

*How was your day?*

It was interesting. I got tired, then talked to you and applied what you told me and, come to think of it, everything changed for the better.

*High energy and a good outlook. All these principles, if applied, work. My word is with power. That He has assured me of.*

So . . . the secret of your great confidence revealed.

*You sound like you haven't heard this before. God told me my word was with Power. I told you your word was with Power. I cannot lie and I cannot be wrong, so where is your great confidence?*

Feels pretty high right now.

*Our message is in a transitional stage. It's changing to a higher vibration level. We're catering to those beings who have chosen to move up. These are tied down no longer. These have wings, and their flight is with vision. Aren't you tired of pampering? Aren't you sick of the sickness? Nature itself cries out for these to be delivered. This IS the manifestation of the sons of God, and it IS happening now. Some will see it and grieve, many will see it with joy unspeakable—and there's a few who won't notice at all.*

Guess you're getting into the meat of it now.

*It is all now and it's all meat and there is a certain logic to the order. It is something like a stair-step program, somewhat like Jacob's ladder. The angels were ascending and descending. This is something to deeply consider. It speaks of a partnership. And of a give and take into oneness. I'll tell you again, there is no end to this we're speaking of. That's something else I was told. This is not opinion.*

*Time for you to go.*

To dreamland.

*Some call it that.*

### September 14

### 9:00 AM
*The earth works WITH you. SEE IT as working with you. All things are yours.*

### 6:26 PM
Hello!

*Hello to you.*

I feel like you've got something to say.

*I do. I also feel like you've got something to say.*

Probably, but you know what you've got to say, and I'm wondering what I do.

*You underestimate yourself.*

Maybe, but maybe you could give me a nudge; my mind's blissfully blank at the moment.

*And that's usually when the inspiration comes.*

Then I could be in danger of overflowing with inspiration.

*You are, but it's really not dangerous.* ☺

(G took a drink of orange juice).

*That's another one of life's simple pleasures, isn't it?*

Yes, orange juice is pretty good.

*When you can enjoy and really appreciate life's simple pleasures, you're really living and in the moment too. That being in the moment is being in the now, where all is complete.*

It's amazing what you can find out from a sip of juice.

*It's amazing what's revealed in the moment, which is everything.*

Satori, instant realization of truth, enlightenment.

*Well said, and your Buddha nature.*

Never heard you talk about Buddha before.

*That's because I've never talked to you about it before. There is a train that you need to ride.*

Where's that?

*You'll know it when you see it.*

What else about that?

*That's it.*

*Now, there are specific people we are going to address here and this will be for these individuals. Not that others can't learn and be blessed by our message to them by residual effects, because they will, but it's important to know that much of this hereafter will be directed towards them and some things particularly for certain individuals. Everyone on this train is not on the same car.*

Sounds like a narrow track.

*It is.*


**10:13 PM**
I see that there are different lessons in different cars, aren't there?

*It is. It depends on where they're at as to what they receive. And there aren't different levels. It all is now. It's all a holy and wondrous oneness. Different levels speaks of, entails, separation. That illusion is non-existent here.*

*Momma, that's the best explanation that I can give you now. Someday you will see clearly what I mean. I love you. I like the pants you bought!*

> Talia's last sentence, "I like the pants you bought," was special to me. Just a few hours earlier I was shopping. While in the dressing room trying on some pants I thought to myself, *Wow, Talia would really like these!* And then she responded to me via G just a few hours later!

*September 21*

**12:44 PM**
Hi, Talia.

*Hi! How was your training?*

G attended a special class.

I enjoyed it. Some of the things that were said were what you had said before. The truth verifying itself. You said that I would learn from it. I learned more that I realize right now. Still digesting it.

*That's truth. Receive the truth and it grows in you. It's alive. Living.*

I appreciate you more than I can ever say.

*I know you do.*

That "if you control yourself you control your situation" has great depth.

*That's something I had said to you and you weren't sure it was me.*

Now I'm sure.

*Good, that's that "prove all things" I told you about.*

Thanks for bringing that back around.

*It all comes back around until you get it. This happens to everyone. The lessons return again and again until you've gotten it, then you move on and grow. New lessons begin. A new beginning. This takes place with that shift in consciousness from the engrafting of the living word. The lesson received and made a part of you. That's the light expanding.*

Oh, yes, the instructor said, "Practice what you preach." Same thing you said the other day.

*That's good advice.* ☺

**8:30 PM**

*We are all of one. I have the power of an endless life.*

I know you do.

*But do you know what it means?*

I thought so but apparently not.

*It means I can change the law.*

How so?

*The law is not written in stone; it is written in the hearts of man.*

Incredible.

*It's the perfect law of liberty.*

### September 22

**1:44 PM**

*There are some things you need to know.*

OK.

*It has nothing to do with my approval. It has to do with your life as you live it. You can only fool yourself. That's where your conscious comes in and your consciousness. When you feel the check, don't go there. Let everything be done for the building up, for edification. Unnecessary problems arise from not heeding it (the check) and rushing forward. Sometimes untold misery. You don't need that. Let's move beyond it. In your weakness is His strength perfected. It's time to awake out of slumber.*

I feel better.

*That's because you're awake.*

### September 23

**8:24 AM**
Good morning, Talia.

*Good morning, G.*

Help me to hear you.

*You do. You think I'm holding back; I'm not. Our core message is complete. That pyramid spoken of is narrower at the top, ending in a point. Our lessons now are specifically for those determined to move on in the pure light. Those who have chosen to forsake all for the Kingdom. These are a chosen few. These see the illusion of loss in this world equates to the fabulous and incomprehensible gain in the next. No trinkets in this world will detour them from the next. They perceive the difference between shadow and substance.*

So . . .

*Deep answers unto deep. These have cast off from the shallows despite the warnings. The wind is in their favor regardless of the direction.*

I just saw that plain as day. They're sailing out of the harbor, past the warning signs and advice of friends, into the stormy sea. Victory assured.

*That's my vision I gave you.*

That was so clear. I saw a cliff on the shore, rocks in the water.

*It's safer in the deep and much more fulfilling.*

I see there are so few and some alone, but they are helped.

*They always have been, and they always will be.*

Talia, are we done?

*With this book?* (Talia and G both said this at the same time).

Yes.

## 11:58 AM
Talia, thank you so much, this has been the most awesome journey and experience.

*It's not over yet. You're just entering into something new. The placement of these truths is ordained. You've enjoyed the sacrifice?*

Immensely.

*Excellent! And I knew the answer before I asked. It's important for you to know. The ones who've read this and heard about it are a microcosm.*

I suspected as much.

*You knew as much. I AM just confirming it for you.*

That vision I had of hands tying strings around presents this summer was you, wasn't it?

*It was what was happening. You saw my hands joyfully tying it all together for the finish. As I've said, it's all a gift. Remember when it's misunderstood what it means.*

I will.

*So you say. Did you really believe this could not be done?*

No, I believe all things are possible.

*All things are possible. All things are what they are, and our message has been to convince some that what they really know is real is real. All are born with the knowledge of truth and your life on earth is to remember that truth and live it. That's wondrous discoveries, and that's the wonderful discovery that I spoke about uncovering in my life. My joy was uncontainable. That's why it overflowed to others, and that's another reason why I said that my life was an example of how to live. It was my gift and my gift to share with others. You must see your life as a gift and a gift to share with others or you're not fully living it, not at all.*

I can never express my gratitude to you for being you and who you are or to God for creating you.

*Live these truths. That's expression enough and gratitude enough.*

# Epilogue

Though this book has come to an end, Talia's communications with G, others and me have not stopped. In fact, they have continued and expanded. The moment after Talia told G that her messages for this first book were complete, she continued to speak. G kept recording their communications, and in time there will be a second volume.

Talia was clear that her words should be published so that as many people as possible could read them, but that this book was the foundation for the next book, so it was important to keep them separate. Book Two will be for those people who want to expand their awareness and delve deeper into the words spoken by Talia.

For me, a great deal has changed since I wrote the first chapter of this book.

Since Talia's body died, I have experienced the great shattering that opened me up instantaneously to a new belief system. I have become much quieter in my mind and have been working on hearing Talia myself. Since the plane crash I have wanted nothing more than to be able to communicate directly with my daughter, and now I can honestly say that I too can hear her.

As Talia stated many times in her communications with G, all people have the ability to communicate with the spirit world; they just need to believe, and to quiet themselves. She said that communication between the spirits and us is as normal and natural as any conversation that two people in our realm would have. I'm here to tell you she's right.

But until you actually experience it for yourself, there's always a bit of doubt. Honestly, even in the beginning there's doubt. You hear but you're not sure you're actually hearing; you think it's your imagination. There are many, many instances where G expressed to Talia his doubt that it was she he was hearing. She constantly reassured him it was in fact she.

When I started to hear Talia, I too doubted. I asked her for confirmations over and over again—so much so that she probably was annoyed at me, though she never let on to that! I would say, "Talia, is this really you?" And within minutes, G would tell me that Talia had asked him to tell me, "It was me."

How do I hear Talia? A bit like G hears her. I hear her in my head. I hear her thoughts, in my voice but in her voice too. It's hard to explain, but I talk to Talia in my head, and I hear her responses in my head. The answers to my questions just flow, and when they flow I know it's she. When the answers cut off my questions, I know it's she. I don't even have to state my question in word form; I just think it, and before the thought is truly formulated, I hear her answer in my head. If I have to think about it, I know it's not Talia, but me. There's a big difference.

How was I able to start hearing Talia? First of all, I truly believed that I could and that I would. Belief is the ultimate requirement. If you doubt, you will not hear. Also, over the last year I have done a lot of work to get where I am. I went to spiritual healers who helped me open up my channels of communication and quiet my mind so I could hear Talia. I went into a quiet place in my mind, a sort of meditation, in order to be free of outside noise so that she could get through to me.

Going to these healers is not necessary; I just felt it would help me speed up the process of learning how to quiet myself and gain confidence in what I was hearing. At this point I have seen Talia and spoken to her, and in a couple of cases I have touched her.

Another thing I did this past year was to have my astrological chart read and compared to Talia's, to her dad's, and to G's. The results of that reading were stupendous.

First of all, Stephanie, the astrologer, pointed out to me where in *my* chart it showed that my daughter would die instantly, in the air, with her father. She had seen it when she read for me years ago, but because I hadn't asked about Talia, she hadn't told me (I agree with her decision). Stephanie also pointed out where *Talia's* chart showed her dying in the air instantly with her dad. She then pointed out in Michael's chart where it showed he would die instantly in the air with his daughter.

When I saw the three charts together, it was undeniable. Then Stephanie showed me where G had a direct communication link to Talia, *once she was in spirit,* which had opened up the moment Talia "died." Stephanie went on to tell me a great deal more about my purpose in life once Talia was in spirit, my relationship with Talia before and after the crash, my relationship with G, and Talia's relationship with G. *All of it* was already known by me, in my heart, but hearing it confirmed was mind-blowing.

Talia was and is the most important person in my life and always will be. She is still in my life; I know it for a fact, though her body is not with mine. I can't see her sitting next to me, or driving with me, or lying down with me. I can't take her to horse shows or to the movies, or hear her blasting her music from her room. I can't make her dinner, or see her sitting there, smiling at me. But I know she is with me, all of the time. She has told Rebecca, G, and me that she will always be with me—and she is. I feel her.

Sometimes I feel her more strongly than at other times, but I always know she is here with me. This is what I want people to understand, so that they too can feel at peace and know that their loved ones who have "died" are OK. Talia has said it herself a few times. People don't die; their spirit, their energy, is alive after the body dies—even more alive than when in the body. It's the separation between us who are still here in our bodies and the spirits we love—who are here also but without their bodies—that is hard for us to deal with.

Besides coming to realize that there is NO DEATH, I have also learned that no matter what our path, we all get to the same place. No matter what choices we make here on earth while in this body, we really are on a path already set out for us. We meet whom we meet for a reason. We do what we do for a reason—especially if we know our soul, listen to our inner voice, and follow that voice in how we live and what we do. Our inner vision knows the truth, but it's not always easy for us to hear that inner voice and see that inner vision.

Being able to hear from Talia, either myself or though G, has changed my life. I can make it through the day, through the night, through the week, and somehow, I have made it through my life since the plane crash without really wanting to leave this world myself.

Being able to hear and speak to Talia, and knowing that she is with me and watching over me and helping me with my every endeavor is more than an inspiration to me; it gives me peace. She gives me peace.

# A Message from G

WHEN I FIRST STARTED HEARING Talia speak to me, I thought all she wanted was for me to get a message to her mom—a message letting her mom know that she was all right. As it turned out, Talia had much much more to say to her mom and me than just the simple statement, "Tell my mom I'm OK." Talia had a message, and she wanted to get that message out to the world.

I always knew that there was much more to this universe than we see with our eyes, more to life, death and the spirit than I was taught in school. And though I have always been able to hear from the spirit world whenever someone wanted to get through to me, I never realized the depth and extent of what there was to learn from the other side until Talia started to reveal herself, her words, and all the information she has given me to pass on to others.

The more I heard from Talia, the more she spoke to me. The more she spoke, the more I wanted to hear. I spent every available moment of every day and evening being quiet, listening to her, and writing down everything she told me and everything I said to her.

I am truly honored to have known Talia before she "died," and even more honored, grateful, and humbled to have been able to help her get her messages—the universe's messages—out to you, the reader, and the world.

# About Kim Klein

Raised in Southern California, Kim Klein attended the University of California, Santa Barbara. After graduating with a B.A. in Political Science, attending law school and being admitted to the California State Bar, Kim worked with her then husband in real estate investments and their high-tech companies. After having her daughter, Talia, Kim became a stay-at-home mom, devoting all of her time to raising her only child.

Just after her thirteenth birthday, Talia was killed when the small private plane she was on crashed into the side of a volcano. The event devastated Kim's heart and shattered her entire belief system—and from the moment of Talia's death, Kim's motherly devotion shifted from raising Talia to learning to communicate with her in the afterlife.

Kim now spends her time writing about her experiences surrounding the death of Talia and the many communications between Talia from heaven and the spirit world to us here on earth in the physical. She is learning how to heal others from the grief of losing a loved one, as well as studying primitive living skills. She currently resides in Nevada, where she enjoys the peaceful desert scenery and continues on her path of healing, learning, and spiritual awakening.

Kim can be reached via her website:
*www.kimberlyklein.com.*

For more information about this book:
*www.theuniversespeaks.com*

To order Kim's other book, *Hummingbirds Don't Fly In The Rain:*
*www.hummingbirdsdontflyintherain.com*

# Resources

THERE ARE MANY GIFTED and powerful astrologers, mediums and psychics in the world. There are also a great number of not-so-gifted ones. Then there are the fakes.

I have tried nearly every medium and psychic that's come across my path—from the world famous to those that advertise on the street. The people I've mentioned throughout this book are those that have proven to be extremely gifted, honest and reputable. Over time they have become my favorite sources of spiritual communications, guidance for my own awakening—and very special people in my life.

Though each client and reading is different, and everyone relates differently to different people, I am very comfortable recommending these people to my family, friends, and you, the reader. I want to help those of you that are searching for a way to communicate with your loved ones but don't know where to look for it. Providing these names and contact information is also way for me to give back to them for the great blessing they have been and continue to be in my life.

**Astrologer**

Stephanie Jourdan, Ph.D.
Astrologer, Author, Lecturer
Higher Self Communications, Inc.
Woodland Hills, CA
818-340-4099
*www.HigherSelfCommunications.com*
*www.LifeIsAGiftShop.com*
*info@HigherSelfCommunications.com*

**Medium**

RonaLaFae Thapa
*ronalafae@msn.com*

**Pet Psychic**

Laura Stinchfield
*www.ThePetPsychic.com*
*Laura@thepetpsychic.com*

**Memorial and Celebration Jewelry**

In order to keep a part of Talia with me physically, I had a few custom jewelry pieces made to hold her ashes. Everyone who saw these pieces loved them so I decided to offer them to the world at: *www.memorialandcelebrationjewelry.com*

**Editor**

This book was edited by Jennifer Read Hawthorne.
*www.jenniferhawthorne.com*
*jennifer@jenniferhawthorne.com*

If you would like to read more about Talia before the crash, or about the author's extraordinary journey before, during and after Talia's transition, please read *Hummingbirds Don't Fly in the Rain.*

You can buy *Hummingbirds Don't Fly in the Rain* on the authors website, *www.kimberlyklein.com,* at *Amazon.com,* as well as from other retailers and online bookstores.